Brent D. Taylor in an engineer and businessman, specialising in quantitative research and statistics, including benchmarking studies for management in the private and public sectors. His focus on Thomas Blamey stems from a keen long-term interest in military history and high-impact leaders. He is a member of Military History & Heritage Victoria and has been mentored on this project by senior military officers. Brent lives in Richmond in Melbourne.

BLAMEY

BRENT D. TAYLOR

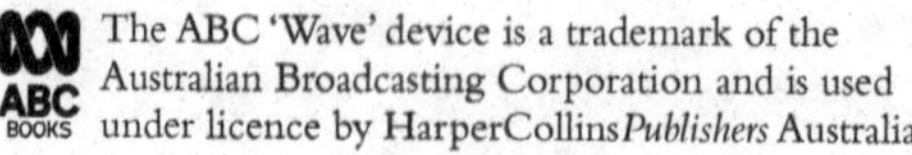

The ABC 'Wave' device is a trademark of the Australian Broadcasting Corporation and is used under licence by HarperCollins*Publishers* Australia

HarperCollins*Publishers*
Australia • Brazil • Canada • France • Germany • Holland • India
Italy • Japan • Mexico • New Zealand • Poland • Spain • Sweden
Switzerland • United Kingdom • United States of America

HarperCollins acknowledges the Traditional Custodians of the lands upon which we live and work, and pays respect to Elders past and present.

First published on Gadigal Country in Australia in 2025
by HarperCollins*Publishers* Australia Pty Limited
ABN 36 009 913 517
harpercollins.com.au

Copyright © Brent D. Taylor 2025

The right of Brent D. Taylor to be identified as the author of this work has been asserted by him in accordance with the *Copyright Act 1968*.

All rights reserved. Apart from any use as permitted under the *Copyright Act 1968*, no part may be reproduced, copied, scanned, stored in a retrieval system, recorded, or transmitted, in any form or by any means, without the prior written permission of the publisher. Without limiting the exclusive rights of any author, contributor, or the publisher of this publication, any unauthorised use of this publication to train generative artificial intelligence (AI) technologies is expressly prohibited. HarperCollins also exercises its rights under Article 4(3) of the Digital Single Market Directive 2019/790 and expressly reserves this publication from the text and data-mining exception.

HarperCollins*Publishers*
Macken House, 39/40 Mayor Street Upper
Dublin 1, D01 C9W8, Ireland

A catalogue record for this book is available from the National Library of Australia

ISBN 978 0 7333 4373 5 (paperback)
ISBN 978 1 4607 1821 6 (ebook)

Cover design by Luke Causby, Blue Cork
Cover image by Universal History Archive / Getty Images
Maps by Laurie Whiddon, Map Illustrations, www.mapillustrations.com.au
Indexer: Don Jordan, Antipodes Indexing
Typeset in Sabon LT Std by Kirby Jones

Printed and bound in the United States

Contents

Foreword

General Sir Peter Cosgrove AK CVO MC (retired)

Most of us are enthusiastic readers. Your enthusiasm and, not least to say, your attention are particularly focused when you are asked to write the foreword for a book, especially when it is in one of your major areas of interest: military history, especially of Australia and our involvement in the Great War and World War II (the generations of my maternal grandfather and my father). The combined military history and biography of a famous Australian wartime general – and Australia's only field marshal – is a potent mix.

There have been a number of other historical and biographical accounts that tell us about General Blamey but, in my view, Brent Taylor adds a powerful point of view to those who have come before. Like many soldiers and scholars, I carried into my reading certain perceptions and predispositions about Australia's commander in chief of our military forces (that is to say our army) during much of World War II. It seems precisely because Taylor came to believe that there was so much jaundiced opinion about Blamey that he embarked on this comprehensive account of Blamey's early life, his military career, and some detail of his life and times between the crucibles of the Great War and World War II. I must say, I came to feel somewhat chastened for my previous perceptions, which tended to focus on particular incidents, episodes and relationship issues, and cast shadows across his considerable years of military experience and accomplishments.

Taylor's account does not shrink from describing these issues but helps us to see context, understand overriding concerns and consider the very important part that interpersonal relationships and cultural differences between key Australian and British and US leaders played in the exercise of high command. Taylor strongly asserts that Blamey was the man for his times, both for his operational and strategic judgement, and his determination to preserve the troops under his command.

Much has been made about Blamey's private life and aggressive and occasionally ruthless behaviour. Taylor does not reject that Blamey was hard-nosed but wants us all to understand that he needed to be if he was to achieve military outcomes without decimating his precious Australian forces. Taylor persuasively points to Blamey's very significant experience in World War I as being influential in his overall dedication to this end and his time as commander in chief.

He poses the question of how we judge a senior leader who is extraordinarily capable in virtually every necessary domain of his or her leadership but who on occasion displays less reputable behaviour. I should note here that every leader will have observant critics who will be enthusiastic in their broadcast of that leader's lapses and, heavens above, even sometimes embellish them in the telling! No leader can be perfect and Taylor concedes that Blamey was an imperfect, if exceptionally able and accomplished, leader. There is no doubt history would have been much more generous to him if he had provided less opportunity to his critics.

I am glad to have been asked to participate in this fascinating biography of Thomas Blamey. Although other senior Australian military figures of the 20th century have received abundant accolades, there is no doubt that this eloquent, persuasive and occasionally pungent biography shines a different light on Australia's highest-ranking military officer. I congratulate Brent Taylor most warmly and commend this book to all readers.

General Sir Peter Cosgrove was Governor-General of Australia (2014–2018), Chief of the Defence Force (2002–2005), Chief of Army (2000–2002) and leader of the International Force for East Timor (1999–2000). As a lieutenant, he won the Military Cross for leading action in Vietnam in 1969.

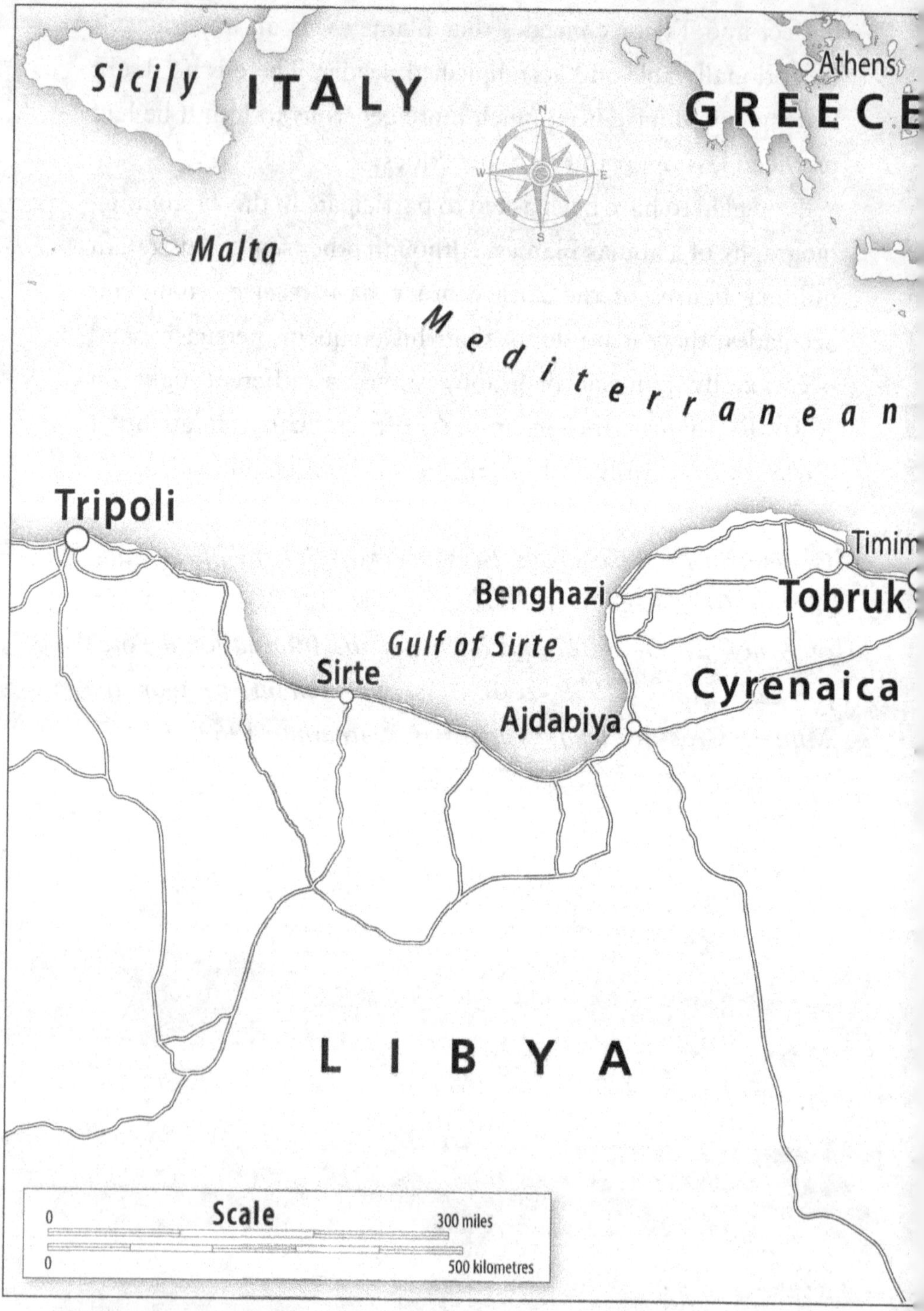

Sicily
ITALY
Athens
GREECE
N
W
E
S
Malta
Mediterranean
Tripoli
Timimi
Benghazi
Tobruk
Gulf of Sirte
Sirte
Cyrenaica
Ajdabiya
LIBYA
Scale
0
300 miles
0
500 kilometres

Cyprus
Nicosia
rakleiou
Crete
Sea
Beirut
Damascus
Nazareth
Jerusalem
Gaza
Sidi Rezegh
Bardia
Sollum
Mersa
Matruh
Alexandria
Halfaya Pass
El Alamein
Suez Canal
Suez
Cairo
Red
Sea
EGYPT

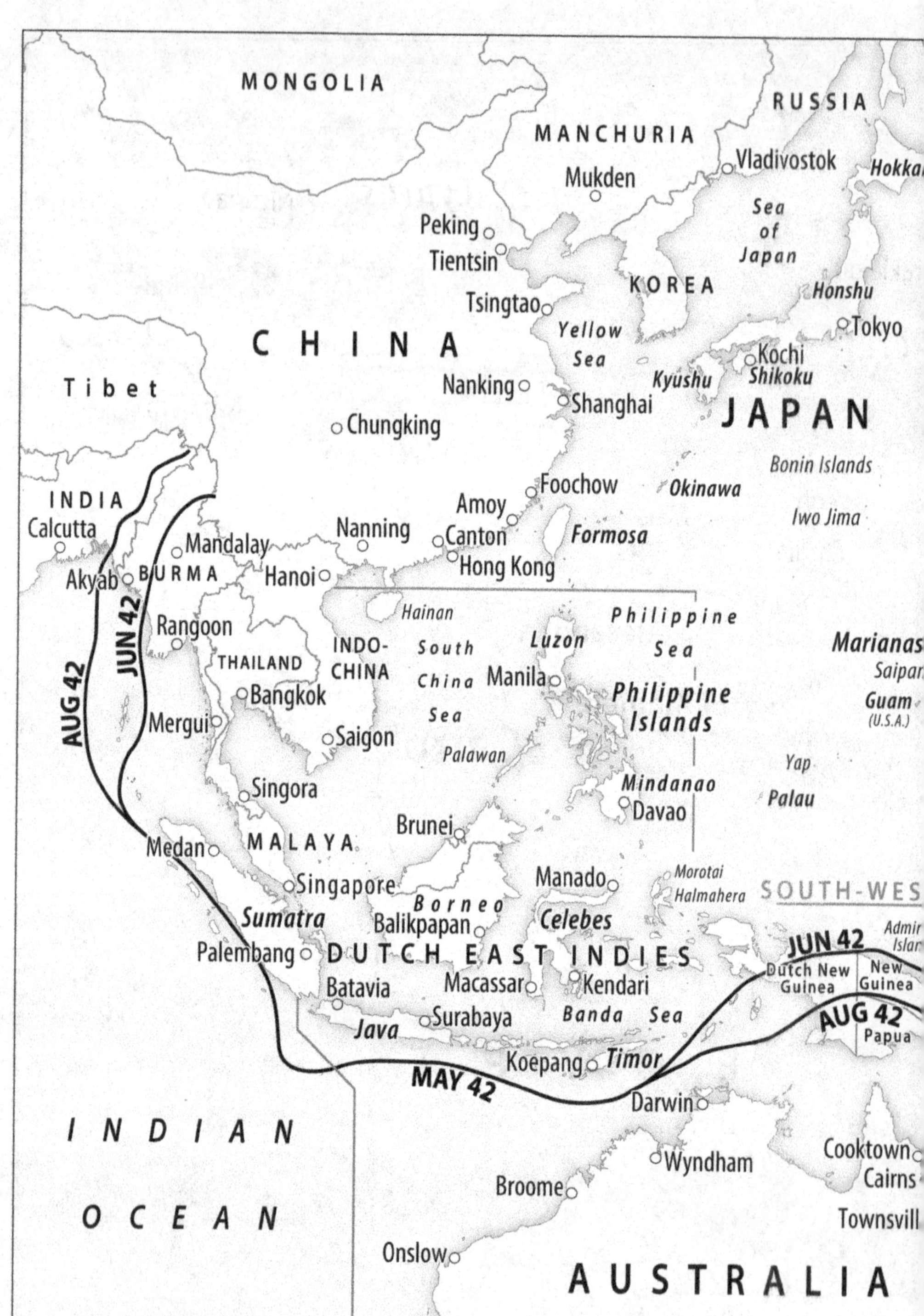

MONGOLIA
RUSSIA
MANCHURIA
Vladivostok
Hokka
Mukden
Sea of Japan
Peking
Tientsin
KOREA
Honshu
Tsingtao
Tokyo
CHINA
Yellow Sea
Kochi
Shikoku
Kyushu
Nanking
Tibet
Shanghai
JAPAN
Chungking
Bonin Islands
Foochow
Okinawa
INDIA
Amoy
Iwo Jima
Calcutta
Nanning
Canton
Formosa
Mandalay
Hong Kong
Akyab
BURMA
Hanoi
Hainan
Philippine Sea
Rangoon
Luzon
Marianas
INDO-CHINA
South China Sea
THAILAND
Saipan
Manila
Philippine Islands
Guam
(U.S.A.)
Bangkok
AUG 42
JUN 42
Mergui
Saigon
Palawan
Yap
Singora
Mindanao
Palau
Davao
Brunei
MALAYA
Medan
Morotai
Manado
Halmahera
SOUTH-WES
Singapore
Borneo
Sumatra
Balikpapan
Celebes
Admir
Islan
JUN 42
Palembang
DUTCH EAST INDIES
Dutch New Guinea
New Guinea
Batavia
Macassar
Kendari
AUG 42
Surabaya
Banda Sea
Java
Papua
Koepang
Timor
MAY 42
Darwin
INDIAN OCEAN
Cooktown
Wyndham
Cairns
Broome
Townsvill
Onslow
AUSTRALIA

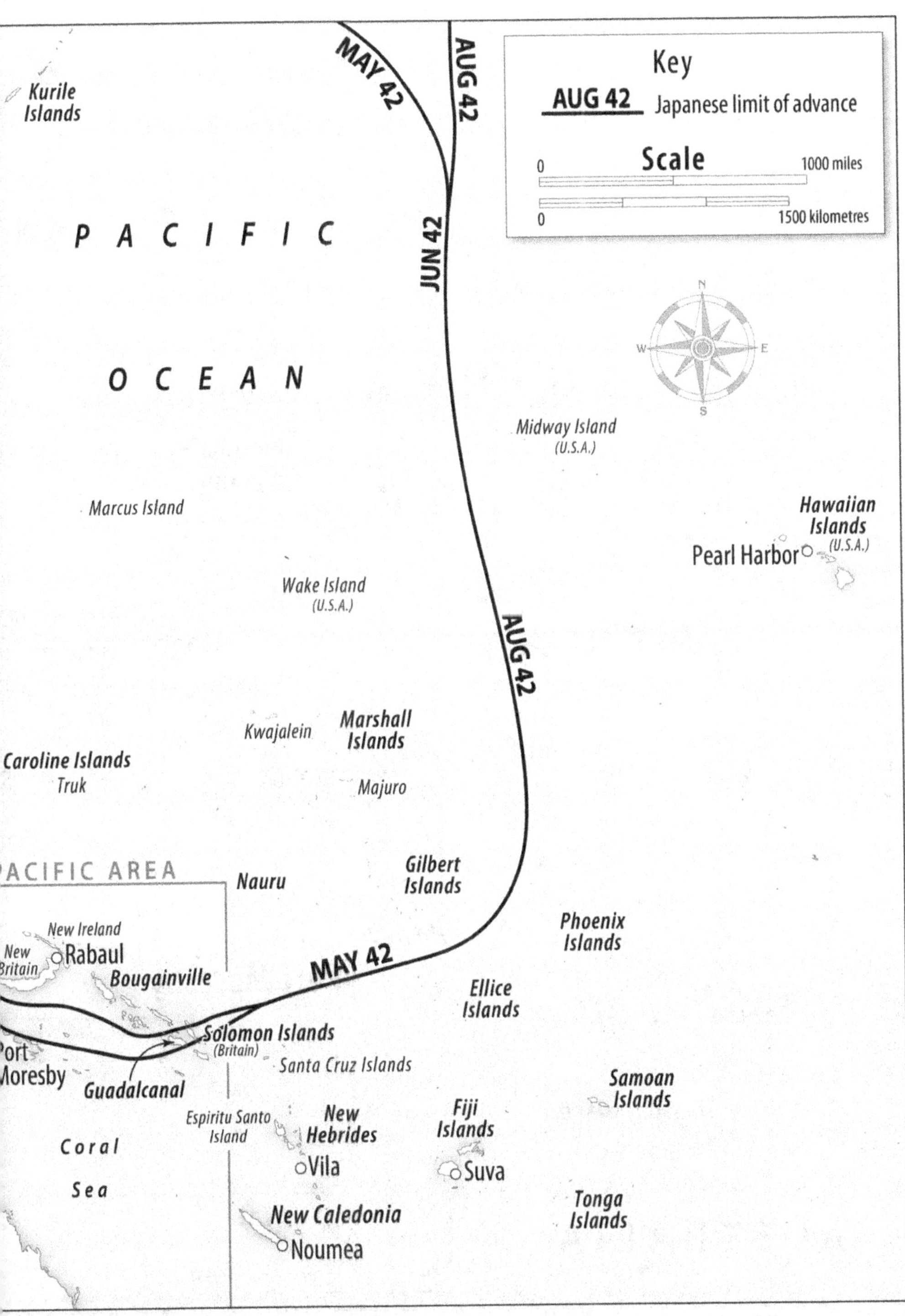
Kurile Islands
PACIFIC
OCEAN
MAY 42
AUG 42
JUN 42
Key
AUG 42 Japanese limit of advance
Scale
0
1000 miles
0
1500 kilometres
N
W
E
S
Midway Island (U.S.A.)
Marcus Island
Hawaiian Islands (U.S.A.)
Pearl Harbor
Wake Island (U.S.A.)
AUG 42
Kwajalein
Marshall Islands
Caroline Islands
Truk
Majuro
ACIFIC AREA
Nauru
Gilbert Islands
Phoenix Islands
New Ireland
New Britain
Rabaul
Bougainville
MAY 42
Ellice Islands
Solomon Islands (Britain)
Port Moresby
Santa Cruz Islands
Guadalcanal
Samoan Islands
Espiritu Santo Island
New Hebrides
Fiji Islands
Coral Sea
Vila
Suva
New Caledonia
Tonga Islands
Noumea

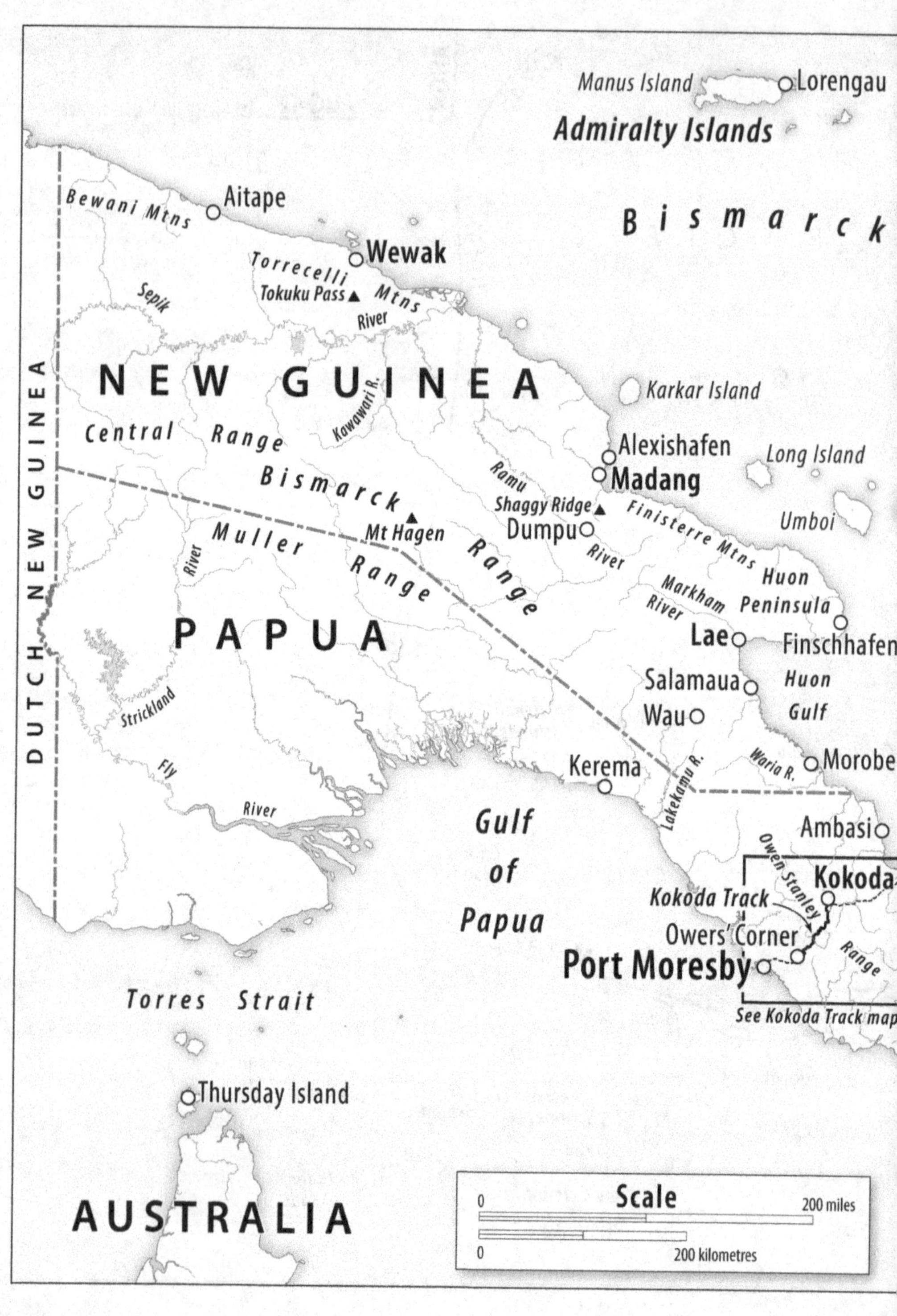

Manus Island
Lorengau
Admiralty Islands
Bismarck
Bewani Mtns
Aitape
Wewak
Torrecelli Mtns
Tokuku Pass
Sepik
River
NEW GUINEA
Kawawari R.
Karkar Island
Central Range
Alexishafen
Long Island
Madang
Bismarck Range
Ramu
Shaggy Ridge
Mt Hagen
Dumpu
Finisterre Mtns
Umboi
Muller Range
River
River
Huon Peninsula
Markham River
PAPUA
Lae
Finschhafen
Salamaua
Huon Gulf
Wau
Strickland
Waria R.
Morobe
Fly
Kerema
River
Lakekamu R.
Gulf of Papua
Ambasi
Owen Stanley Range
Kokoda
Kokoda Track
Owers' Corner
Port Moresby
See Kokoda Track map
Torres Strait
Thursday Island
DUTCH NEW GUINEA
AUSTRALIA
Scale
0
200 miles
0
200 kilometres

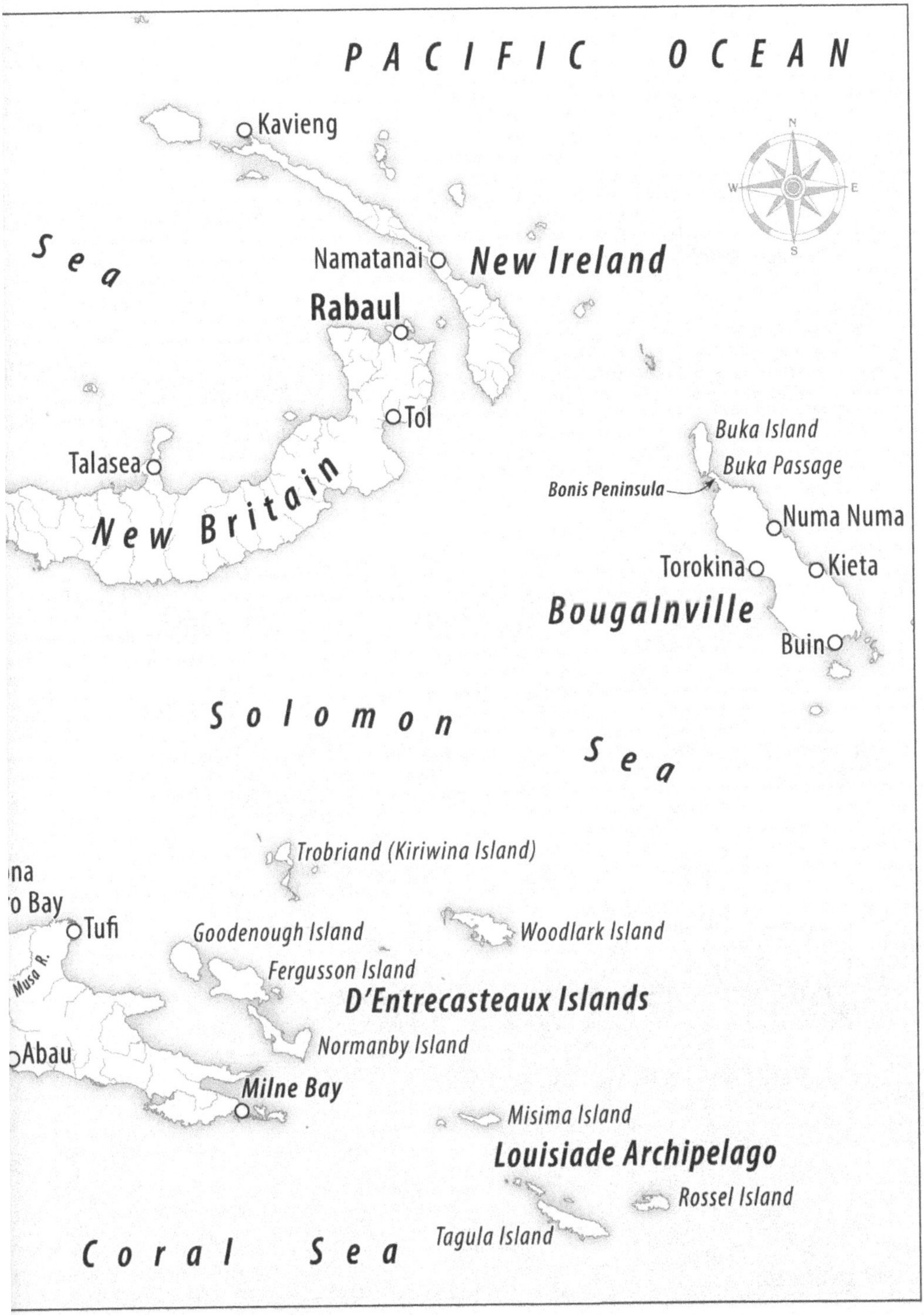

PACIFIC OCEAN

Kavieng

Sea

Namatanai

New Ireland

Rabaul

Tol

Talasea

New Britain

Buka Island

Buka Passage

Bonis Peninsula

Numa Numa

Torokina

Kieta

Bougainville

Buin

Solomon Sea

Trobriand (Kiriwina Island)

na

o Bay

Tufi

Goodenough Island

Woodlark Island

Fergusson Island

Musa R.

D'Entrecasteaux Islands

Abau

Normanby Island

Milne Bay

Misima Island

Louisiade Archipelago

Rossel Island

Tagula Island

Coral Sea

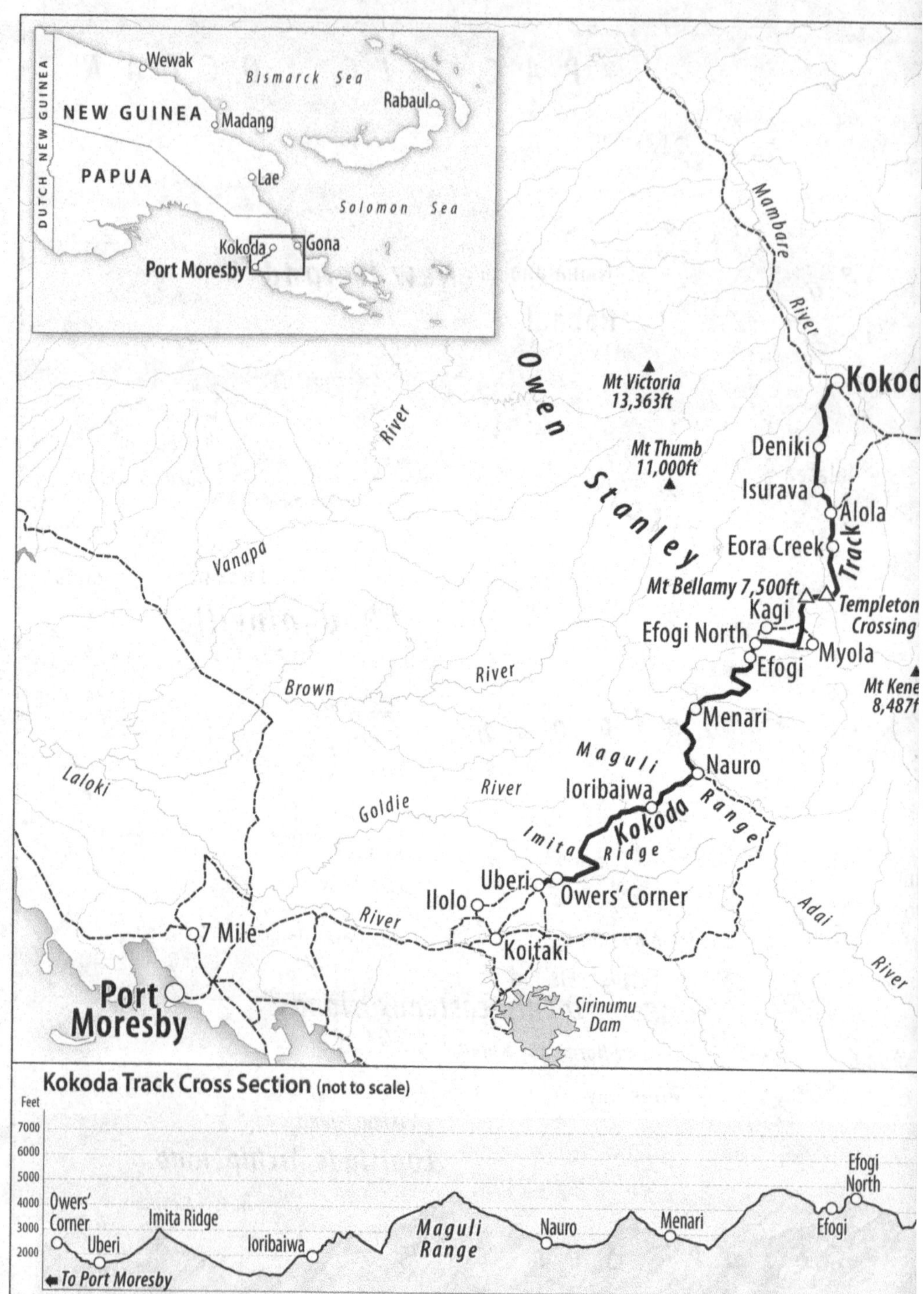
DUTCH NEW GUINEA
NEW GUINEA
PAPUA
Wewak
Bismarck Sea
Rabaul
Madang
Lae
Solomon Sea
Kokoda
Gona
Port Moresby
Mambare River
Kokod
Owen Stanley
Mt Victoria 13,363ft
Mt Thumb 11,000ft
River
Deniki
Isurava
Alola
Eora Creek
Track
Vanapa
Mt Bellamy 7,500ft
Kagi
Templeton Crossing
Efogi North
Myola
Efogi
Mt Kene 8,487f
River
Brown
Menari
Maguli
Nauro
Laloki
River
Ioribaiwa
Goldie
Kokoda
Range
Imita
Ridge
Uberi
Ilolo
Owers' Corner
River
Adai
River
7 Mile
Koitaki
Port Moresby
Sirinumu Dam
Kokoda Track Cross Section (not to scale)
Feet
7000
6000
5000
4000
3000
2000
Owers' Corner
Uberi
Imita Ridge
Ioribaiwa
Maguli Range
Nauro
Menari
Efogi
Efogi North
To Port Moresby

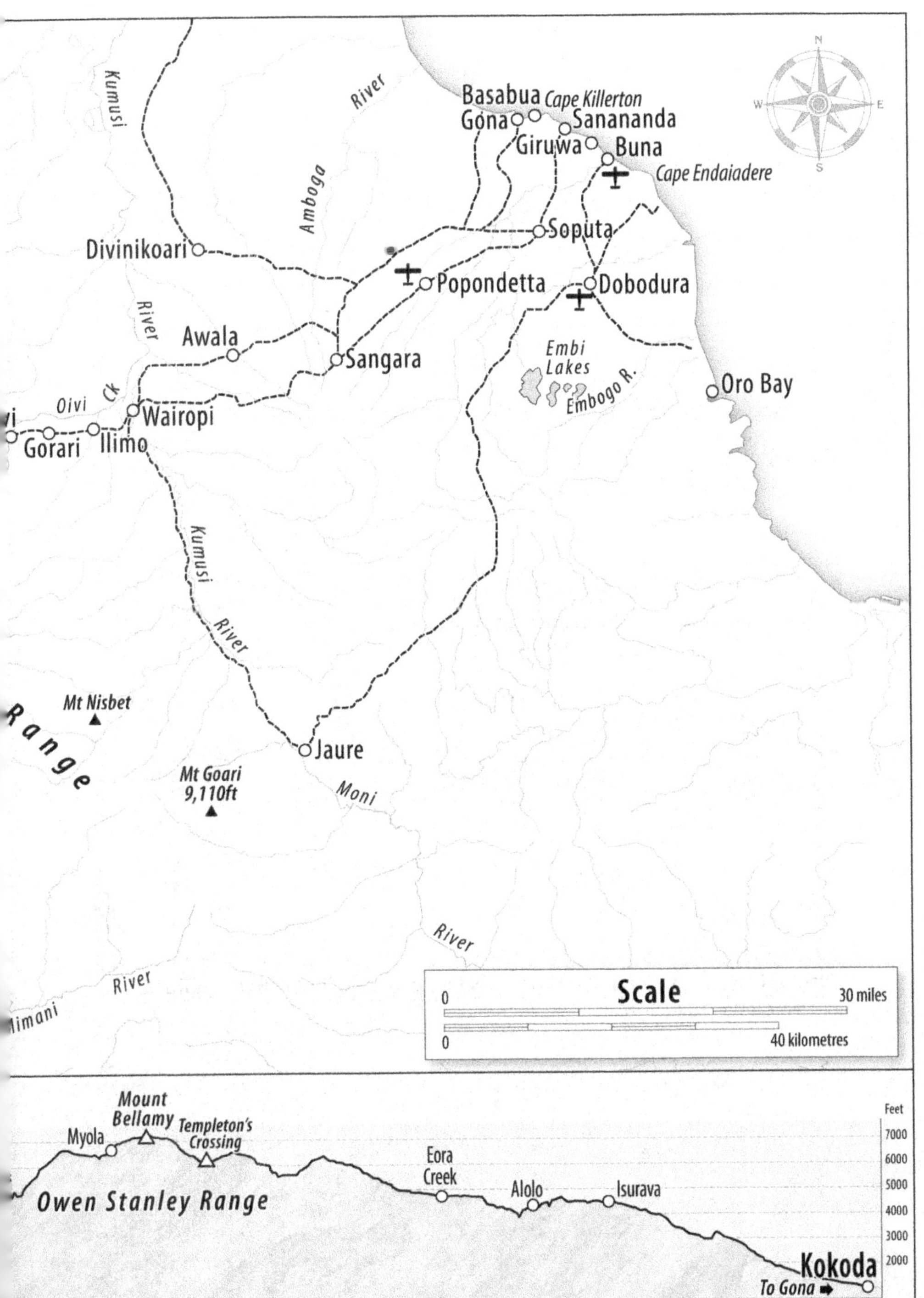
Kumusi
River
Amboga
Basabua
Cape Killerton
Gona
Sanananda
Giruwa
Buna
Cape Endaiadere
Soputa
Divinikoari
Popondetta
Dobodura
River
Awala
Sangara
Embi
Lakes
Embogo R.
Oro Bay
Oivi
Ck
Wairopi
Gorari
Ilimo
Kumusi
River
Mt Nisbet
Range
Jaure
Mt Goari
9,110ft
Moni
River
River
Mimani
Scale
0
30 miles
0
40 kilometres
Mount
Bellamy
Templeton's
Crossing
Myola
Eora
Creek
Alolo
Isurava
Owen Stanley Range
Kokoda
To Gona
Feet
7000
6000
5000
4000
3000
2000

Blamey inspecting part of 7th Division before they head to the Kokoda Track, c. September 1942. (AWM 015714)

INTRODUCTION

Blamey: A Flawed Hero

On 9 November 1942, the 21st Brigade of the Australian Army assembled at the Koitaki cricket field, close to the start of the Kokoda Track in Papua. The field was generally used for recreation, but today the men gathered in a hollow square, on orders from General Sir Thomas Blamey.

They had marched the 37 minutes from the brigade barracks at Sogeri, outside Port Moresby. Anticipation was running high. They knew that two other brigades had recently been reviewed and congratulated by Blamey, and expected that their brigade would also be praised.

It was a month since they had been relieved from vicious jungle fighting on the Kokoda Track, delaying a Japanese advance on Port Moresby. Some 222 of their comrades had fallen in battle, and another 272 had been wounded. A large number had been stricken by malaria and other jungle-borne diseases – probably around 1240 men – and the strength of the brigade was now catastrophically low. What had started as an advance had become a fighting withdrawal.

The 1000 or so officers and men formed up at 3 pm. Sweating under the hot tropical sun, they dressed in their regulation open-neck shirts, shorts and puttees, with hats brim-down to provide a modicum of shade. Blamey had specified that there would be 'NO march past'.

The general arrived 45 minutes late. The assembled crowd were beginning to shuffle.

Opinions vary as to what happened next.

Certainly, Blamey addressed the assembled men in stern tones. Brigadier Ivan Dougherty, who had assumed command of the 21st Brigade just 17 days earlier, recalled hearing a complicated story that first described the enemy as gorillas and finished by describing the Japanese as being like rabbits that had to be driven out of their holes and made to run before the man with the gun could get them.[1]

The men, however, recalled something different. It sounded to them as if Blamey were accusing *them* of having run like rabbits. To top it off, Blamey reportedly growled that *the brigade* had been defeated, *he* had been defeated and *Australia* had been defeated.[2] Journalist Raymond Paull, who interviewed many ex-soldiers, wrote in 1958:

> Blamey's words fell with stunning effect on all ranks, and without exception, they resented every syllable he uttered. The substance of his speech spread like a grass-fire borne on a summer gale. It travelled overnight from one end to the other of the Port Moresby area, and sped along the signal lines to forward troops and scattered outposts. Whatever Blamey hoped to gain by his diatribe at Koitaki is unfathomable.[3]

Blamey's actual words and his intended meaning are lost in the mists of time, but their effect was to diminish his reputation for decades to come. Since the late 1950s, the 'rabbits' incident has grown in prominence and is often the only thing that people remember about Blamey, other than that he commanded the Australian forces in World War II.

Yet Blamey's contribution to Australia's defence was immense. He was our highest-ranking officer ever, commanding our largest-ever army, in which more than 700,000 served. He was called to this position firstly as Commander of the Second Australian Imperial Force (AIF) under British command from late 1939. He continued as Commander in Chief when Australia was threatened by an advancing Japan, while operating under US protection via the capricious command of a much less battle-hardened General Douglas MacArthur. But for Blamey's fine sense of diplomacy in gaining the trust of, and influence over, a series of British commanders and later MacArthur, the Australian Army might well have been subsumed into a foreign command whose overall strategic goals were not the defence of Australia, but defeating an enemy in Europe and Asia. This would have had dire consequences for the troops because Australian officers at all levels would have lost the power to protect them from the often bloody-minded battle demands of British and US commanders.

There is no doubt that Blamey was a flawed hero. For all his diplomatic skills, he could act forcefully and, at times, brutally, creating enemies inside and outside the army. Many of those enemies and rivals have fed the Blamey narrative with an outrageously inaccurate caricature of the general as a fat, drunken, incompetent buffoon. Indeed, a number of contemporary military histories have largely focused on controversial incidents involving Blamey, including the Koitaki parade, but also accusations of drinking and womanising, fraud and corruption. They have also amplified charges of cowardice.

Blamey's tarnished reputation has effectively led some individuals and organisations to 'cancel' him. For example, in December 2024, under pressure from concerned citizens, the City Council of Wagga Wagga, the town Blamey grew up in, transferred a portrait of him from a prominent position in the council chambers to the council museum.

But is his tarnished reputation deserved? How do we judge a commander's performance? By his personality and morals, or by some other measure of success? Prime Minister John Curtin – no fan of Blamey or his political leanings – commented that 'the Government was seeking a military leader not a Sunday School teacher'.[4]

The negative commentary about Blamey has prompted some former and current military leaders to seek a more balanced view. Some of those I spoke to in the course of writing this book were keen that I 'put the record straight'. One recent military leader, General Sir Peter Cosgrove AK CVO MC, has written a supportive foreword to this book.

I hope these advocates of Blamey are pleased with the result. I firmly believe it is his significant military contributions that should define his legacy – that is, how he avoided catastrophic defeats and won battles without wasting the lives of too many of his troops. The Diggers under Blamey had a creditable string of successes in the Middle East and won all their campaigns against the Japanese.

This is not a story that seeks to whitewash the past; rather, it seeks to put the negative issues into context, and question what is required of a successful military leader in his country's hour of need. In my view, Blamey's significant contribution to Australia's military record far outweighs the impact of some of his more questionable behaviours.

* * *

One of my interests is understanding what goes into creating great leaders. I am not a historian, and in compiling this account of Blamey's life and his military achievements, I have relied very much on the work of others – particularly that of historian David Horner, whose biography *Blamey: The Commander-in-Chief* remains the most comprehensive account of the commander in chief. His book – as well as *I Remember Blamey* by his aide-de-camp Norman Carlyon, and John Hetherington's *Blamey: Controversial Soldier* – was a tremendous resource in compiling the sequence of events that occurred in Blamey's life and establishing many of the aspects that contributed to his personality and informed his decision-making.

My interest in Blamey derives from my experiences in business and leadership. My first book was about self-made billionaires. I found no trouble in choosing subjects to study for that book, nor in quantifying their achievements by measuring their wealth, because that kind of performance data is in the public domain. It is not so easy to assess the performances of generals, the criteria for which are murky.

In any endeavour, good leadership is what makes the greatest difference to the results. While that might appear an obvious statement, all too often public attention regarding military efforts is on the men and the action on the ground. To the external viewer, a general's work looks dull, and much of it is. But the most important decisions in a military conflict are made at the various divisional headquarters – and, to an even greater extent, at general headquarters, or GHQ, where the commanding general works.

Quite obviously, a commander's level of responsibility rises with the number of people they command. It also rises in proportion to the degree of freedom they have to make decisions. The consequences of good or bad decisions are much greater when they are made at the top of the hierarchy. Blamey has been criticised for being tough on officers. Yet the hard lessons of war show that if leaders aren't tough, both the results and the troops will suffer. Small errors at the top can compound into catastrophe at the bottom.

Unless it is measured, good leadership can be hard to identify, because when efficient and effective systems are peopled by competent staff, they are taken for granted. Bad leadership, on the other hand, stands out because catastrophe can follow catastrophe. Curiously, soldiers are often poor judges of leadership because they are not aware of the full story: they often confuse likeability, heroic speechmaking or rugged appearance with good leadership, but there *is* no relationship between them.

So, to understand the impact of Blamey's leadership, I have applied the same rigorous methods I used as a senior analytical researcher in the world of business. I always begin by questioning whether a leader, as the head of an organisation, has achieved that organisation's objectives effectively and efficiently.

In the civilian world, high levels of material or labour waste are key indicators of poor management. Combat death rates are an obvious wartime equivalent. By my calculation, Blamey's greatest achievement was saving tens of thousands of Diggers' lives during World War II: much more than the number expected.

I reached this conclusion after applying a typical business benchmarking analysis. The attrition rates of the Allied countries of the UK, the USA, Canada and Australia were compared for both World War I and World War II, making allowance for differences in equipment and tactics between the two wars. (The details of the benchmarking method are outlined in the Epilogue.) Using these performance calculations, I have estimated that Blamey saved 35,000 men: the equivalent of two out of the six Australian divisions that served overseas.

In a book this size, it has been necessary to compress aspects of Blamey's story. In the discussion of his World War II role, I have kept very much to examining Blamey's leadership in relation to the safety and conduct of the men under his command. As AIF Commander and later Commander in Chief, Australian Military Forces, Blamey was responsible for the resourcing, training, logistics, budgeting and other functions of a large organisation, and answerable to senior commanders, politicians and bureaucrats. I have omitted much of the sometimes-rocky negotiation involved, which frequently did not go Blamey's way. It certainly took a toll on him, and often created conflict with Labor politicians ideologically opposed to his conservative values. It also contributed to his lack of support once the war was over, but it is less relevant to an examination of his conduct regarding the men under his command.

* * *

Blamey saved Diggers' lives by applying two cast-iron rules. The first was to keep control of his army. In World War I, the Australian Government ceded too much control of its forces to the British for too long. That lack of control cost Australia significant casualties.

To protect Australian servicemen in the next war, Blamey negotiated conditions with the government that gave him greater authority over the forces under his command. Nevertheless, when fighting overseas, the Australian Army operated as a junior partner to more powerful Allied leaders. In the early years of the war, the Australians were under British command, and later in the war under the Americans. Yet Blamey was generally successful at 'managing up', maintaining cordial relations with Allied leaders in order to win their support for his initiatives, which included dedicated supply and transport for Australian forces.

Blamey's second rule was that battlefield command must receive priority attention. Blamey chose his subordinates carefully, and promoted officers who had demonstrated capability and who shared his purpose and values. Initially, these were all World War I veterans, but later they were recruited from the peacetime officer corps and from the ranks. Blamey's promotions were made with great care and were merit-based. One of his key criteria for selecting officers – as he told a group of his appointees at a dinner at Melbourne's Naval and Military Club in late 1939, just as the first deployments of Australian soldiers were about to embark for war in the Middle East – was that they would look after the troops.[5]

* * *

To fully appreciate the impact of Blamey's leadership, it is critical to understand the context in which he was operating. When Prime Minister Robert Menzies appointed Blamey to lead the army in late 1939, he was not interested in making a political appointment. Menzies not only wanted someone with intelligence and experience, he wanted a commander with toughness and the willingness to take on anyone. Blamey fitted the bill perfectly.

In choosing toughness as a criterion rather than, say, political acceptability, likeability or social standing, Menzies showed himself to be acutely aware that the demands of leadership during wartime are quite different from those required in times of peace. A senior commander's orders affect the lives of thousands of men and women, and the fates of nations. Speed, accuracy, decisiveness and assertiveness are critical skills. Menzies made an inspired choice in Blamey, whose pugnaciousness and capability were well known. When the Coalition government lost power in October 1941, new Labor Prime Minister John Curtin also recognised Blamey's value and retained him as commander.

Blamey's well-known personal habits and interests were not part of either leader's decision. Menzies and Curtin were both aware of the conflicts and scandals in which Blamey had been involved during his time as Victorian Chief Commissioner of Police between 1925 and 1936. They didn't need to like him; they just had to agree that he was the best man to lead Australia's forces during the war.

Blamey was willing to confront anybody to achieve his goals. He stood up to British Prime Minister Winston Churchill and many tough Allied generals, men whose decisions could directly damage his troops. He was aided in this by the authority vested in him by both Menzies and Curtin to make decisions – or appeal to the Australian Government against orders from foreign commanders that, under normal chain-of-command arrangements, he would have had to obey. It was only during the Kokoda Track and beachheads campaigns that his power was completely circumvented. It is hugely ironic that Blamey is widely criticised for slighting Australian troops when in fact he consistently demonstrated an overwhelming concern for the safety and welfare of the people under his command.

Blamey was disliked by various Australian ministers of the day, as well as colleagues and rivals. But it wasn't his job to be liked; he was there to do the nation's work. Blamey kept his job, leading the Australian Army for the whole of the war, under both Labor and conservative governments. This is a great achievement indeed.

Whatever Blamey's faults, nothing should detract from his record as Australia's greatest general, whose primary concern, within the constraints of military operations, was always the preservation of his troops' lives. And surely that is one of the highest accolades a wartime leader can receive.

1

Building Character

1884 to 1914

On a bright September day in 1950, Governor-General Sir William McKell made a special visit to a seriously ill Thomas Blamey in the Heidelberg Repatriation Hospital, in the eastern suburbs of Melbourne. The purpose of McKell's visit was to bestow on Blamey the title of field marshal, and present him with a field marshal's baton in honour of his contribution to the Allies' military success in World War II.

This honour has never been given to any other Australian Army commander. Blamey would never have anticipated, growing up in country New South Wales, that he would one day attain such a rank. Yet there was much in his childhood that contributed to the man he became.

* * *

Take charge, work hard, never complain, never explain and keep going under all conditions. During his hardscrabble rural upbringing, these maxims were etched into Blamey's character.

Life was tough in country New South Wales in the late 1800s, as farmers battled droughts, floods, bushfires and recession. The effects of these catastrophes were magnified for the Blamey family because Thomas's father, Richard, had a knack for business failure.

Richard Blamey was born in Cornwall. In 1861, at age 16, he arrived in Brisbane alone but with high hopes. Yet fortune would elude him his whole life. After odd-jobbing as a coach driver, shearing assistant, shopkeeper and drover, he managed to scrape together enough capital to buy an isolated cattle-grazing property in harsh country where droughts sometimes lasted for years. There he met Margaret, whom he married in 1871. The farm failed, and they were forced to sell up in 1878.

The next move was to another modest and inhospitable property at Lake Albert, just outside Wagga Wagga in the Riverina region of southern New South Wales. Wagga Wagga was a prosperous and growing service town on the banks of the Murrumbidgee River. The area was renowned as one of the fattening grounds for cattle that had been driven from the drought-stricken region to the north. But it was the Wild West, where the last of the bushrangers still roamed. Just after the Blamey family settled at Lake Albert near Wagga Wagga in 1878, Captain Moonlite and his band went through the district and held up 39 people.

Thomas Blamey was born on 24 January 1884, the seventh of 10 children and the family's fourth son.

Although the Riverina was a food bowl, drought, bushfires and low cattle prices put paid to the Blameys' farming venture at Lake Albert and they moved to town when Tom was three.

Richard reverted to work he knew he could do. He assembled a team of horses for contract droving and cartage and did other jobbing work as he could find it. It was a struggle to support his growing family, so the children also laboured to help put food on the table. The effort to overcome adversity put grit into Thomas Blamey's character.

The Blameys' home in Wagga Wagga flooded twice in three years, and both times the family escaped with little more than they could carry. Finally they moved 5 kilometres out of town to a 28-acre block on higher ground. The children walked the long stretch to town every day to attend school.

The Blamey family were deeply religious, attending Wesleyan Sunday school. Around 1892, Thomas and several siblings sat the statewide examinations. Of the five Lake Albert students who passed, four were Blameys, with eight-year-old Tom scoring 91 per cent.

For a family that had achieved precious little so far, religion and academic achievement were a pathway out of difficult circumstances. According to biographer John Hetherington, who interviewed Blamey's brother and son, Margaret Blamey was a cultured and intelligent woman who made learning fun for all the children. Learning became Tom's lifelong obsession, and advancement though exams was the vehicle for his early success. When he was too old for Sunday school, he joined Bible class; at 17, he became a lay preacher and began ministering to local congregations.

Like many high achievers, Tom had few close friends outside his family. His closest companion was his brother Jim, with whom he spent a lot of time riding, hunting and fishing.

All the Blamey children went to the grandly named Wagga Wagga Superior Public School, where exceptional students were often bullied. Nine-year-old Tom, who would later stand up to chief commanders, was playing marbles when two boys, older and larger, tried to get the better of him. Blamey was having none of it. He came out swinging and was giving as good as he got when a teacher broke up the skirmish.[1]

Sport provided the social glue for the town and the school, and Tom Blamey did what was required to fit in. He was a handy rugby player and later played Australian rules football, but he was no star.

Horses were an important part of country life and, according to Hetherington, Blamey was a capable rider and fearless in the saddle. One time the call came that his father needed help, and Tom, at the age of 13, rode his horse alone over 200 kilometres through the blistering heat to reach him. He could read the land, which is a great asset for a military vocation that depends on it. He was also a tenacious horse-breaker, willing to take the hard falls and keep remounting, again and again, until he dominated the spirited animal. In time, his horsemanship would enable him to socialise as an equal with the horse-mad British officer class.

In 1897, Thomas transferred to Wagga Wagga Grammar School, where he joined the cadet corps. At this stage he did not stand out and was not seen as someone likely to make a career in the military.

The Second Boer War began in October 1899, and 15-year-old Tom and 18-year-old Jim were fired with patriotism and yearning for adventure. The pair fronted the local recruitment table to enlist for the army, each adding years to their age.

But the recruiting officer, a local saddler, wasn't fooled. The minimum enlistment age for the war was 20. He sent them back to their mother to grow up.

That same year, Tom passed the New South Wales Education Department's entrance examination to become a pupil-teacher. He took up a position at Lake Albert School and rode to classes on a brumby he had broken in himself.

Two years later, he was moved to nearby Newtown (South Wagga) Public School. It was here that he first took command of a group of cadets when the gentle, elderly staff sergeant took ill. Now in his natural element – in command – Blamey's enthusiasm for leadership came to the fore. He put some bark into the orders and some steel into the drills, and the cadets responded. Blamey's powerful voice made his 1.7-metre frame appear to grow, and it was just as effective when used on cadets in 1901 as it would be on Churchill's generals in 1940.

While Blamey was at Newtown, he became friendly with a cultured teacher named Louis Stone, who would go on to become a novelist. Stone was an important influence on Blamey, introducing him to literature and music, thus adding cultural appreciation to Blamey's intellectual accomplishments and outdoorsmanship. As a result, when Blamey eventually became an officer, he could just as easily mix with refined generals as with common soldiers.

In 1902, Blamey took the Education Department's exam for an advanced training course in Sydney. There were only 25 pupil-teacher places available, and he finished 27th. His next posting, in early 1903, was to a tiny school at Rosewood near Tumbarumba, 86 kilometres southeast of Wagga Wagga.

But there were opportunities elsewhere. Blamey was told by a second cousin, Henry Wheeler, that Western Australia was desperately seeking teachers. Sensing a golden opportunity, he quickly decided to go west, arriving in mid-1903. He was soon appointed as a temporary teaching assistant at the Fremantle Boys' School.

The 19-year-old Blamey passed the exam to become a full-time assistant teacher with honours, and volunteered to be given a difficult, undisciplined class. It quickly became clear that he was both a born teacher and a disciplinarian. With his strong voice and quick tongue, he soon had the class under his thumb.

Not satisfied with just one possible career path, Blamey tested out cadet leadership and Methodist lay preaching, while improving his teaching qualifications and considering a university degree. In the cadets, he attended various camps and began an upward path, firstly training to be a cadet officer and passing his Teacher's Drill Certificate – First Examination. He also considered becoming a missionary because, as he wrote to his brother, he was attracted to the life of a minister. While there was little money to be made, there were other, more meaningful rewards for a devout Methodist.

It is clear that Blamey, from an early age, was drawn to leadership, good deeds and the exercise of power, but not to money. All three career options he tested were based on public service, and had clearly structured hierarchies. All three also offered him the opportunity to project power – or, in modern parlance, to lead.

During the just over three years he spent in Western Australia, Blamey became firm friends with Charlie Middleton, another pupil-teacher from New South Wales. Blamey remained a practising Methodist, which brought certain social benefits. As non-smoking teetotallers, both Blamey and his pal were taken under the wing of a large Methodist family. With them, they enjoyed some good, clean, inexpensive fun, including tennis, boating on the Swan River and camping. Much of their leisure time was focused on the Church. Thomas Blamey delivered sermons from time to time, and threw himself into organising and stage-managing concerts. Making use of his prodigious memory, he recited whole pages of books, error-free, for the amusement of his friends.

His future began crystallising when, in May 1906, the army advertised for young men to apply for a commission in the Cadet Instructional Staff of the Australian military forces. With only five weeks to prepare for the examination, Blamey wired to Sydney for the appropriate texts, which took two weeks to arrive. He got to work, studying hard. Blamey later wrote to his brother Jim that he hadn't gone to bed, or even taken his boots off, for the whole time, and that a number of mornings he had woken slumped over his books.

It was lucky he had such a superb memory. After sitting a marathon 23 hours' worth of exams, Blamey achieved the third-highest score in the nation.

There were only four vacancies to fill, but none in Western Australia; Blamey was denied a place. Incensed at this injustice, he wrote a letter threatening legal action if the unfairness wasn't rectified.

His threats worked – or perhaps it was his sheer gall in sending what appeared to be a professionally prepared letter.

Whatever the reason, Deputy Assistant Adjutant-General Major Julius Bruche was so impressed that Blamey got his commission and soon found himself in Melbourne, being fitted for his lieutenant's uniform. It was not the last time Blamey would resort to using civil law to solve his career problems.

It is interesting to note the similarities between Blamey and other Australian generals – and indeed other high achievers, including self-made billionaires. He was bright, had to fend for himself at an early age and had little attachment to either people or places, making it easy for him to move in order to take up opportunities. Bright country kids in Australia often do this, which gives them an advantage over their more anchored urban competitors. A disproportionate number can be found high up in organisations. Blamey, who was more a rugged individualist than a true outsider, found in the army a place to belong and a structure within which he could advance.

In late 1906, Blamey joined the Administrative and Instructional (A&I) Staff of the Commonwealth Military Cadet Corps in Melbourne. He was now a permanent lieutenant, and with this progression came modest pay and a potential career path. His long and illustrious career in the Australian Army had begun.

* * *

Blamey started in the army as he intended to carry on. He was a relentless worker with a driving ambition to get ahead. Naturally, this didn't make him popular, but it did gain him respect.

Not that the army was much in those days, a mere five years after Federation. It had a few permanent staff officers and a small number of others manning fixed defences, while the balance of the force was made up of part-time militia who were not allowed to serve overseas.

The cadets constituted a national school-based training scheme that acted as a feeder for the army. Blamey's task was to supervise training across Victoria. Teaching and training would be fundamental to his leadership throughout his long military career.

In 1908 and 1909, he studied signalling and military engineering and passed his captain's exam with distinction.

Despite his full schedule, he found time to go courting, and in September 1909 he married Minnie Millard, nine years older than him. Minnie, the daughter of a Toorak stockbroker, met Blamey through the Methodist Church. Their first son was born five months later; clearly Blamey's strict religious practice had waned.

In April 1910, he was transferred to the A&I Staff of the Citizen Military Forces, where he provided instruction and set exams. When his captain's promotion came through in December of that year, he was sent back to the cadets to work in the universal training program. After a short training course with over 200 other inductees, Blamey returned to Victoria as brigade major for the 12th Brigade Area, in the south-east of the state.

In 1905, the British Army had replicated their Surrey staff college in Quetta, in the hills of what was then British India and is now Pakistan. Entry to both staff colleges was by a difficult examination; many experienced British officers passed it only with the assistance of crammers or specialised tutors. As a concession by the British, four Australian officers had already been admitted to the colleges despite failing the exam. Blamey sat the exam in 1911 and became the first Australian to pass and enter a British staff college on merit. He may have crammed, but he did not have the assistance of a crammer, or the luxury of much time to study.

Blamey travelled to Quetta, arriving in mid-February 1912. His wife and son Charles, nicknamed 'Dolf', followed a year later.

Blamey was one of the youngest and least experienced junior officers there. He had no trouble with the course content; the greatest lessons he had to learn concerned the British officer class. All his classmates came from British regiments and were of a higher social standing.

British officers were typically dismissive of 'colonials', but Blamey had a secret weapon: what he lacked in elegance he more than made up for in grit and daring on a horse. The brumby-busting country boy from Wagga Wagga frequently won a leading place in the officers' riding contests.

Since the British were horse-mad and the cavalry was the elite arm of their army, Blamey's riding skills were the social leveller he needed, particularly when accompanied by a few drinks in the officers' mess. Blamey's teetotalling ways quickly went out the window, never to return. He made important connections with men who would soon be prominent figures in the British Army.

His time at Quetta wasn't all outdoor exploits and boozing at the bar, however. Blamey relished hard work and he passed

Blamey (left) as a cadet officer in Melbourne. (Blamey family)

Blamey (seated) and his older brother Jim. (Blamey family)

his course with a B. This was not at all bad for a man who, as his final report from Quetta said, 'came here uneducated (in a military sense)'. The report identified Blamey as 'a self-reliant man who knows what he wants and means to get it'.[2]

Blamey 'passed out' from Quetta in December 1913 with the all-important letters 'PSC' ('Passed Staff College') following his name, indicating that he was a man on his way up the officers' ranks. For an aspiring senior military commander, this was an important milestone.

Following the course, Blamey spent nearly six months in postings to various Indian battalions. He noted that Australians worked much harder on their training in India than the British soldiers did.[3] Training for war, in all its aspects, is one of the key activities of any peacetime army. If an army is not preparing for the next war, there is little point in its existence. It was a sad indictment of the British forces in India if Australia, with its much more limited size and budget, was in better shape.

Minnie had endured her husband's absence for months and now decided that enough was enough. She was missing her family in Melbourne, she had a lively three-year-old son and she was pregnant with their second child. She wanted to go home before Blamey finished his Indian rotation. Minnie and Dolf sailed for Australia at the end of 1913. The family would not be reunited for the best part of six years.

Blamey's next assignment from the Australian Army was to travel to the United Kingdom so he could gain experience with British Army regiments, and he sailed for London in May 1914. En route, he passed through the Dardanelles, catching glimpses of areas of Turkey in which he would soon be fighting.

While passing through Europe, he made expeditions to various historical battlefields; his curiosity saw him arrested by the Germans for being too interested in the strategic fortifications of the ancient city of Metz, on the German–French border. He was held for 24 hours then sent on his way.

After arriving in England, Blamey spent two weeks attached to the Dragoon Guards. He had just begun a series of rotations with the British Army when, on 28 June 1914 in far-off Sarajevo, Archduke Franz Ferdinand of Austria was assassinated.

War was coming to Europe.

2
Hard Lessons
August 1914 to April 1918

By the time Britain declared war on Germany on 4 August 1914, Captain Blamey had found a temporary place for himself on the staff of the Wessex Division as it prepared for its annual camp. Once the five battalions were on the move, Blamey performed the duties of railway control officer at Exeter for over 24 hours, then assisted in setting up camp on the Salisbury Plain. Both activities earned him praise from the divisional commander.

With the war effort suddenly ramping up, there was a demand for capable, unattached officers, and on 20 August Blamey was plucked from the Wessex Division and assigned to the Intelligence Branch at the War Office. In his new job, he worked from six in the morning until 10 at night, six days a week. Once a week, he worked through the night to prepare the daily intelligence report for Field Marshal Lord Kitchener, Secretary of State for War.

Capable intelligence officers were thin on the ground in the Australian forces too, and Blamey's home-country commanders had not forgotten him. Promoted to major, he was ordered to join the first contingent of the Australian Imperial Force (AIF) when it arrived in Egypt in early December 1914. The AIF was a purely volunteer army, separate from but related to the Australian Army. There, he filled one of the three general staff positions for intelligence officers under two levels of Australian command, with the top commander of the Australian and New Zealand Army Corps (Anzac) being British Lieutenant General Sir William Birdwood.

Blamey, now nearly 31 years old, was coolly efficient and unsmiling, an officer who drove himself hard and expected the same of his subordinates. He was not popular, but he was respected.[1] His cool demeanour applied just as much outside the office as it did inside, and a tendency not to fraternise with his colleagues during wartime became evident. Even when he went out on the town in Cairo, he went alone.[2]

When naval attacks failed to secure the Dardanelles Strait for Britain and its allies in early 1915, the British command decided to mount a land invasion of the Gallipoli Peninsula. Birdwood's Anzac Corps was selected to take part.

Major Blamey came ashore at the place destined to be known as Anzac Cove at 7.20 am on 25 April 1915, alongside two other Australian officers, Major General William Bridges, Commander of the Australian 1st Division, and Lieutenant Colonel Cyril Brudenell White. Disembarkation had begun at 4.30 am, and all the men were ashore by 9 am.

As was the case for all soldiers at Anzac Cove, Blamey's life was constantly at risk from Turkish snipers and artillery fire. On the morning of 15 May, during one of Major General Bridges's daily inspections of the front line, a sniper's bullet severed the femoral artery in his right leg. Medical care aboard the hospital ship *Gascon* was inadequate to the task and he died of infection three days later.

Bridges was the first Australian general officer to be killed during the war. Blamey and all his fellow officers could easily have shared a similar fate.

Blamey once crawled into enemy territory at night with two other men in an attempt to locate a Turkish gun position. Their mission was imperilled when enemy soldiers appeared. The Australians dropped to the ground. A Turk stumbled upon one of the men and was about to bayonet him when Blamey killed the Turk with a pistol shot. A wild firefight broke out, but the trio made it safely back to their lines. How many of the enemy they had killed was unknown.

Soon afterwards, Blamey and a Turkish major negotiated a truce so that the dead from that evening's fighting could be retrieved and buried. Hoping to discover how many Turk fatalities there had been, Blamey exaggeratedly claimed that 25 men had been killed. The major responded that the number had only been six. Blamey was doubtless pleased when the major asserted that there had been 25 Australians in the foray, and didn't disabuse him. Blamey was mentioned in dispatches for this operation.[3]

As an intelligence officer, Blamey constantly ranged about under fire to collect information. After he became familiar with the multitude of trench passageways and learned how to avoid the riskiest spots, he was also called on to escort more senior officers to meetings around the dirt maze.

On one such day he was guiding the journalist Charles Bean around the trenches. Bean had been chosen by the Australian

Journalists' Association as its official war correspondent, and would in time become the general editor of Australia's official war history. As Blamey and Bean sidled around the trenches, ducking sniper bullets in exposed places, they came across a Digger with a primitive wooden periscope on the end of his rifle. Bean recorded in his diary that he was inclined to dismiss it as the 'wild brainwave of a man who was rabid keen on keeping out of danger'. Blamey, however, thought otherwise: he could see that the invention had promise and installed the man in a workshop. Prototype testing soon showed that the periscope guns were effective and life-saving, and soon they were in use around Anzac Cove.[4]

This is the earliest reported example of Blamey's career-long passion for adopting technology to save lives and improve efficiency on and off the battlefield. It is also a clear example of how he valued any good idea, no matter who it came from. Blamey would carry this attitude with him into high command in both world wars.

After three months at Gallipoli, Blamey was sent back to Egypt as part of the battle-hardened command nucleus around which the AIF's 2nd Division was to be formed. That division was sent to Gallipoli on 3 September. However, Blamey had a bad case of haemorrhoids that needed medical attention, and he didn't return to Gallipoli until 25 October 1915. He was now Assistant Adjutant and Quartermaster General of the 2nd Division.

The Gallipoli campaign had devolved into static trench warfare, and British command had finally appreciated the futility of forcing more troops into the charnel house that was

Anzac Cove. Blamey was evacuated just before Christmas 1915, as the campaign was coming to its inglorious end.

The campaign, Australia's first of the war, had been a tragedy from start to finish. Between the landing on 25 April 1915 and the final evacuation on 19–20 December, some 50,000 Australians served. Of these, around 8700 men died and more than 18,000 were wounded.[5] Around a quarter of the Australians who died met their end in early August, during the four-day Battle of Lone Pine.

With the apparent willingness of British command to sacrifice Anzacs, it was dawning on the Australians how vital it was that their government should control how their own forces were used. Although Australia was a self-governing nation, it existed within the British Commonwealth, and gaining control of its own military would require time and concerted political effort. As we will see, it took far too long for that effort to be made.

The withdrawal of the Anzac sector without further casualties is considered the most successful operation of the whole campaign. Blamey was responsible for the administrative planning of the Australian 2nd Division's withdrawal. By this time, despite the horrors and futility of the Gallipoli campaign, Major Blamey had gained tremendous experience.

* * *

I Anzac Corps, including Blamey and the 2nd Division, was transferred to the Western Front in mid-March 1916, where the following month it took up position close to Armentières,

France. This location, 250 kilometres north of Paris and 75 kilometres south-east of Dunkirk, was relatively quiet, meaning that the newly arrived AIF forces had time to get accustomed to trench warfare without being subjected to the full onslaught of battle. For this reason, the sector was known as 'the Nursery'.

After three months and a small amount of action, the 1st, 2nd and 4th Divisions of the AIF moved 100 kilometres south, to a more active area around Pozières and Amiens, some 150 kilometres north of Paris and immediately adjacent to the River Somme. During the move, Blamey was transferred to the 1st Division as General Staff Officer Grade 1 (GSO1), under the command of Major General Harold Walker.

Walker had reputedly been the best divisional commander at Gallipoli, known for standing up to his superiors when the lives of his men were needlessly put at risk. This was particularly significant given that the 1st Division of the AIF had the misfortune of being commanded by Lieutenant General Hubert Gough in the Reserve (later Fifth) Army. 'Thruster' Gough was, as his nickname suggests, an old-school cavalry man with a penchant for charging. Unfortunately, charging across open ground obstructed by barbed wire, especially after alerting the enemy with days of bombardment, guaranteed a catastrophically high casualty rate.

Gough did not wait for I Anzac Corps headquarters to arrive and instead took direct command himself. This was problematic, because a properly constituted headquarters in a corps manages everything required to wage war, from the provision of food and uniforms to the complex business

The 1st Division headquarters at Anzac Cove, 3 May 1915. Major Blamey is standing on the right. This position was exposed to shrapnel fire. (AWM G00933)

Colonel Blamey on his horse at Saint-Sylvestre-Cappel, near the Western Front, France, c. May 1918. (AWM E02288)

of coordinating the large number of men. If coordination disintegrates, chaos and catastrophe can ensue.

Naturally enough, in the absence of a proper command structure, order broke down when Australian and British divisions were thrown into the Battle of Pozières in quick succession. Years later, Major General Walker called General Gough's determination to launch a frontal attack 'the very worst exhibition of Army Command that occurred in the whole campaign tho' God knows the Fifth Army was a tragedy throughout'.[6] In his official history, Bean described the fighting as 'in some respects the heaviest they had ever experienced'.[7] Casualties from the Australian 1st, 2nd and 4th Divisions totalled around 23,000 men.

Walker, assisted by Blamey and others, did his best to cope with the poor orders he was receiving in a situation over which he had little control. He struggled valiantly to bring a semblance of order to the chaos Gough caused within the Australian 1st Division. Blamey was central to divisional planning and Walker praised his efforts, saying, in recommending him for a Distinguished Service Order (DSO), that he had a 'clear conception of a situation, and his attention to detail contributed to the success of the Division' in helping take and hold Pozières.[8] Blamey was awarded the DSO on 1 January 1917, and was mentioned in dispatches.

Both Walker and Blamey were deeply frustrated at being under British command. Yet Blamey, as he stoically followed orders that he disagreed with, was learning some hard lessons. As depressing as it was, he understood that it was better for him to remain on the job, doing his best for the men, than to abandon them.

Foul weather during the winter of 1916–1917 in the trenches around the Somme made life miserable. Both officers and men were falling sick in droves. During that bitter winter senior officers were constantly being replaced due to illness.

Blamey agitated to be given a field command. He wanted a chance to command as brigadier, but was denied by General Birdwood because he had not yet commanded a battalion. On 3 December 1916, Birdwood directed him to lead a battalion that was training close to the trenches.

Such was the turnover of officers from sickness and battle that Blamey soon became the acting commander of a brigade. Then, to his chagrin, his career on the front line was aborted when General Headquarters (GHQ) discovered that Blamey had a field command while a less-qualified officer was acting as his staff officer. GHQ's view was that, with a shortage of graduate staff officers, such men should only command in the field if they had performed their staff duties poorly.

Blamey was disappointed to be sent back to the office, but he was promoted to colonel in April 1917, with the promotion backdated to December 1916, disproving his belief that the only route to promotion was direct combat command.

While he no longer had direct command of fighting men at the front, Blamey believed that a good staff officer should get out of the office and walk around. In upbraiding Captain John Rogers, a more junior staff officer, Blamey reportedly said, 'It's not only your job to write orders ... It's your job to see the orders are carried out.'[9] How much walking around Blamey did once he reached the rank of colonel is unknown, but it's likely that he left all but the most critical checks to his subordinates.

By February 1917, the Germans had withdrawn between 15 and 50 kilometres to the defensive position known as the 'Hindenburg Line', a complex of solidly constructed trench fortifications. In doing so, they straightened their line, which allowed them to defend it using fewer men and resources. For a short time the Australians were able to conduct mobile operations as they pursued the enemy's rearguard to the new defensive line.

The Australians were still part of the Fifth Army during the various battles around Bullecourt, and the Diggers were now calling their commander 'Butcher' Gough. The 4th Division was the first engaged, on 10 April, in a force that was meant to be supported by tanks. None arrived and the Australians were withdrawn. Against the advice of General Birdwood, they were ordered in again the next day. This time the tanks did arrive, but they were so poorly made that most broke down before they could get into position to support the troops. Three thousand men in the division were killed or wounded, and the survivors lost their faith in tanks.[10]

On 3 May, Gough tried again at the same location, this time with the 2nd Division. After early success, the Germans counterattacked, as they usually did, and the division was pushed back. Gough ordered them to hold an impossible position. After taking heavy casualties, they were relieved by the 1st Division – for which Blamey was staff officer – and the 1st was in turn relieved by the 5th. The bungled operation of the Second Battle of Bullecourt commanded by Gough cost the AIF 7482 casualties.[11]

Gough was a favourite of Field Marshal Douglas Haig, commander of the British Expeditionary Force (BEF), which included all the British imperial forces on the Western Front.

Gough and Haig were cavalry officers who shared some decidedly pre-industrial views. They were both believers in attritional warfare, the practice of sending masses of infantry across no man's land into the face of an entrenched enemy, in the belief that the enemy would run out of men or morale before they did. In addition, they held the bizarre view that the more casualties their own side incurred, the more it proved that their soldiers were trying. According to this perverse logic, high levels of Australian or British casualties were more likely to win Gough praise and honours than criticism from Haig.

While not in the line of fire himself, Blamey must have felt the almost crippling weight of preparing plans for battles that he knew would result in disaster for the Diggers, and his health suffered. In mid-September 1917, he was sent to England and hospitalised after a bout of coughing and vomiting; he was also suffering from psoriasis, a debilitating skin disease.

He returned to the front a month and a half later. His 1st Division, which had been withdrawn for extended rest after suffering more than 2300 casualties, was fortunate to have missed the catastrophic series of onslaughts ordered by Haig that comprised the Battle of Passchendaele.

Haig's BEF had started as six divisions and grown to five armies. (Generally, an army, consisting of 100,000 to 150,000 people, comprises two or more corps with up to 50,000 each. A corps is made up of two or more divisions, each including up to 15,000 people. A brigade is a third of a division, and a battalion is a third of a brigade.)

Colonial forces were assigned to various armies. In the British way, whole colonial forces or parts thereof were moved around willy-nilly, which was incredibly disruptive to the chain of command. While poor organisation of forces was a serious problem, this was not the main issue at Passchendaele. The main concern was that, after a dry start, the weather turned wet and stormy, leaving the ground hopelessly waterlogged. Haig pushed on against strenuous advice to the contrary, including from Major General John Monash.

Troops fought amid a sea of mud churned up by artillery fire. The quagmire was so deep that men, horses and wagons sometimes sank without a trace. Drownings were commonplace and mobility hideously difficult in the face of hostile fire. By the time the fighting stopped in the late autumn of 1917, the cost was some 250,000 BEF casualties, of which 38,000 were Australians.[12]

Early in 1918, both Walker and Blamey were appointed CMGs (Companions of the Most Distinguished Order of Saint Michael and Saint George) for their work in 1917.[13] Staff officers and indeed senior officers are not often awarded for physical bravery, because that is not part of their remit. Yet, while it is not always obvious, great staff work makes the system run well, and a well-run system feeds into success in battle. During peacetime, poor staff work may just be irritating, but in war it can result in excess fatalities.

Clearly Blamey was attracting positive attention, for within six months he would be elevated to the rank of brigadier general and take up a new position as Monash's chief of staff in the newly formed Australian Corps. Coming under the tutelage of Australia's most successful commander to date would not only be character-building for Blamey, but would also hone his instincts for running wars efficiently and preserving soldiers' lives.

* * *

It was Monash's application of logic, technology and planning that set him apart from most career officers. During his time rising up through the militia hierarchy, he had brought professional engineering practices to military situations.

If he planned and executed badly in his construction business, his business suffered. Monash's business did even better if he innovated, reducing accidents and saving on labour, equipment and time. The more he innovated, the greater the benefits.

A business could not afford to squander its resources, and neither could an army. Monash understood that the conditions on the ground mattered, as did the equipment the men were given. He believed that planning and technology were the weapons that would maximise damage to the enemy and minimise damage to his own force.

This didn't mean Monash was soft on his troops. He understood that their survival depended on their being as tough and as well trained as they could be. Nor did it mean that he wasn't prepared to send men to fight and maybe die. But if they were going to fight, then he believed they must be given the best possible chance of victory and survival. Monash hated wanton losses. A war of attrition was not acceptable to him.

His first experience of battle had come at Gallipoli in 1915. He was appalled, because the campaign was unnecessary, badly planned and wasteful. At the outset, there were no topographical maps and no information about Turkish defensive positions, and that would barely improve during the campaign.

Time and again, the British command – with the Australian Government's acquiescence – ordered ill-planned attacks. Brigadier Monash was too junior to argue and went with his men on these suicide runs. After one such assault, his brigade was reduced from 4500 men to 1750, yet he was ordered to produce more soldiers.[14] He despised the British commanders' contempt for the men at the front, who were condemned to do and die. And those generals seemed as indifferent to their own soldiers as to the Anzacs. Monash pleaded for them to come and see the conditions for themselves, but his invitations were declined; the leaders preferred to observe the battles from the safety of their ships out at sea.

Despite the heated differences he had with the British command, Monash followed orders. Rather than descend into pessimism and defeatism, as some officers did, he developed a characteristic cheerfulness, aided by his determination not to worry about what he'd been ordered to do, because both his orders and the consequential losses were beyond his control.

Blamey had briefly interacted with Monash the day after the Gallipoli landings in 1915, as he escorted him to a meeting of Australian brigade commanders with their senior officer, General Bridges. That first meeting between Blamey and Monash had left little impression on either man. They likely bumped into each other around the trenches and dugouts, but there wasn't any particular attraction.

At Gallipoli, Monash had been in the thick of the action and had been exceptionally lucky to survive unwounded. Many of the middle and lower ranks of officers had been killed and replaced by those in still lower ranks. In that uncompromising situation, promotions were virtually self-selecting. If a lower-ranked soldier took over from his fallen superior, there was a strong probability that he would be promoted to the position permanently.

When replacing field officers, Australians gave little weight to class or education; what mattered was performance under battle conditions. And Gallipoli had been the toughest possible test of competence. By the time the Australians had been evacuated, two-thirds of the officers in the AIF had been promoted from the ranks.

As author Roland Perry has observed, the British looked askance at this class-free promotion system, claiming that bank managers and people with degrees couldn't be commanded by working-class men.[15] In the British system, men of a lower social rank rarely, if ever, became officers.

Unhappy with the Australian losses at Gallipoli, which were soon replicated on the Western Front, the government began pushing for overall Australian command of its army. As an interim measure, it was agreed that all Australian divisions should be led by Australians. The British would continue to command above division level, so they could still do as they pleased with the structure of the force, how and when it was deployed, and the battles it fought.

The AIF was expanding at this time, and needed experienced leaders. As the size of the AIF doubled, existing combat units were broken up and reformed, with a core of experienced men retained to absorb and train new recruits. Officers from experienced units were identified and put in charge of novice units.

With British support – principally that of William Birdwood, under whom he had served at Gallipoli – Monash was promoted to major general in July 1916 and appointed leader of the new Australian 3rd Division.

Monash began preparing the division in England. His recruits arrived fresh off the boats from Australia and had to be trained from scratch. He constantly winnowed his officers, moving them on if he perceived any lack of performance. Importantly, Monash had no truck with politics or privilege: one former state politician was summarily fired for incompetence and drunkenness. The British made requests to break up the division and send Diggers to the front, but Monash rebuffed them all.

While in England, Monash familiarised himself with modern weapons developments, including artillery, aircraft and the still very unreliable tank. His training manoeuvres were considered masterful by the British, who sent 120 generals and senior officers to learn from him. He impressed with his use of clear planning and debriefing, among other things.

Monash demanded his officers do everything possible to protect the men in battle, and stressed that they should not be used as machine-gun fodder. His men had to be well fed and equipped. Most of all, he emphasised, clear and accurate communication was essential: every man had to know exactly what he was meant to do in every contingency. There was to be no haziness, as there had been in Gallipoli.

These were fine principles, but it would be some time before Monash was senior enough to control the timing or circumstances of the major actions in which his force was involved. The whole of the Australian force was grappling with the same problems.

* * *

The 3rd Division moved to France in late 1916. Monash was fortunate that his division was attached to General Herbert Plumer's Second Army because Plumer held similar views about planning, technology and the treatment of soldiers. The two men and their staff officers quickly established a rapport.

Senior staff of the Australian contingent were shuffled around in January 1917 and Monash became the most senior commander of the five AIF divisions in France. Monash and the 3rd Division were posted to a relatively quiet sector, close to the Belgian border. Monash broke with the official media blackout and distributed printed news reports among his soldiers to build their *esprit de corps*. Monash's division had the lowest crime and illness rates of all the Australian divisions.[16] The division's losses were relatively light and morale was high.

Plumer included Monash in the preparations for the Battle of Messines in June. After a huge cache of explosives was set off to devastating effect at 3.10 am on 7 June 1917, Monash's men had control of their target within 45 minutes and consolidated the gain during the day. It was the first major victory of any Australian division in the conflict.

As Monash's star continued to rise, his men, alongside the only New Zealand division, were put back in the line at Passchendaele to attempt a second success. The divisions were ordered to go over the top on 9 October 1917. Monash, ever the engineer, understood exactly what would happen to the battlefield once the autumn rains arrived. Whole platoons, stuck in the mud and caught on barbed wire, were obliterated by artillery and machine-gun fire. Some even drowned in the quagmire. Good planning by Monash could only do so much to lessen the much larger impact of bad planning by Haig.

From July to October 1917, the BEF lost 250,000 men for a gain of 8 kilometres. Even though this gain was in fact large by previous standards, the price paid was too high, and the tide of opinion began to turn against Haig.

Australian soldiers had been put into the hottest battles, and disproportionately high numbers had been killed all along the Western Front. Not even rigid censorship at home could conceal the horrendous losses from the public.

* * *

In September and October, Blamey, as we have seen, was recuperating from illness in England. The 1st Division had gone on the attack without him on 20 September 1917 and had great success at the Battle of Broodseinde on 4 October. His position was filled for about a month by Colonel John Dill, and then by Major John Lavarack, until his return on 7 November.

Lavarack stayed on until December, but evidently unhappily: he and Blamey developed an enmity that would play out during the next war. As author Brett Lodge writes in *Lavarack: Rival General*: 'their time serving together would have provided opportunity enough to establish that, although both were able and professional, they were essentially different in character and so the chance of any deep rapport developing between them was remote'.[17]

The Hindenburg Line went quiet over winter, with both sides resting and regrouping, before the Germans began a spring offensive, Operation Michael, on 21 March 1918. The Germans attacked through the Hindenburg Line and the Allies were pushed back. Monash was ordered to bring his troops back into the line. Lacking information about the battle site, he personally went on reconnaissance forays to the front, coming close to being shot a number of times.

The Australians counterattacked on 25 April 1918, Anzac Day, and retook the small town of Villers-Bretonneux, capturing 1000 prisoners. This was considered by many to be a turning point in the war, because it demonstrated that a relatively small band of soldiers could beat the German Army.

With intransigent optimism, Haig had been betting that his peculiar philosophy of attritional warfare would defeat the Germans. It was because of Haig that sending out infantrymen to charge at enemy trenches was still the primary method of warfare, even if the land was so waterlogged that soldiers and horses drowned in it.

British Prime Minister David Lloyd George had become so disillusioned with the BEF's performance that he planned to dismiss both Haig and Gough. He eventually relieved Gough of his Fifth Army command but demurred on removing Haig, concerned that he had too much public and political support.

On 26 March 1918, France's Marshal Ferdinand Foch was appointed Supreme Allied Commander, which put him in charge of all Allied forces, including the BEF. Yet since Haig remained at the head of the BEF, this compromise made little difference to the men serving under him.

For the Australians – and indeed for all servicemen on the Allied front lines – the real change would come when Monash, ably supported by Blamey, developed and employed a highly effective new way of defeating the foe.

3

Monash's Apprentice

June to November 1918

While they might not have realised it at the time, 1 June 1918 was a momentous day for the Diggers on the Western Front. That was the day Monash became commander of the new Australian Corps, which brought together Australia's five infantry divisions on the Western Front. That day, the Diggers gained a leader with enough influence over the British command to change the way things were done, a leader who was devoted to the task of winning while saving the maximum number of Diggers' lives. And win they did, consistently and in spectacular fashion. So much so that Monash's innovations would provide the template for winning the war.

Blamey was by Monash's side for the whole of that time, breathing life into his plans. He would develop a very close relationship with his commander, who, like him, was somewhat aloof. Within a short time, Monash was writing to a fellow Australian general that he and Blamey 'get on most excellently'.[1] Blamey shared Monash's vision of using planning and technology to win with minimum casualties. Indeed, so closely did they work together that it is not possible to say which innovations were Monash's and which Blamey's, or indeed which came from elsewhere.

Innovation is a critical capability, but even more important for Blamey were Monash's lessons on how to 'command up' – in other words, to persuade the more senior commanders of the alliance to order sensible and timely actions. Blamey would take the Monash ethos into the next war.

In taking command of the Australian Corps, Monash was promoted to the rank of lieutenant general under the British Fourth Army commander General Sir Henry Rawlinson. Monash was now the highest-ranking officer in the Australian Army.

Consolidating the Australian forces into a corps under Monash made a difference in three important ways. Firstly, Monash now had sufficient rank and power to influence high command. Secondly, he was now privy to high-level intelligence. Thirdly, with that intelligence he could identify and propose campaigns. Monash immediately set about influencing the course of the war, proposing actions to Haig through his commander, Rawlinson.

Monash kept the five-man executive team he had inherited from Birdwood. All but one were Australian. Since the corps was now an Australian force, most of the high-level British officers left, although a number remained in artillery and logistics positions, along with some American engineers. Eighteen of the 20 high-level officers were Australian citizen-soldiers (men who were not part of the permanent army before the war started).

As he set up his command, Monash insisted on diversity, mixing experienced career officers with more recent promotions. Blamey would do likewise in World War II.

Blamey had been chosen by Major General Brudenell White to replace White as Brigadier General of General Staff (BGGS) when he transferred to the Fifth Army. Blamey joined White as an understudy on 15 May and formally took on his role on 1 June. While Blamey was not officially chief of staff, Monash used him in that role, giving him the job of organising staff throughout the corps.

Attitudes to Blamey varied considerably. Official historian Charles Bean observed that 'his capacity was outstanding and no other available officer of the general staff in the Australian divisions had anything approaching his experience'. Bean added that perhaps Blamey's only failure was an absence of tact.[2] Birdwood thought Blamey 'an exceedingly able little man, though by no means a pleasing personality'.[3] Corps Chief Engineer Brigadier General Cecil Foott found Blamey 'a pleasure to work with', because he consulted the heads and the branches of the corps extensively about any operation under consideration. He understood what was required and made sure everyone else did too, then left them to get on with the job.[4] Those of the lower ranks were not so sanguine. Lieutenant Jack Stevens, signal master of the corps HQ, called Blamey 'brusque and inaccessible', someone who would not accept excuses when errors were made.[5]

According to John Hetherington, Blamey worked 'sixteen hours a day, sometimes longer ... He was absorbed in the study of ... detailed experiments in parachute dropping of ammunition to isolated posts, in the evolution of tactics that succeeded in the most spectacular manner. In short, he was playing no small part in digging the grave of the German Army.'[6]

But it wasn't all work for Blamey. His search for relief from stress also gained him a reputation for playing hard. He was renowned for boozing, womanising and frequenting Parisian brothels. He was often seen in the same pleasure places as other soldiers. Some Diggers approved, others didn't; it didn't matter to Blamey. Monash, who himself had a mistress in London, certainly had no objections.

* * *

With new authority, Monash began planning his first solo operation, the Battle of Hamel. It would be a relatively small engagement, involving around 7000 men, mostly Australian infantrymen and some US servicemen too. It also included British tanks and more than 600 British and French artillery pieces. The assault had limited geographical objectives: capturing the village of Le Hamel and the surrounding area. But it would have important consequences, as Monash's battle plan would demonstrate effective new tactics for attacking an entrenched enemy that would serve as a model for the remainder of the war.

Not surprisingly, Monash the accomplished engineer treated the campaign almost as he would a huge engineering project. To the extent that he could, he assessed the condition of the ground and developed his plans accordingly. To gain more information about the enemy's disposition, Monash innovated by pressing aeroplanes into service to photograph the terrain, then developing maps that showed every enemy trench, gun and strand of wire, along with geographic features.

Consistent with his belief that every soldier should know what they were doing and where they were going, Monash had huge topographical models made of the attack zone, which large numbers of troops were able to study prior to battle. This was important not only for the fighting men but also for the porters and medical staff, who had the difficult and dangerous job of delivering a huge amount of materiel to the advancing troops and carrying out wounded men on litters.

In what had already become his standard practice, Monash held planning conferences. He later wrote that 'very great importance was attached to the holding of conferences, at which were assembled every one of the Senior Commanders and heads of Departments concerned in the impending operation. At these I personally explained every detail of the plan, and assured myself that all present applied an identical interpretation to all orders that had been issued.'[7] While Monash's was undoubtedly the key voice, he was happy to take suggestions, particularly from Blamey, whose role was to integrate the components of the overall plan. Monash considered all criticisms and ideas, but he made the final decision. Importantly, he refused to consider late revisions, no matter how tempting, which allowed his commanders to plan their attacks with confidence.

Constantly on the lookout for any psychological or technological advantage, Monash explored the use of the recently improved Mark V tanks. His plan was for his infantry to advance under a 'creeping barrage' of artillery fire that moved forward in small increments, just ahead of advancing troops. The tanks would then follow in support. If the infantry encountered local resistance on the way, be it entrenched enemy or physical barriers such as wire entanglements, the soldiers would lie down and summon the tanks to clear it as planned.

Monash was acutely aware that the Diggers of the 4th Division had been badly let down by tanks at Bullecourt more than a year previously: the failure had been related to poor reliability, inexperienced tank crews and poor coordination with the infantry forces. Both services would need to work together more effectively; to achieve this, Blamey organised tactical learning sessions.

The Tank Corps set up a realistic mock-up of a battleground, with trenches and barbed wire. Infantrymen of the 4th, 6th and 11th Brigades were bussed to the ground and spent the day working with the tanks, rehearsing tactics. The role of the Tank Corps would be to follow closely on the infantry, ready to be called into action if the way became blocked by wire, trenches and gun emplacements, and so on.[8]

Perhaps all the camaraderie left the British tank commander feeling a bit cocky, for he proposed that the army dispense with artillery fire altogether. Blamey and the field artillery commander opposed this vehemently, saying in a memo that victory in the upcoming battle was certain with artillery and no tanks, but that the reverse was very *un*certain.

On 21 June, Monash had his plan for taking Le Hamel approved by a somewhat sceptical Lord Rawlinson, commander of the British Fourth Army. Monash set the attack for 4 July 1918, the Americans' Independence Day. After some negotiating, it was agreed that 1000 US troops would take part.

The day of the attack started much like any other day for the Germans, with a pre-dawn artillery barrage. But it wasn't like any other attack day. There had not been the usual days of intensive extended bombardment, intended to soften up the enemy but which in fact alerted them to an impending attack.

As the British tanks came up to their starting positions, their sound was masked by 600 Allied guns shelling the enemy. The barrage intensified just after 3 am, and the troops and tanks advanced under their creeping barrage. Elsewhere in the line, diversionary raids and barrages were coordinated to disguise the main event. Monash had even arranged for imitation German signal flares to be fired to confuse their artillery.

The innovations and decoys worked. The tanks, operating under control of the infantry, proved themselves valuable. Planes dropped bombs and provided updates on the forces' progress, while ammunition supplies were dropped by parachute to speed up delivery and save the lives of porters. In addition, older tanks were pressed into service to deliver ammunition and supplies up to the moving front, reducing the normally expected number of 1200 porters while increasing the speed at which materiel was distributed during the battle. In addition, Monash experimented with deceptions to confuse and demoralise the enemy. For example, he innovated with artillery fire that mixed coloured mustard gas bombs with normal artillery rounds. When he launched a raid or attack, he removed the mustard gas from the coloured bombs so his men were able to attack without their cumbersome masks, but the Germans were fooled into keeping theirs on, and so were much less effective.

The result was the first modern battle, in which all services worked together in a coordinated fashion.[9]

In addition to his meticulous pre-action planning, Monash also engaged in extensive post-action debriefing. He believed that the opinion of a private could be just as valuable as that of a general, so he consulted broadly. Without fear or favour, he learned what went right and what went wrong.

A short time after the battle was won, Blamey commented to Charles Bean that the idea for staging the battle at Hamel had been his.[10] This might sound arrogant, but it was common for trusted senior officers to propose campaign opportunities to their superiors. Naturally, the senior officer took the credit if the campaign succeeded, because they carried the risk of its failure. Blamey and Monash would have been discussing where to stage an ideal battle to test his ideas. Le Hamel fitted the bill, particularly as a battle in that location was conceptually simple. But it was not simple in execution, and they spent a great deal of time planning every step. This was a new and untested concept: a surprise attack with shelling starting just before the attack got underway, incorporating close coordination of all arms and using innovations to protect infantry and porters with tanks to clear the way and transport materiel. So if they made mistakes in implementation and failed to deliver the promised results, they would likely never get a second chance.

Monash had used every means at his disposal to confuse and shock the enemy. According to Bean, 1600 Germans were taken prisoner.[11] Monash was particularly pleased to see that his coloured gas deception had worked, because half of the captured Germans were wearing gas masks. The Battle of Hamel, although not a large encounter, was unusual in that the attacking side lost fewer men than the defending side, and the ground captured wasn't lost again.

Before the battle, Monash had claimed that Le Hamel would be captured in 90 minutes. In the event, it was accomplished in 93 minutes. On the Australian side, there were 1062 casualties, including 800 killed, while the Americans suffered 176 casualties, with an estimated maximum of 26 killed.[12]

* * *

Monash became a hero along the Western Front and in England. His annotated orders of the day were published and distributed to all Allied commanders, and he was visited by a constant stream of Allied commanders and non-Australian press. Because of Australia's severe censorship rules, however, he was not feted in his own country.

The British commanders were not the only ones learning from Monash's methods. The French, too, had observed the outcome of the battle and began coordinated attacks with aircraft, tanks and artillery, with great success.

Although more German troops were fast arriving, the German infrastructure was now struggling to absorb them, and at long last the German spirit was beginning to crumble, which spurred on the Allied effort.

The Monash command had grown to nearly 160,000 men, which, at its peak, was comprised of five Australian divisions of some 110,000 men[13] and two US divisions consisting of a total of 50,000 soldiers.[14] Monash and Blamey were now actively included by General Rawlinson and his chief of staff, Major

General Archibald Armar Montgomery-Massingberd, in their planning for the next campaign. Blamey and Montgomery-Massingberd worked closely on the detailed planning, and the latter had only praise for the Australian's efforts.

The Battle of Amiens was launched on 8 August 1918, as part of a major Allied offensive spearheaded by Australian and Canadian corps. It would not be a set-piece battle, as the Battle of Hamel had been – limited and pre-planned – but a running battle, ongoing and unpredictable, with the aim of piercing the German front and pushing forward as far as possible.

Maximum surprise was required, so the build-up of the force was carried out with all the guile Monash could muster. The roar of tanks being brought up to the line was disguised by the noise of aircraft flying close to the German trenches. The artillery was set up without any preliminary registration fire.

It was a shock to the Germans when the 550 Australian big guns opened fire at 4.20 am in the thick morning fog, followed close behind by a casualty-saving, leapfrogging infantry attack behind a creeping barrage. By 7 am it was already clear that the attack had been a success.

When the order to halt came, the Australians had advanced 12 kilometres on a 7-kilometre front; the Canadians' achievements had been similar. The Allies had punched right through the German lines and opened a gap of some 24 kilometres. This was another attack with a lower casualty rate for the attacker than defender: the Australians lost 2000 men and captured 7925 prisoners.[15]

The attack had incorporated many of Monash's and Blamey's innovations. Monash was once more the man of the moment and was made much of by Allied commanders. Marshal Foch came to pay tribute. Speaking to Monash and Lieutenant General Arthur Currie, commander of the Canadian Corps, Haig was so overcome that he broke down in tears. The King came to France and, on the steps of his field headquarters, elevated Monash to Knight Commander of the Order of the Bath: Monash's second knighthood.

Despite the celebrations, the war wasn't over. Monash had to keep planning and fighting, but the tactics he had developed – with considerable input from Blamey – had become a partial blueprint for the British Expeditionary Force.

Monash's men pushed on to take Peronne and Mont Saint-Quentin. By now, these battle-hardened soldiers were operating as a close-knit team. More than eight Victoria Crosses were later awarded for bravery. But their exuberant heroism came at a price: there were 3000 Australian casualties, including 600 dead.[16] The Germans fell back to the Hindenburg Line, their position before their break-out in March. By the time the Australians had taken Mont Saint-Quentin on 3 September 1918, they had captured 14,500 prisoners and 170 guns.

The Australian part of the Amiens campaign climaxed in the attack on the Hindenburg Line. Again Monash innovated, this time causing chaos behind German lines as a battalion of Rolls-Royce armoured cars raced around firing at the enemy's rear areas. While it didn't do much damage, the tactic spread uncertainty and fear: such penetrations are usually a signal that the front has collapsed and the rear will soon be overrun too.

As the Allies began fighting along a wider front, their tanks were spread more thinly, so Monash doubled the number of machine guns to compensate. He later recounted what he was told by one captured German battalion commander: 'The small-arms fire was absolutely too terrible for words. There was nothing to be done but to crouch down in our trenches and wait for you to come and take us.'[17] The Nazi field marshal Erwin Rommel would use the same tactic to great effect in World War II. Recognising that the Australians were tiring, Monash ordered the last of his countrymen out of the front line on 5 October 1918.

Monash was rightly proud of his corps' achievements. His five divisions had defeated around 39 divisions of the enemy. According to Monash, the Australians had taken more than 29,000 prisoners, and liberated more than 116 towns over 394 square miles.[18] There is no reliable estimate of German fatalities, but later figures indicate that around 45,000 Germans at Amiens were killed or wounded by all Allied forces.

The Australian dead between 8 August and 5 October totalled nearly 5000 and the wounded just over 16,000, which Monash claimed was extraordinarily moderate, given the strenuous nature of the fight and its the great results, and in comparison with the disastrous losses of previous years.[19] Monash also calculated that, in terms of prisoners, territories and guns taken, the five Australian divisions achieved around 2.4 times the results of the 53 British divisions at Amiens.[20]

The Amiens attack contributed significantly to the nervous breakdown suffered by defeated German leader General Erich Ludendorff, and thus to the breakdown of cohesive German command. Ludendorff reportedly said later that the first day of the battle was a black day for the German Army.[21] It was at about this time that the German high command gave up hope of winning the war.

After their set-piece success at Le Hamel, there had been much conjecture about whether Monash and Blamey could plan, execute and win a running battle. The evidence was in: they could, and would continue to do so.

Even though the press in England saw the victory at Amiens as a British one, Monash was lionised in London for breaking the years-long deadlock on the Western Front. The Australian troops under Monash took part in three victory parades in the British capital.

Censorship spared Prime Minister Billy Hughes from having to laud Monash – a man he believed might become a political rival – for his victories in 1918.[22]

* * *

The war years had been an incredibly formative time for Blamey. He had experienced the powerlessness of being ordered by high command into horrific, pointless battles in which his soldiers were ordered to do and die. Then, like opening a door onto another, more benign world, he had had the rare good fortune to become the understudy and protege of a great leader. He had learned a great deal about command, innovation and how to save the Diggers.

Most of all he had discovered the value of achieving power beyond that conferred by rank. The ground-breaking win at the Battle of Hamel had set the standard for the series of winning battles that led to the end of the war.

This gave Blamey a powerful precedent. In World War II, he would successfully strive to put these principles into effect.

Lieutenant General Sir John Monash (seated) posing for a photo with senior Staff Officers of the Australian Corps at Chateau de Bertangles, near Amiens, France, in July 1918. Brigadier General Blamey is in the centre of the back row. (AWM E02750)

4

Between the Wars

November 1918 to October 1939

When the armistice bringing the Great War to a close was signed on 11 November 1918, there remained a great deal of work to do.

Australia's focus was primarily on shutting down its operations in Europe and bringing its men home. Prime Minister Hughes remained concerned about the attention being showered on Monash, and conspired to keep him away from Australia for a further year, assigning him the job of repatriating the troops. Monash's aspirations were in fact more modest than Hughes suspected: he hoped to take over the permanent leadership of the AIF but had no political ambitions. Nevertheless, with Blamey at his side, he loyally took to his new role. The repatriation proceeded with typical Monash–Blamey efficiency. Much more efficiently, in fact, than Hughes had wanted, because there was little work at home for the returning servicemen.

Meanwhile, there was ignominy ahead. As was traditional in the British Army, to which the Australian Army was beholden, promotions earned during wartime were not retained in peacetime: those who had been promoted were expected to be slotted back into their pre-war rank without protest.

Blamey had entered the war as a major and so he reverted to that rank. If he remained in the service, he would be in for a long, dull grind, working daily for more senior but less capable officers. Worse, some of his subordinates during the war would be his time-serving superiors in the peacetime hierarchy. Unless something changed, Blamey's future in the Australian Army looked intolerable. To add insult to injury, he had been left off the honours list for a Companion of the Order of the Bath (CB), an award second only to a knighthood.

Blamey was aggrieved and, being combative, took the unusual step of protesting both slights. In a letter to Monash, he wrote: 'I shall no longer be able to work either in the same relative standing as regards colleagues as at present.'[1] With Monash's support, he was almost immediately installed as a permanent lieutenant colonel and put back on the list for the CB. This was not the brigadier general's rank he had held during the war, but it mollified him for the time being. Later in 1919, he finally received his honours in acknowledgement for his role as corps chief of staff. He was also awarded the French Croix de Guerre and was mentioned in dispatches twice more, bringing his total number of mentions to seven. The delay in rank and honour was brushed off by the British as a 'clerical error'.

Blamey was discharged from the AIF on 19 December 1919 and returned home to his family, who were now living in the Melbourne suburb of East Malvern. Dolf, by this time aged nine, had only a vague recollection of his father. Young Tom, aged five, had never met Blamey and was somewhat overawed and a little frightened by this strange man. Blamey's friends noticed a change in his demeanour. He was much more serious and sadder than the enthusiastic young officer who had left for India eight years previously.

Blamey re-entered the Australian Army as a full colonel. He was made Deputy Chief of the General Staff to Major General Brudenell White, on the understanding that he would step into that position when White retired. He considered this arrangement fair, because White had outranked him throughout the war.

In January 1920, the Australian Minister of Defence, Senator George Pearce, called a conference of five senior officers, Monash among them. The purpose of the conference was to review the wider aspects of Australia's defence. Blamey wasn't senior enough to be consulted, but he was tasked with managing the conference and reporting its outcomes. It found that while Australia's security was still tied to that of the British Empire, it must have the ability to hold an invader at bay until help arrived from the British.

The senior commanders had Japan in mind as the most probable threat. The Treaty of Versailles following the war had not given Japan all the territory it wanted; nor did the final treaty include a provision affirming the equality of all nations, as Japan had urged. In addition, the Japanese military was rapidly becoming an independent political force, and was aggressively increasing its capability. As a result, Japan had begun expanding its empire, capturing German territories in China and the Pacific. The conference recommended that Australia develop a national force of 180,000 servicemen, organised into divisional headquarters with permanent staff.

Blamey was put in charge of military intelligence, army signals and the Directorates of Operations and Military Training. He was particularly interested in military intelligence. Among other things, this involved national security matters, including the always-important business of tracking illegal immigrants, espionage, counterespionage, and dealing with fifth columnists and revolutionaries, particularly the burgeoning communist threat following the Russian Revolution in 1917, and the newly identified threat from Japan.

He also served on an interservice committee with responsibility for forming a separate Australian air force. At the Washington Naval Conference between late 1921 and early 1922, attending nations agreed to limit the number and size of their battleships. The Australian Government, which was already struggling under war debt, savagely cut into the personnel numbers and equipment of its navy and its army. Having reduced its pool of officers, thus perpetuating its reliance on Britain, the Military Board (the army's governing body) decided to fulfil a request from the British to send them a senior man who could speak with authority on Australian matters. So, in late 1922, Blamey headed to England with his family as Australia's representative on the Imperial General Staff, fully expecting to be made chief of Australia's general staff when he was recalled.

The British military, however, was undergoing much the same sort of painful transition as the Australian military, and little work of note was being carried out. Blamey found it to be moribund, with his position lacking in purpose. Never one to sit on his hands, he expanded his watching brief, working his contacts from the war as hard as he could and relying on his reputation as Monash's former chief of staff.

His major interest concerned the evolving military arrangements for the defence of Singapore, especially the naval base that was due to be built there. According to Britain's 'Singapore strategy', should the Japanese attack any of its territories in the Pacific – including Australia – a Royal Navy fleet would make its way from Britain to the new base to mount a defence. A decade earlier, in his major essay at Quetta, Blamey had argued that such an attack was 'unlikely except in the case of complication in Europe. In this case naval assistance in the Pacific may not be available.'[2] Blamey also assessed that the Japanese were capable of defeating the British fleet in Asian waters. His conclusion was that the British simply could not defend Australia against the Japanese.

Blamey continued to expand his network of contacts and keep up with the latest military thinking and practices. As always, he was interested in the most recent technological advances, and closely followed developments in wireless and signalling, motorised transport, aircraft, anti-aircraft guns, and tanks.

In mid-1923, Major General Brudenell White was persuaded to retire as Chief of the General Staff (CGS). Blamey became anxious that he would not be given White's position, particularly as others were campaigning for it. Opposition to his appointment centred on the fact that Blamey, as a colonel, was junior to at least seven rival officers, whose appeals to politicians invariably stressed their senior rank and underplayed Blamey's superior experience.

White managed to salvage half the job for Blamey by convincing Prime Minister Stanley Bruce to split it in two.

When Blamey returned to Australia in early 1925, he was given the more junior CGS role.

The senior CGS, Inspector General Sir Harry Chauvel, was not likely to step down anytime soon, and even then Blamey might miss out on the role. That, along with the fact that the army was still in steady decline, forced him to rethink his position.

Idling in a defunct organisation with limited opportunities for advancement, Blamey began making good on his 1919 threat to move to greener pastures.

* * *

Late on the evening of 31 October 1923, a third of the Victorian Police Force went on strike. This was the latest episode in a long-running dispute over pay and conditions. During the strike, more than 600 police officers were dismissed as mutineers and never re-employed by the force.

With too few police on duty, there were riots, looting and violence in central Melbourne. The rioting was especially bad over the weekend of 3 and 4 November, ahead of the running of the Melbourne Cup on the Tuesday. Three people died and a tram was overturned. The culprits were not criminals but opportunistic young men and boys out to make mischief, perhaps having consumed too much Cup Carnival cheer. As an immediate result of the police strike, the army was called in – but, aside from guarding their own property, they declined to help contain the civil disorder.

Monash had retired from the army in 1920 and was asked by the Victorian government of Harry Lawson to organise a volunteer constabulary force, composed mainly of returned soldiers, to restore order. This force was placed under the command of Major General Sir James McCay. It restored civil order and remained in service until mid-1924.

In the meantime, the Nationalist Victorian government had given some ground on police employment conditions, but it botched getting the force back to full strength, refusing to reinstate the dismissed men and rushing the recruitment of others. Public confidence in the police was at rock-bottom.

In 1924 Monash was commissioned to review the Victorian Police Force. His damning report, delivered early the next year, pointed to the failings of the incumbent chief commissioner, Alexander Nicholson. Politics being politics, the incumbent's tenure was extended, but as fate would have it, he fell ill in late 1925 and resigned. With the vacancy open, the decision was taken to appoint the best man who could be found from *outside* the force.

Monash worked strenuously behind the scenes to get Blamey appointed. There were a few tense moments as Blamey sought to negotiate the inadequate salary up to an agreeable level, but he was duly appointed Chief Commissioner of the Victoria Police on 1 September 1925. Blamey was not to have an easy time of it; his years as commissioner would be politically and economically turbulent. He would serve under eight premiers and nine Victorian governments, and be required to keep the peace during the upheaval of the Great Depression and the rise of a militant Australian Communist Party.

Almost before he had warmed his seat, Blamey became the centre of a public scandal. In October 1925, during a raid of a sly-grog shop that doubled as an illegal brothel, his uniquely numbered service badge was found. The man in possession of the badge was not charged, and the badge was posted back to Blamey.

Inevitably, this juicy bit of scandal was leaked to the press and Blamey was accused of, among other things, being a patron of the brothel. It was all very exciting for the media, and the story wouldn't go away, even as the government backed Blamey in his denials.

Offered an open public inquiry, Blamey opted instead for an investigation to be carried out by two detectives. The detectives confirmed that, although he had been out earlier in the evening, Blamey was at home at the time of the raid. Blamey said he had lent his badge to a friend who wanted some alcohol from his locker at the Naval and Military Club.[3] He refused to name the friend and the man was never identified.

The fact that the investigation was carried out in-house and so was potentially subject to interference by Blamey left enduring suspicions that it was a cover-up, and that Blamey himself had been caught during the sting.[4] The matter would plague his tenure as Police Commissioner, and throw up moral criticisms of him that persist to this day.

Putting the drama behind him, Blamey rolled up his sleeves and set about rebuilding the police force.

Reformers are rarely popular. Inevitably, the changes they introduce disrupt entrenched power structures, leaving them with a fight on their hands. This proved to be the case for Blamey, who found the situation as chaotic as Monash had warned him it would be.

Being a great believer in benchmarking, he discovered that the ratio of officers to people in Melbourne was well below that in Sydney, which in turn was well below that in New York or London. He constantly agitated for greater numbers of recruits. He had some success in this, against the backdrop of a rising crime rate, probably due to the volatile economy and increasing unemployment. Intent on raising standards, he introduced rigorous training for new recruits, with examinations at the end of the first year.

When he took the job, police pay was well below that of a labourer, which inevitably affected the quality of recruits the force could expect. It also raised concerns about corruption, because there was a clear temptation for officers to augment their incomes by selling information or favours. Blamey argued hard for wage increases for his officers, but he had to fight with the government of the day. It would take him 10 years to bring police wages in Victoria up to a suitable level.

He also worked to improve non-monetary conditions for his men. Innovations included a benevolent fund, partly paid for by the proceeds of an in-house discount store, and the establishment of a police hospital. As we have seen, Blamey's war command had convinced him of the importance of up-to-date technology, so he embarked on a program to modernise police equipment. Wireless communication was introduced, along with high-powered patrol cars and motorcycles.

The issues Blamey pursued as Police Commissioner influenced the kind of army commander he would become during World War II. Yet he was about to discover that the leadership style that had worked for him as a wartime

Victorian Police Commissioner Blamey (second from right) with police vehicles and officers, c. 1936. (VPM7836)

commander on the Western Front did not work nearly as well in a peacetime democracy.

Blamey didn't care what anybody thought of him, and consequently often rubbed people the wrong way. Particularly dangerous was the fact that he did not care what the press or politicians thought of him. Those in the Labor Party considered him an agent of the establishment, and so did not trust him. His attitude to his own public image and his way of reforming earned him many enemies, whose resentment would dog him for the rest of his life.

Blamey had improved the quality of the police force's recruits, but things became more difficult when, in early 1929, he moved to introduce a merit-based promotions system, to replace the existing time-serving model. This obviously had benefits for talented staff, for the organisation and for the public. However, there was a substantial number of powerful officers in senior positions who weren't very capable and who were used to being promoted because it was their turn. These officers needed to be displaced if Blamey were to make room for the more capable younger officers.

Unfortunately, playing politics was not high on Blamey's agenda. He rammed through the changes without consulting the Police Association, which predictably made both it and the soon-to-be-displaced senior officers hostile.

With an election looming, the Police Association instructed its members to vote for the Labor Party, despite the fact that endorsing a political party was a direct contravention of its role according to the *Police Regulation Act*. The Labor Party duly won government in December 1929, and it repaid the Police

Association for its support by suspending Blamey's police seniority changes, pending review.

Blamey's tenure was due to expire in 1930, and he expected it to be renewed without discussion. But Premier Edmond Hogan was not enamoured of Blamey's command-and-control approach to industrial relations, and he declared the position of Chief Commissioner of Police vacant. The government also substantially reduced the salary for the position.

Ever pugnacious, Blamey reapplied, and after a drawn-out and somewhat humiliating process he was reappointed. The following year, with the Great Depression biting government revenues hard, his salary was again reduced in line with public service austerity measures.

This public humiliation and the obvious challenge to his authority enraged Blamey, who went to war against the Police Association. Invoking the *Police Regulation Act*, he declared the Police Association an illegal organisation and instructed its members to resign. Its civilian secretary was charged, convicted and sentenced to a month's jail, which was reduced on appeal to a fine. Blamey introduced merit-based pay and sent the poorly performing senior police to the outer reaches of the state.

Naturally, all this further enraged both the government and the broader union movement, and Blamey was branded anti-Labor. The Labor movement has a long memory, and Blamey's relations with it would remain fragile for the rest of his life. The enmity of the political left would dog him later, when Labor was in power in Canberra too, and especially when left-wing politicians held key wartime portfolios.

The situation was hardly improved by Blamey's heavy-handed approach to the communist threat and his tendency to turn a blind eye to police violence during demonstrations. According to his biographer John Hetherington, Blamey did not understand the art of compromise. If he wanted something, he would destroy everything in his way in order to get it.

Naturally, this is not the way to make friends and influence people.

* * *

Meanwhile, Blamey had not abandoned the army altogether. Taking on the role of Chief Commissioner of Police had meant that he was forced to resign from the permanent army and go on the Unattached List. But soldiering was his first love, so he had immediately joined the Citizen Military Forces (CMF), often called the militia: part-time reserve units of the Australian Army, organisationally separate from the permanent regular army but answering to the same command. Although he was vastly overqualified for the role, Brigadier General Blamey had taken command of the 10th Brigade on 1 May 1926, for which he was paid a modest stipend.

In 1931, Major General Harold 'Pompey' Elliott – a distinguished war veteran and Commonwealth senator who commanded the CMF's 3rd Division – suicided, most likely as a direct result of post-traumatic stress disorder from his experiences during the Great War. Blamey was promoted to major general and took over Elliott's command while still leading the police force.

By the early 1930s, as the Great Depression took hold, the world was beginning to look like a more dangerous place. There was great unrest and nations were mobilising their military forces. In September 1931, Japan invaded the Manchuria region of China, and from March 1932 began a series of border conflicts with Soviet Russia.

Blamey's move to the militia was to his advantage, as he ducked the unpleasantness experienced by permanent army officers as a result of constantly diminishing budgets, cuts in manpower and consequent squabbling between service chiefs and federal politicians. While Blamey had a national reputation, his political problems were largely confined to Victoria.

When Monash died in October 1931, however, Blamey joined the federal government's Council of Defence, whose membership included several senior AIF commanders. Blamey's accession to the position over officers with greater seniority was never explained, but most likely it was due to Monash's influence. The council, which had been inactive since the Great War, barely met before 1929, and not at all from 1929 until 1935, but membership meant that Blamey retained the stamp of approval from the giants of the old guard.

In 1932 the Victorian Labor government resigned and a government led by the conservative United Australia Party, under Sir Stanley Argyle, was installed. A young politician named Robert Menzies became Deputy Premier. It is not known whether Blamey and Menzies had any direct professional contact at that time, but as conservatives in Melbourne they would have been well known to each other. On 15 September

1934, Menzies was elected to the federal parliament and quickly became Attorney-General of Australia and the Minister for Industry in the government of Joseph Lyons.

As the pressures of the Great Depression eased in the mid-1930s, civil unrest declined and Blamey's salary reverted to its previous higher level. With fewer external demands, the Chief Commissioner of Police was able to resume his reforming task. He continued to work hard, having taken only seven days' leave in five years. There was plenty to do and he thrived on the challenge.

Consistent with his belief in rewarding achievement, Blamey recommended that the police be paid for their efforts during the centenary celebrations for two of Victoria's foundational events: the establishment of the first white settlement in Victoria on 19 November 1834, and the founding of Melbourne on 8 June 1835. The extensive festivities would encompass more than 300 events during the nine months from October 1934 to June 1935.

Blamey's recommendation to award the police back pay was accepted. Blamey himself was knighted on the recommendation of the Argyle Government in 1935.

During these years, though, Blamey had experienced two personal tragedies. His eldest son, Dolf, had graduated from the Royal Military College, Duntroon, and had been in the Royal Australian Air Force for two years when he tragically died in an aeroplane crash on 6 December 1932. Blamey was extremely fond of Dolf, and the young man's death affected him deeply. He remained sentimental about his son and kept a photograph of him until the day he died.

The second tragedy was that Blamey's wife Minnie had suffered worsening illness since 1930. Her condition became chronic and she died in October 1935.

But further distress, of an entirely different kind, was coming the following year.

* * *

It was the practice of newspaper correspondents to ring or visit police stations for their news scoops. Some journalists disrupted police work as they roamed around as if they were in their own workplace. This also created an opportunity for critical information to leak, often in return for payment. The talkative police got publicity and other rewards, while the more discreet did not.

Blamey did not like uncontrolled access by the media at all. In November 1935, he appointed a publicity officer to field queries and issue daily press releases. Simultaneously, and without warning, he denied the press direct access to police stations and police officers. All press requests now had to go through the centrally controlled press office.

The news outlets didn't like the new arrangement one bit. There were heated exchanges between the press and Blamey in the media, and eventually Blamey sued for libel. He won the suit, but he had made yet another powerful enemy, which would be ready to pounce next time he slipped up.

On the night of Friday, 22 May 1936, an incident occurred at Royal Park, Parkville, that would scandalise the city of Melbourne. Police Superintendent John Brophy, the head of the

Criminal Investigation Branch, was waiting for an informant in a car, accompanied by a driver and two female friends. The group was set upon by two masked assailants; Brophy fired two shots but the assailants got away after inflicting three wounds on him. He was taken to hospital and, keen to protect the force's reputation and keep the presence of the women secret, made the improbable claim that he had shot himself by accident three times.

Blamey visited Brophy the next day, then told the newspapers Brophy's preposterous story, leaving the women out as instructed. The papers weren't buying it, and correctly judged that Brophy had been attacked by crooks. The following Monday there was a more in-depth newspaper report, and a police spokesperson released information to the press, withdrawing the statement that the shooting had been an accident and confirming that Brophy had been attacked by robbers. Blamey then wrote a report to the government on 28 May, in which he repeated Brophy's robber story. The press had a field day. There was speculation as to who had been responsible for the inaccuracies and why.

But for yet another change in government, Blamey might have toughed out this incident as he had others. Yet just over a year earlier, in the Victorian election of 1935, Stanley Argyle's conservative government had been replaced by a Country Party government headed by Albert Dunstan, who formed a coalition with Blamey's old enemies in the Labor Party. It was now open season on Blamey. With the government, the Police Association and the press lined up against him, he didn't stand a chance.

The government was so keen to dispense with Blamey that it called a royal commission into the Brophy affair a mere fortnight after the event. Commissioner Hugh Macindoe called 44 witnesses, including Blamey and Brophy.

Ultimately, Commissioner Macindoe found nothing amiss with Brophy's behaviour. He was sympathetic to Blamey's attempt to protect the reputation of the force but put it to Blamey that he had lied in his initial press interview. Blamey maintained under oath that he had not set out to deceive the press. The commissioner tried to move him from that implausible stance by asking him if he felt justified in issuing an untrue statement to the press to protect the reputation of the force. Blamey became pig-headed and was unwilling to answer yes or no. Had he not been so headstrong, he could have corrected his statement, justified his actions and suffered only mild embarrassment. He did not, and the commissioner had no choice but to find in his report that Blamey's replies were not strictly in accordance with the truth.

Despite the furore, no one could establish how Blamey would have made any personal gain from the deceit. (There are rumours, accepted by author Roland Perry,[5] that Blamey was in the car with Brophy that night, both of them accompanied by prostitutes, but most historians adhere to the story revealed at the royal commission.) It might have been a lie for the right reasons, but Blamey had been caught out. What made all the difference was that the lie was made under oath.

There were no legal ramifications for Blamey, but word got back to him that the government had lost confidence in him. A King's Council friend urged him to resign. The friend warned that if Blamey were dismissed, it would put an end to any prospect he might have of leading the army or achieving any other high office. Blamey had a phone conversation with a member of the government in which it was confirmed that it was seeking to remove him. For once, he resisted the urge to fight back and resigned on 9 July 1936.

Blamey had been a change agent at the Police Force of Victoria, and such people inevitably stand on many toes as they renovate their organisation. They are trouble-shooters, not people made for managing the steady state. It speaks volumes about Blamey's toughness of character that he had remained as a reforming head of the Victoria Police for 11 years. But his time was up and he had to go.

Blamey took the loss of his job hard. Whenever he spoke about it in later years, he would mention that it might have been character-building. That may be true, but it was a double blow for Blamey to lose both his high-status job and his Police Commissioner's salary. He applied for compensation for holidays he had not taken and for rent allowance, and settled for slightly over half of the value. He had superannuation, some savings and a small rental income, plus his CMF stipend. Even so, he was earning less than a third of his previous income. While he was hardly living rough, his reduced status was a shock for a man used to far better circumstances.

Time now hung heavy for Blamey. While a few people had stood by him, he was shunned by people he had considered friends. He tried his hand at writing for newspapers but had no success. He attempted to become a politician and approached the United Australia Party, whose conservative manifesto aligned with his values, but failed twice to be accepted by the UAP. His public reputation was too hot to handle. He toyed with going into business but was undercapitalised, and was not really interested in business anyway. And he had no chance of getting a Victorian Government board position while Albert Dunstan remained Premier.

The 3rd Division had occupied some of Blamey's time since 1931, but his command ended on 31 May 1937 and he was once again added to the army's Unattached List. It is not clear whether he kept his stipend. At least he could indulge in fishing, his favourite recreational pastime.

* * *

The clouds of personal misfortune finally began to part for Blamey in early 1938, just as the worldwide political situation was deteriorating rapidly. Five years earlier, Adolf Hitler had become Chancellor of Germany, and would annexe Austria and the Sudetenland in 1938 then invade Poland in August 1939, precipitating World War II. Germany and Italy were involved in the Spanish Civil War between 1936 and 1939. In 1937, war had also begun between China and Japan.

The Council of Defence had been reconvened in 1935, which had put Blamey at the heart of the strategic discussions about the looming threat of war with Germany and Japan. For the first time, it also put him in direct contact with Frederick Shedden, the council's assistant secretary, who would soon be a driver of Australian policy as Secretary of the Department of Defence. Shedden would become a great supporter of Blamey.

Another of Blamey's few loyal friends, Alfred Kemsley, the general manager of Melbourne radio station 3UZ, convinced Blamey to broadcast a series of Sunday-night talks on international affairs – but anonymously, under the name 'The Sentinel'. Kemsley, a veteran of the Australian Corps, had become concerned about the complacency of Australians in the face of the growing belligerence of both Germany and Japan. This dovetailed with Blamey's own view – and he was pleased to have the extra income.

The broadcasts started in March 1938 and continued for about 18 months, until just after the outbreak of the European war in September 1939. Blamey's subjects included the Germans' role in the Spanish Civil War; Hitler's rise to power; Hitler's manifesto, expressed in his book *Mein Kampf*; and German expansionism. He also paid attention to the Sino–Japanese conflict, explaining Australia's vulnerability to a southward move by the Japanese. Only when the broadcasts finished was it revealed that 'The Sentinel' had been Blamey.

In September 1938, in a decision influenced by Shedden, Blamey was appointed Chairman of the Manpower Committee and Controller General of Recruiting. Thus Shedden ensured that Blamey would be seen by politicians and the public as being close to the centre of war planning. The committee's role was to expand Australia's militia forces and develop a system that ensured men with critical civilian skills were not enlisted. The Recruiting Secretariat that Blamey would also lead would assist in this task. In the year to March 1939, the recruitment effort headed by Blamey would double the size of the militia to 70,000.[6]

Around this time Blamey, now 54 years old, met Olga Farnsworth, a 35-year-old fashion artist (an important occupation in an era before fashion photography became widespread). They married on 5 April 1939 and rented a house at 486 Punt Road, South Yarra, not far from Melbourne's Royal Botanic Gardens. Their home was nearly opposite the historical house 'Airlie', which had been owned by a series of rich families before the war. From 1942, at Blamey's suggestion, an intelligence unit called Z Special Unit, tasked with organising secret raids against the enemy, would use 'Airlie' as its headquarters.

The Blameys always lived well. Blamey bought whisky 9 litres at a time and rented a year-old Oldsmobile car.

* * *

As war loomed, a great deal of consideration was being given to who should command the newly formed Second Australian Imperial Force (AIF). It was planned that the AIF would be Australia's key force in the coming war, expected to grow in size and importance from a division to a corps and possibly to an army. Under the *Defence Act*, only volunteer personnel could belong to the AIF. Any part-time militia or permanent military staff had to resign from their positions and volunteer for the AIF instead.

There were seven generals on the active list, but of these, only Lieutenant General John Lavarack, Major General Gordon Bennett and Blamey were in serious contention.

Lavarack had been a general staff officer in two different Australian divisions during the Great War. Blamey had more direct wartime experience than Lavarack, while Lavarack had been more senior in the permanent army during the interwar years, in a role that had essentially been political and budgetary. But wartime experience trumps peacetime experience every time. Many considered Lavarack volatile: Blamey had experienced his wrath in 1917, after Lavarack filled in for him in the 1st Division, and Blamey had seen him rub others the wrong way many times since. Lavarack was also politically inept, and made such a nuisance of himself in the selection process that he effectively disqualified himself for the job.

Bennett had been a brigadier general commanding the Australian 3rd Infantry Brigade during the Great War. Apart from his tendency to act on his own initiative, his fighting record was impeccable. He did not, however, have the depth of wartime staff experience Blamey had. During the interwar years, Bennett, then in the militia and never shy about expressing his opinions, had become increasingly outspoken in the media about the permanent army staff. Such indiscretion was deemed to render him unfit for office, and he was transferred to the Unattached List in 1932. He compounded his errors by being publicly critical of national defence policy. He was considered temperamentally unsuited to any command in which there was a need for diplomacy, particularly if it involved subordination to British command: he was even more scathing of British officers than he was of Australians.

As Germany grew increasingly aggressive, with troops massing on the border of Poland, the decision about who would lead Australia's troops became ever more urgent.

* * *

Britain declared war on Germany on 3 September 1939. At this time, any declaration of war by the United Kingdom also applied to its Dominions, so Australia too was now at war. Menzies announced the formation of a war cabinet on 15 September 1939, consisting of Commonwealth Government ministers, with the three chiefs of staff – army, navy and air force – attending in an advisory capacity. It would be Australia's key decision-making body during the war.[7]

Blamey's old supporter Robert Menzies had become Prime Minister on 26 April 1939. Menzies had been acquainted with Blamey and his work during the years when Blamey was reforming the Victorian Police Force, and was aware of his work for the Council of Defence, as well as his effectiveness in increasing the size of the militia. Though he was cognisant of the damage Blamey had done to his own reputation during that period, he recognised Blamey as a skilled and intelligent staff officer. He knew he needed a tough reformer to lead the tiny, under-equipped peacetime Australian army through a modern global war.

Blamey was appointed to command this force on 13 October 1939. Menzies wrote in his foreword to John Hetherington's 1973 biography *Blamey: Controversial Soldier* that none of the other candidates 'matched [Blamey] in the power of command – a faculty hard to define but impossible to mistake when you meet it'.[8]

But Menzies needed more than this. The man he chose to command the AIF had to deal not only with Australian politicians but also with higher-ranked Allied commanders. Menzies, in an interview with journalist Gavin Long, said he thought Blamey's 'toughness' was his most valuable quality, and that 'He will take on anything or anybody.'[9] Time would prove Menzies right. To the great benefit of the Diggers, Blamey was indeed prepared to take on anybody.

Blamey also had the requisite experience: he had the highest command experience of the Australian officers under consideration. That said, the presence of politicians and the aspirations of the candidates meant that there was no certainty he would get the job – and he probably wouldn't have if Labor had been in power, thanks to the enemies he had made as Police Commissioner.

Menzies stipulated that the commanders of the AIF be selected from the militia rather than the permanent army. Neither Menzies nor Blamey was ever fully wedded to this edict, however. Menzies is believed to have directed this only to block the rise of Lavarack, in whom he had lost confidence on account of his political incompetence.[10]

Almost as a consolation prize, the War Cabinet inserted Lavarack into Blamey's operational command structure, giving him command of the 7th Division. Blamey was furious: he considered Lavarack technically capable but unsuitable for divisional command because of his violent temper. Lavarack willingly reverted to the rank of major general to accept the command, but he was on borrowed time.

Blamey's first challenge as the commander of the AIF was to turn men into soldiers. He needed to build an army and prepare it to fight overseas against a much more experienced enemy that had already annexed large swathes of Europe. The expanding Australian force had to be fed, clothed, trained, equipped, transported and cared for in the hundreds of ways a modern army needed.

There was everything to do, and little time in which to do it.

5
Australian Commander

October 1939 to March 1941

On 13 October 1939, a month after the war began, Blamey was promoted to lieutenant general and took command of the 6th Division, which became the first formation of the Second Australian Imperial Force (AIF).

Blamey was ready for action. There was a mountain of planning and administration to climb as the size of the Australian armed forces ballooned. No problem – he had done this before. As for the actual role of command, he could pick up from where he had left off at the end of the last war – except that he needed to solve the vexed issue of British control of Australian formations.

Getting the best commanders in place was relatively easy. Blamey knew them all from his time as Chief of Staff of the Australian Corps in World War I, as well as from his more recent contact with the permanent army and the CMF. His infantry brigade commanders would be Brigadiers Arthur 'Tubby' Allen, Leslie Morshead and Stanley Savige, while Brigadier Edmund Herring would command the artillery. These were all officers from the militia whose capability was well known to Blamey from World War I. In addition to capability, Blamey chose men who he believed would look after the Diggers. He knew some personally, and all of them through the extensive reports that were made.

Ignoring the loosely mandated militia-only edict, Blamey selected Colonel Sydney Rowell as his chief of staff, and Lieutenant Colonel George Alan Vasey as Assistant Adjutant General and Quartermaster General, responsible for logistics.

While all these men would be promoted during the war, only Morshead and Savige would remain in operational command right to the end. Vasey would die in a plane crash just months before the war's conclusion, while Herring, Allen and Rowell would be relieved of their operational duties in the course of the war – in the last two cases thanks, somewhat controversially, to Blamey.

As he made decisions about manpower and resources, Blamey wrote to Menzies predicting a long, hard war that would require a large number of men. He did not believe in salvation by the 'wonder-weapons' of aircraft and tanks. He rightly predicted that aerial bombing accuracy would decline as planes were forced to fly higher to avoid defensive fire. And while tanks would have their place, they wouldn't replace the need for infantry and artillery. He also anticipated that, thanks to technological developments since the previous war, front lines would move too quickly to become static, as they had then.

On 15 December 1939, an advance party was sent to Palestine to prepare a location where the AIF would train. In the meantime, training began in Australia. Matters small and large benefited from Blamey's long experience in the permanent army and the CMF. For example, the Military Board banned alcohol in overseas camps. Blamey countermanded the order, saying the men should not have their rights as adult Australians taken away from them. In his view, controlled drinking in the camps was far preferable to having men go off base searching for grog. He also made sure that Australians would run their own canteens. That way, operating profits would be used to benefit Australian soldiers, rather than British soldiers, as had happened in the previous war.

Even as Blamey proved himself more with each decision he made, not everyone thought he was the right man for the job, and old controversies would continue to dog him. The first of these concerned the recently appointed ABC journalist Chester Wilmot.

In October 1939, a laundry contractor set up operations at Puckapunyal army base north of Melbourne. Lieutenant Robert Vial, a 6th Division cipher clerk, was called in front of Blamey, who said that Chester Wilmot had started a rumour that he, Blamey, was taking a slice of the takings. Vial had been spreading that rumour too. Blamey concluded by saying that he had cancelled Wilmot's accreditation as a war correspondent, and urged Vial to 'think about it'.[1]

In an interview with journalist Charles Bean in 1953, Melbourne-born Wilmot exposed his bias. He pointed out that Blamey's record as Police Commissioner had affected the loyalty of Victorian soldiers: 'Knowing that Blamey had the reputation of being a crook they did not serve happily under him.'[2]

Wilmot was denied accreditation until September 1940, when he was given permission to go to the Middle East. This would not be Blamey's final stoush with the press, nor would it be the last time he locked horns with Wilmot. Later criticisms against Blamey would have Wilmot banned from all Australian theatres of the war.[3]

* * *

It was clear to Blamey that the AIF would serve overseas under the British. He feared a repeat of Britain's ad-hoc use of Australian army formations and constant undermining of Australian command during World War I – with excessive casualty rates as a consequence.

Charles Bean had also identified this issue. He wrote to the Army Minister Geoffrey Street, alerting him to this problem of cooperating with Britain. There was no evidence that the British had changed their ways during the interwar years.

Blamey was not taking any chances. In order to achieve maximum success with minimum losses, he wanted explicit authority to deny British commanders unfettered control over the Australian force. Sir Brudenell White, the former chief of the army's general staff, had operated under the British at a higher level than Blamey during the previous war. (White had retired in 1923, though he would be reappointed Chief of the General Staff in March 1940 after the incumbent, Lieutenant General Ernest Squires, died in office.)

Blamey sought White's advice. White concurred that being under British command was a problem, and that the Australian

Government should grant its army commanders reserve powers to modify or oppose British orders.

To this end, White drafted a charter that Blamey took to legal and military experts for advice. By February 1940, the War Cabinet had agreed on a charter document, to which the British Government acquiesced in March. The charter was formally adopted in April 1940.

To summarise the most important provisions: the Second AIF must be recognised as being under its own commander, who had direct responsibility to the Australian Government and the right to communicate with the government directly. The force could not be broken up, moved or deployed without the commander's consent. In general, the Australian and British Governments had to agree on how the Australian force was to be used, but the Australian commander could act in an emergency if he informed the Australian Government of his actions. Operational control was to be through the Australian commander in chief of each theatre of war.

This was a brilliant contract, in that it set out clearly the way in which the Australian command expected to be treated. Similar charters were given to other Australian commanders when they operated independently of Blamey.

Its greatest flaw was that it could not be enforced through recourse to law. There would be times when the Australian Government intervened at Blamey's behest, but also some critical times when it didn't. Nevertheless, the British assent to this charter was symbolically important, because it gave Lieutenant General Sir Thomas Blamey additional authority beyond his rank.

* * *

Recruitment and training got underway apace, and more divisions were formed. On 11 April 1940, Blamey was made commander of I Corps, which incorporated the 6th Division and the newly formed 7th Division; in 1941, the 9th Division would be added to those going to the Middle East. Major General Lavarack would retain control of the 7th Division, which was forming up in Australia, while Major General Iven Mackay took command of the 6th Division, which sailed to Palestine in April 1940 to set up headquarters. The 8th Division, formed in late May 1940, would have the misfortune of being sent to Singapore, and so would not be under Blamey's command.

In April 1940, it was still unclear whether some of the 6th Division would be sent to fight in France while the remainder went to the Middle East. The British evacuation at Dunkirk in early June 1940 and the surrender of France in late June made a decision unnecessary, because the Middle East was now the only part of the world in which the British Army was fighting. Italian leader Benito Mussolini had joined the German side as very much the junior partner, declaring war on Britain and France on 10 June 1940. Libya was an Italian colony, so Britain now had a belligerent enemy-controlled power bordering its own colonial possession of Egypt.

The failure to prevent France from falling into Hitler's hands had been a great embarrassment to the Allies. France's fall and the installation of the Vichy puppet government had unforeseen impacts in the Pacific region too. French Indochina – modern-day Vietnam, Laos and Cambodia – fell under the new government's authority. The Japanese had joined the 'Axis' powers of Germany and Italy on 27 September 1940, and had growing designs on French Indochina, thanks to its strategic importance in their war with China. The Australian Government was becoming increasingly worried about the Japanese threat to the Pacific region in general, and to Singapore and Malaya in particular.

* * *

In Palestine, the British had quickly begun putting pressure on Mackay, which neither he nor his 6th Division staff had the experience or authority to resist. It was clear that Blamey's presence was required.

He and a coterie of officers left Sydney in a Short Empire flying boat on 12 June 1940, flying the Horseshoe Route to Cairo via Singapore and Calcutta. This route had 28 stops and took over a week. While the flying boat was luxury travel for its day, by modern standards it was anything but: slow, noisy and uncomfortable.

Soon after arriving in Cairo, Blamey met with British general Archibald Wavell, whose command took in the Middle East, East Africa, Greece and the Balkans, and seven nominal divisions, not one of which was complete. Under pressure to defend so much with so little, Wavell requested that Blamey provide a brigade if necessary to help quell internal strife in Cairo. Blamey reluctantly agreed to put his men on standby, but instructed Mackay not to move the 16th Brigade unless Blamey gave the go-ahead.[4] In any event, they weren't called upon. It would in fact be six months before any Australian was sent into combat.

* * *

Most of Blamey's time during this period was spent on all the other tasks, large and small, that go along with bringing three divisions into a war for the first time. These included administrative arrangements related to establishing the various headquarters, ensuring that weapons and other supplies were provided by the British, and training. Blamey behaved as he always did, tirelessly devoting himself to the administrative detail and expecting the same commitment of his staff.

As he attacked his task of building the corps, Blamey never forgot that he had to keep his troops active and interested. He organised activities to prevent Diggers from becoming bored and disruptive. A brass band was set up, and while the AIF was garrisoned in Syria he arranged for a ski school to be run in the mountain snowfields of Lebanon. Later, artists were enlisted to record both significant and mundane events for posterity.

Blamey worked for long days, then went out for rich meals, drink and – as his aide-de-camp Norman Carlyon observed – pleasure-seeking. Blamey was attracted to young women. When opportunity rose, he had no inhibitions, enjoyed himself to the full, and then moved on.[5] Blamey had long held a fondness for 'fleshpots'. In this, of course, he was hardly alone. But hard work followed by rich living with little exercise played havoc with his health. He briefly checked himself into hospital after being advised by his medical officer that he would wear out and be invalided back to Australia if he didn't change his ways.

Within the corps, like in any large organisation, the senior staff competed for promotion, particularly Lavarack and Rowell. Most of this was fuelled by resentment among permanent army officers, who felt they should receive preference over CMF officers for higher positions. Selection was weighted somewhat to their experience in the Great War, whether they were in combat or staff positions, and whether they could look after the men. Militia officers had the advantage over permanent army officers at that time because there were more of them, and more of them had commanded brigades and divisions in peacetime.

Then there was the natural gossiping about the boss and his predilections. These officers perhaps felt they had something to gain by stirring up outrage at Blamey's drinking and womanising. But Blamey's hide was thick, and neither Prime Minister Menzies nor his successor, John Curtin, ever considered Blamey's moral lapses a barrier to his command of the AIF.

Since January 1940, Blamey had been hoping that Olga would accompany him when he left to join the troops. In October, in what seems like bloody-minded obstruction, the Australian Government refused her a passport, despite Blamey's appeals that it would improve his wellbeing. The wives of some other Australian officers had already arrived, and most of the senior British officers were accompanied by their spouses. Blamey also argued Olga's presence would improve his social standing with the British, because their officers' wives were influential behind the scenes.[6] Lady Blamey's passport was eventually approved in December and permitted her to do voluntary welfare work.

Above left: Lieutenant General Blamey inspecting AIF recruits at Melbourne Showgrounds, December 1939. (AWM 000325)

Above right: Prime Minister Robert Menzies (centre) and 7th Division's Major General John Lavarack (right) with Lieutenant General Blamey at a parade in the Middle East, February 1941. (AWM 005797)

General Blamey discussing operations with Minister of the Army Percy Spender and Brigadier Sydney Rowell in Palestine, January 1941. (AWM 004852)

Blamey had always had a taste for amorous flings with willing women, alongside his predilection for 'pleasure-seeking'. He had engaged in these flings before Olga's arrival, and would continue afterwards. Carlyon and other personal assistants worried that the indiscreet way Blamey went about these liaisons might lead to trouble, but apparently it did not.

* * *

In the meantime, on 13 August 1940, a plane carrying three government ministers and Sir Brudenell White, Chief of the General Staff, had crashed near Canberra. In White, Australia lost one of the only remaining senior officers who fully appreciated the difficulties facing the AIF in overseas operations under the British. Blamey volunteered to come home and do the job, saying that the task in the Middle East only required a major general, as the corps was slow to build up in Palestine and to be armed and trained. However, Menzies ordered him to stay put and Lieutenant General Vernon Sturdee was appointed to replace White instead. As it turned out, this was the right decision: Blamey would not easily have managed the British misuse of Australian forces from that distance.

Immediately prior to his appointment as Chief of the General Staff, Sturdee had taken a demotion to major general to assume command of the 8th Division as it prepared to head to Singapore to serve under British command. Like Blamey and many other senior officers, he had little faith in the British Government's 'Singapore strategy'.

Now, Sturdee's elevation led to an immediate reshuffle. To Blamey's chagrin, Major General Gordon Bennett took over the 8th Division as it came up to strength in Australia. Given Bennett's impetuosity and frequent criticism of British officers, this appointment would have catastrophic consequences. Rowell later recalled seeing Blamey's knuckles go white when he heard the announcement on the radio as he clutched the arm of the chair he was sitting in. Vasey would recollect that Bennett's elevation was a terrible shock to everyone present.[7]

* * *

Blamey was still spending considerable time batting away requests from Wavell to use chunks of the Australian force for ad-hoc assignments. Through vigilance and force of character Blamey was mostly successful in keeping the Australian forces together under Australian commanders. The divisions were being equipped by the British and trained by the Australians. To push them into battle prematurely would have resulted in excess casualties, Blamey believed, especially if they were under British command.[8]

In September 1940, Blamey uncovered a British plan to send the 16th Brigade of the 6th Division to the Western Desert without his agreement. He was furious. Unable to travel because of gout, he sent Rowell to Cairo with a copy of his charter. Lieutenant General Henry Maitland Wilson, acting in Wavell's position, confided to Sydney Rowell that he, Wilson, had been a 'naughty boy', and backed down.[9]

By now New Zealand commander Major General Bernard Freyberg was also in the Middle East. He confided in Blamey that he had lent his Divisional Signals group to the British and was having trouble getting them back. In a typically frank exchange, reported by Freyberg's son and biographer Paul, 'Blamey told Freyberg he had been a fool to lend anything [to the British], and that it had been the cause of the major rows in the First World War between Monash and Haig'.[10] For the time being, despite the robustness of his interactions with the British commanders, Blamey managed to remain on good terms with them – just like Monash before him.

* * *

By December 1940, the Australian corps in the Middle East comprised three combat divisions and ancillary units: around 56,000 men in total. In addition, there were hospitals, extensive stores depots, workshops and other administrative services.

Blamey was still only officially in charge of the 6th Division, as that had been the entirety of the AIF when he first went to the Middle East. With the arrival of the 7th and 9th Divisions, his title no longer reflected the job he was doing. On 10 December 1940, he received an official promotion to General Officer Commanding the AIF, backdated to June.

That same day, at Sidi Barrani, 60 kilometres from the Egyptian border, the 6th Division under Major General Iven Mackay first engaged the Italians in a two-day battle. This was part of Operation Compass, the first of three British pushes that would force the Axis forces west, back into Libya. On this occasion, Blamey acceded to Wavell's request for the 6th Division to join the British Western Desert Force (later known as XIII Corps), under the overall command of British Lieutenant General Richard O'Connor. Blamey had little direct involvement in this action aside from following progress from a distance and seeing to the myriad tasks necessary for preparing the two other divisions for combat.

The Australians made up over a third of the mixed imperial force. The remainder comprised the British 7th Armoured Division and 4th Indian Infantry Division. This force was vastly outmatched by the Italians in terms of men, guns, tanks and aircraft. But for their poor command, the Italians should have defeated the British.

The British attack started during a dust storm, in near-zero visibility, and soon degenerated into chaos. Despite this, Italian morale was so poor that, according to official Australian historian Gavin Long, 38,300 Italian prisoners, including four generals, were captured, as well as 237 guns and 73 tanks. A substantial number of Italians fled west towards Libya. The Indian division suffered 435 casualties: the majority of casualties on the British side.[11]

On 3 January 1941, the Australian 6th Division and its commander Major General Mackay took a lead role in the attack on the coastal town of Bardia, on the Libyan side of the border, to drive the enemy further from Egypt. It was the first battle of the war commanded by an Australian general, as well as the first planned by Australian staff, with the support of British artillery and tanks.

Bardia had been strongly fortified by the Italians with extensive anti-tank ditches, concrete bunkers and barbed wire, and its supposed impregnability lulled the Italian commanders into a false sense of security. Mackay devised a night-time attack that required precision and daring.

The attack was preceded by aggressive night patrolling on 2 January to determine the enemy's positions and weaknesses, and peg out the Allied start line. The men wore heavy clothes against the cold and each carried more than 30 kilograms of gear. All bore white patches on their backs so their fellows could recognise them. They were keen but nervous.

The attack began during the early hours of 3 January. According to military historian I.S.O. Playfair, the artillery pounded the enemy from the desert side, while three battleships and seven destroyers blasted the defenders from the sea. For days British bombers had pummelled the area and their attention was now directed on the airfields. Engineers breached the perimeter wire of the military complex and cleared mines, allowing infantrymen and tanks to pour through. Sometimes the tanks led and sometimes the attacks were led by the infantry. It was highly fragmented fighting.[12]

The British Matilda tanks were virtually impervious to the poor Italian artillery and quickly penetrated deep into the heart of the central defences. On the second day, the Italian position was cut in two, leaving two pockets of the enemy: one to the north and one to the south. On the third day, two infantry brigades worked south and overran the enemy positions there, while the Italians in the north surrendered. The Australians suffered 130 dead and 330 wounded,[13] while the Italian losses were 1000 dead, 3000 wounded and 36,000 captured, as well as 400 guns, 120 tanks and hundreds of motor vehicles.[14]

This resounding victory raised hopes of a conclusive Allied victory in the Middle East. While the British took credit internationally, the Diggers developed a fearsome reputation among the Italians.

This contributed to a collapse of Italian morale during the next battle, at Tobruk, 120 kilometres west of Bardia. The port fell to the Australian 6th Division and the British 7th Royal Tank Regiment on 22 January 1941 with hardly a fight. The captures included 25,000 prisoners (among them 2000 sailors), 208 field and medium guns, and 87 tanks. Total Allied casualties were just over 400,[15] of which 355 were Australians (49 Australian dead and 306 wounded).[16]

The remaining Italian forces fled west along the coast road. The Australians, led by Mackay, were ordered to pursue and clear out any Italian garrisons along the way. This resulted in a series of small battles all along the 600-kilometre coast road from Tobruk to Ajdabiya, including around Benghazi, the biggest town in the area. The intention was for British tanks to support this thrust, but the advance moved so fast that supplies could not keep up and the tanks became marooned. The Italians were forced further back into Libya ahead of the Australians.

When fuel was finally brought up to the tanks, British commander Lieutenant General O'Connor decided to be bold. Rather than catch up to the Australians on the coastal route, he chose to outmanoeuvre the Italians by taking a daring 400-kilometre shortcut over open ground. The armoured force came out of the desert onto the coast road ahead of the Italians.

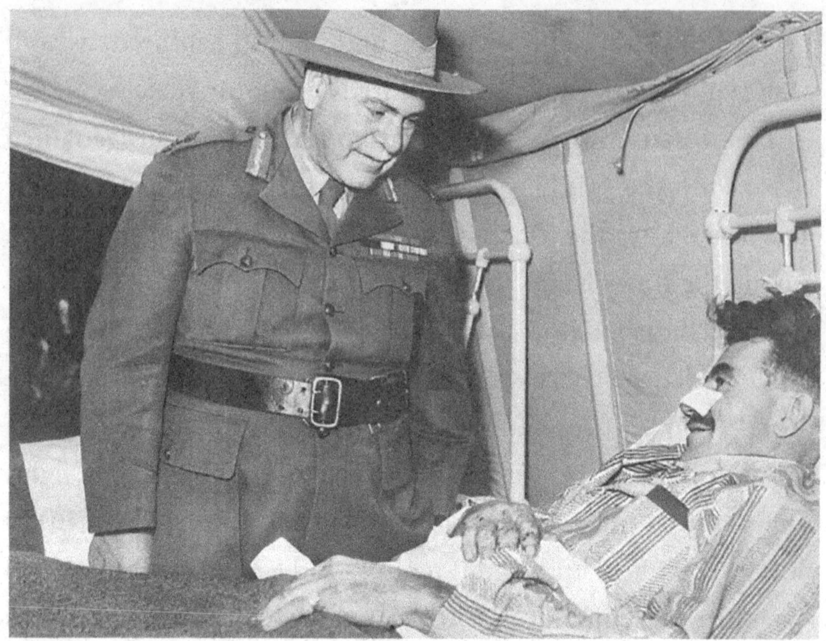

Lieutenant General Blamey chatting to Private Clark of the 2/7th Battalion, who was wounded at the Battle of Bardia in January 1941. (AWM 005226)

Lieutenant General Blamey in his office at Corps HQ in Gaza, Palestine, January 1941. (AWM 006462)

Decisive action began on 6 February 1941, when the Italians realised a trap had been sprung. They initially fought furiously in their attempt to pass the tanks, but very soon surrendered. The Australians took Benghazi that same day. The battle left in its wake a jumbled scene of broken-down and abandoned trucks, guns and tanks extending over 25 kilometres, with wandering groups of Italian soldiers destined to become prisoners. Ultimately, the POWs numbered around 25,000.[17] Included in that haul was their commander, Lieutenant General Annibale Bergonzoli.

This was a crowning victory for O'Connor's force, which had advanced over 640 kilometres and thoroughly destroyed 10 Italian divisions in less than two months, with 500 Allied troops killed, 1373 wounded and 55 missing. The enemy, meanwhile, lost 130,000 prisoners, more than 200 light tanks and 180 medium tanks, and 845 field guns or bigger.

Having defeated the Italian Army, XIII Corps was deactivated, O'Connor was promoted to commander of British troops in Egypt, and – probably because of the good showing of Mackay's 6th Division – Blamey and his staff were given responsibility for holding the captured area of Libya, stretching from Bardia to Ajdabiya.

But the 6th Division would soon be needed elsewhere. Winston Churchill had decided to fight the Germans in Greece, and set about manipulating the Greek, Australian and New Zealand Governments to achieve that result.

Central to this manipulation was the manifest lie that the Allies could be successful in this action.

* * *

Before his losses in North Africa, without consulting Hitler, Benito Mussolini had decided to capture Greece. When the Italians invaded on 28 October 1940, they were both surprised and humiliated to be quickly stopped by the Greeks. To prop up Mussolini, Hitler moved German forces into the Mediterranean in January 1941.

Britain had treaty arrangements with Greece, and Churchill approached Greek Prime Minister General Ioannis Metaxas, offering military assistance. Metaxas declined, suggesting that any force the British sent would be too small to help, and that it would be better used in North Africa, where it could make a bigger difference. After Metaxas died of throat cancer on 29 January 1941, the new leader, Alexandros Koryzis, relinquished and asked for aid.

It was clear to Churchill that Britain, even with Commonwealth support, would have considerable difficulty winning the war unless America was brought in on the Allied side. The British had been humiliated by the Germans in France, and in discussion with General John Dill, Chief of the Imperial General Staff, Blamey thought he 'seemed to be very much impressed by the political necessity of the expedition', particularly the effect on American public opinion.[18]

All along, Churchill had been told by his top military advisers that Greece was beyond help, and that any force he sent would be too small and under-resourced to win. Blamey and Freyberg both agreed that Greece was a lost cause, but neither was consulted – not even by their own governments. Churchill ordered Wavell to take as much of O'Connor's force as he could to fight in Greece.

Menzies now came calling in the Middle East, en route to London. On 7 February 1941, he visited Alexandria and the Mediterranean Fleet, and on 10 February flew to Cairo, where he met with Wavell; historian David Horner considers it unclear whether they discussed the proposed Greek campaign.[19] The next day, near Benghazi, Menzies inspected the troops for the first time.

Menzies travelled with a party of advisers whose composition, according to historian David Day, mirrored his political rather than his military concerns. There were no senior military advisers to give him independent counsel. When Menzies arrived in London on 20 February, almost straightaway Churchill approached him with the plan to defend Greece. Although he believed Churchill was a dangerous warmonger, Menzies fell under the Englishman's persuasive spell and largely agreed with everything he demanded of the Australians.[20]

Blamey had gone to great lengths to ensure Menzies understood the dangers of giving Australian forces to the British, but to no avail. Menzies had every opportunity to refuse the Greek 'adventure'. The Australian Prime Minister had no experience of war, while Blamey was perhaps a little green in managing the information flow between the Prime Minister and his government. A simple order from Menzies to Blamey not to embark troops for Greece would have empowered Blamey to hold the Diggers back, but Menzies didn't give it and neither did Blamey ask for it.

Wavell informed Blamey and Freyberg that the Anzacs would campaign in Greece, and that their respective governments had agreed to this. In fact, in Australia's case, only Menzies had agreed. He had not involved the Australian Government as he should have. On 25 February, Wavell showed Blamey a telegram stating that a British War Cabinet meeting had approved the operation the previous day, and that Menzies had attended this meeting. Again it implies approval but made without the imprimatur of the Australian Government.

Blamey had many concerns about the Greek campaign. In addition to his worries about the superior German enemy, he was perturbed that overall British command had been given to Lieutenant General Henry Maitland Wilson. Nicknamed 'Jumbo', Wilson was the general officer commanding 'W Force', of which the Australian and New Zealand forces were a subset. He had been chosen more for his political compliance than for his military acumen, and Blamey had little regard for his ability to command in battle. Based on his experience both of Wilson and of British command in World War I, Blamey objected to this arrangement and pointed out that, as the ranking Anzac officer, he should be in command. This was overruled, because the stated plan was for the force to comprise 126,000 men, of which less than one-third would be Anzacs.

This logic was irrefutable – or it might have been, if Churchill had delivered the promised men, but as usual he wildly overpromised and under-delivered. Twenty-three squadrons of the Royal Air Force had been promised but only nine were delivered. In this way Churchill checkmated demands for Blamey to have overall command. The Dominion forces were now entirely under British leadership, just as Blamey had feared.

Menzies had been caught in a political trap of his own making, while the Australian soldiers had been caught in

Churchill's. When Blamey finally realised there was trickery behind the order, he informed Canberra that the situation was most hazardous. This caused alarm, but it was too late. For better or worse, the Australians were on their way to Greece.

Blamey had been too slow to blow the whistle on the Greek affair. At the first mention of the campaign, he should have begun communicating with the Australian Government, clearly explaining the hopelessness of the venture and the extreme danger in which the 6th and 7th Divisions would be placed, for no strategic or territorial gain.

He would never make this mistake again.

* * *

Wavell had instructed Blamey to take the inexperienced 7th Division from Palestine first, but Blamey wanted to take the 6th. He felt the experience its men had would be invaluable early in the Greek campaign against the Germans. The 7th could follow later, while the even less experienced 9th would take over from the 6th in North Africa, now that the front on the Western Desert had quietened down. Blamey argued his case in what must have been a fiery meeting; Sydney Rowell would later observe that Wavell's chief of staff was 'very white and glum' and announced to his staff immediately afterwards: 'We've lost.'[21]

Little did anyone know that the fighting in Libya and Egypt was about to become intense. The Nazi general Erwin Rommel had been ordered to North Africa with his Afrika Corps. Rommel was Hitler's propaganda hero, the commander of the famous 'Ghost Division', which had been renowned during the battle for France for its ability to disappear and reappear where it could do the most damage.

Rommel would soon be giving the green, barely formed and woefully equipped 9th Division, under Major General Leslie Morshead, a baptism of fire in the Western Desert and, later, at Tobruk.

Most of the 7th Division would never make it to Greece either. The division would be split up and sent off to fight in different theatres of war.

Blamey's worst fears were being realised: with Menzies's acquiescence, the main Australian fighting force in the Middle East was now scattered.

6

A Lost Cause

March to June 1941

The 6th Division was now headed for Greece against Blamey's better judgment, but he had to make the best of the bad situation. He judged, correctly, that he was most needed on the ground in Greece, because that was where the Allies would face an overwhelming German force.

On 6 March 1941, with preparations for the embarkation for Greece well underway, Blamey was spotted by war correspondent and poet Kenneth Slessor at the Dug-Out nightclub, attached to the Metropolitan Hotel in Cairo, in the company of a young Egyptian woman and surrounded by junior officers. Slessor doesn't seem to have had a moral issue with this, but thought it was unseemly behaviour for a senior officer and liable to lead to disrespect. He was more concerned that Blamey was making an undignified spectacle of himself than he was concerned with the morality of the general. Slessor returned to the nightclub six days later and found Blamey there again.[1]

As Blamey prepared to depart for Greece, he knew he would need all his command experience and strength to prevent the annihilation of the mixed Australian, New Zealand and British forces under woefully inadequate British command. He made the overnight trip by fast cruiser from Alexandria to Athens on 18 March 1941, accompanied by a small contingent of men, including Rowell and Carlyon, his aide-de-camp.

On arrival, Blamey met with W Force commander Lieutenant General Wilson, then with the King of Greece and his commander in chief, General Alexandros Papagos. After that, he and Rowell toured the sites of imminent invasion, 500 kilometres north of Athens, and visited Major General Freyberg at the New Zealand headquarters.

Blamey's fact-finding mission confirmed what he had felt all along: the projected German force of 20 divisions, supported by a large air force, would triumph against such a weak and thinly distributed Allied force. As it transpired, there were 23 German divisions, of which only 10 fought in Greece, while 13 were held in reserve in Bulgaria and Yugoslavia to be brought in rapidly if needed.[2] Experienced, battle-hardened and bursting with confidence from their recent conquests in Poland, France, Bulgaria and Yugoslavia, these divisions were supported by the latest weapons and a surfeit of air power, conventional and self-propelled artillery and Panzer tanks, while receiving generous supplies over land. They presented a formidable threat.

On the Allied side, W Force comprised around 63,000 men: the Australian 6th Division, the New Zealand 2nd Division and the British 1st Armoured Brigade, with a long tail of administrative, medical and logistics personnel.[3] Each brigade had an artillery regiment, and each division had an anti-tank regiment, combat engineers and a machine-gun battalion, but the force was poorly supplied with aircraft. The Greeks had four armies totalling around 430,000 men, but they were poorly trained and equipped, with inadequate leadership. Worse, they had been located in a dangerous position close to the border because the King of Greece didn't want to give up any ground. Neither Blamey nor Rowell expected them to last long as a forward bulwark.

The Allies would be annihilated if they stood their ground, and Blamey knew it. He was prepared to fight for as long as was practical but he also needed to save his men.

His undeclared plan was simplicity itself. The Australian force would hold briefly at first contact with the Germans, then implement a fighting withdrawal. It would be critical to retain as much control during the withdrawal as possible, because fighting with an enemy at your back is difficult and dangerous. An orderly withdrawal can easily collapse into an uncontrolled rout. If this happened, many Australians would die.

There was, however, no point in withdrawing if the men couldn't be evacuated, since there was no part of Greece that would allow such a paltry force to hold out against such a powerful, well-supplied enemy for very long. Even as the 6th Division under Major General Mackay was disembarking in Greece, Blamey was visiting southern beaches, scouting out suitable evacuation sites and marking them on a map. He told no one what he was doing, not even Captain Carlyon, who was travelling with him, and certainly not Wavell or Wilson. It would have been considered defeatist to plan an exit strategy before the fighting men had even established themselves.

* * *

The Australian force moved close to the Yugoslavian border. Blamey went forward and set up his corps headquarters at a point around 60 kilometres from both the Australians in the north-west and the New Zealanders in the north-east.

There, Blamey learned that Wavell, in his absence and without his permission, had split the Australian forces not due to go to Greece. The 18th Brigade of the 7th Division was sent to join the 9th Division facing Rommel at Tobruk, while the remainder were sent to fight in Lebanon and Syria. Blamey was incandescent with rage. It didn't augur well for Lavarack, commander of the 7th Division, that he had allowed this split to happen.

The Germans sprang into action on the rugged northern border of Greece on 6 April 1941. Facing them was the large but ineffectual Greek Army, an inexperienced infantry division of New Zealanders under Freyberg, the battle-hardened Australian 6th Division under Blamey, and a battalion of British armour – a small, outdated air force contingent and not enough conventional artillery.

The British at this time exhibited a strange disinclination for their tank forces to learn new tactics. They employed old-style cavalry tactics, and tanks were picked off individually and destroyed piecemeal. Their out-of-date aircraft were quickly overwhelmed. But the critical weapon in this battle was artillery. It usually is, even if it doesn't get as much attention in war histories due to its slow-moving nature. In World War II, artillery accounted for 58 per cent of battlefield casualties inflicted: only 9 per cent lower than in World War I.[4] The Allied force was proportionally well supplied with artillery and the expertise to use it, but the Germans had much more.

Despite putting up a heroic defence, the Greek force in the mountains collapsed and dispersed quickly, and the Germans poured in through the many gorges. Mackay's force was engaged on 10 April. It was hard fighting. The conditions were freezing cold and miserable. The men battled on through blizzards, and overnighted in waterlogged gun pits chopped out of rocky ground, enduring wet feet and sodden boots for days on end. They were in constant danger of being outflanked.

The Diggers might have been outgunned, but they weren't overawed by their notorious Nazi enemy, spinning about to meet threats coming from many directions. The Germans were relying on the Blitzkrieg tactics that had already helped them achieve military success, involving concentrated, overwhelming force deployed rapidly, but these tactics work best in open, gently undulating country like that found in Poland and France. In this battle, fought along narrow, winding roads, the Allied soldiers had many opportunities to mine, set up ambushes and destroy bridges. All of this slowed the progress of the invading force and added to its losses, but it was never going to stop the overwhelming German force.

* * *

On 11 April, just days into the campaign, Blamey travelled to Wilson's HQ to meet with him and Wavell. It is not recorded exactly what was discussed at the meeting, but it is likely Blamey forcefully impressed upon the two British officers that the current situation was a British foul-up with obvious parallels to Gallipoli, complete with Churchill's romantic warmongering and lack of preparation. Only one of two outcomes could be expected in Greece: annihilation or evacuation. Annihilation was unthinkable for Blamey, and would have immediate and long-term consequences for British manpower, politics and prestige.

Blamey likely made his evacuation plans explicit at this point. Having softened up the British officers for a fighting withdrawal and evacuation, he no doubt ensured that this would become an agenda item at their next meeting, due 10 days later. Such a change of plan had to be authorised by Churchill, and that would take some doing, because the great man, for reasons all of his own, still seemed to want the Anzacs to become a heroic sacrifice.

One outcome of that meeting was that Blamey was given operational control of the New Zealanders in Greece, in addition to his Australians. The newly reconstituted Anzac Corps would last less than two weeks, until the Allied evacuation. Blamey had little interest in New Zealand militarily, as, with the exception of this brief merging, the two forces operated independently of each other during the war.

As Blamey took command, he discovered that suggestions he had made to Wilson about the New Zealand positions in Greece had not been put into effect, and critical positions around key passes had not been taken up. It was too late to fix that omission, but it meant the Germans were able to push into Allied positions sooner than he'd expected.

* * *

By 14 April, the Germans were getting closer to the Allied positions, their air force clearing their path with bombing. Blamey was evacuated from his living quarters just four hours before they were destroyed by Stuka dive bombers.

The next day Blamey called a meeting of senior commanders, including Mackay and Freyberg, to brief them for the first time on his plans for a fighting withdrawal. Up to that point, as reported by official historian Gavin Long, both commanders 'had been impressing on their subordinates that there would be no more withdrawals. "I did not dream of an evacuation," said Mackay afterwards. "I thought that we would hang on for about a fortnight and be beaten by weight of numbers." Vasey was similarly of a mind that "here we bloody well are and here we bloody well stay".'[5]

The Germans continued to advance while the Anzacs, now on the move, fought a frantic rearguard action. Blamey's plans for a fighting withdrawal included precisely timed activities for artillery, infantry, engineers and signals. Units of infantry and artillery would hold the enemy, then leapfrog back past the line that was covering their withdrawal.

As always, the engineers were the last out, and frequently risked being overtaken by the enemy. They had to maintain bridges and roads until the last formations had passed through, before demolishing them to slow the German advance. Signalling was vital to maintain coordination, since constant adjustments needed to be made as the Germans broke through at various places. The rough terrain, cut through by many fast-flowing rivers, provided copious choke points.

Blamey's corps HQ began to move back on 16 April, then was set up 170 kilometres north-east of the designated evacuation beaches. As Blamey's contingent moved, it became almost gridlocked in bumper-to-bumper traffic. German planes had uncontested control of the skies and put the long lines of vehicles under ferocious attack. When these onslaughts began, people would leap from their vehicles and scatter to lie prone in the fields.

In Norman Carlyon's recollection, Blamey exhibited supreme confidence, because he was the only one who did not automatically fall flat on his face.[6] That was not bravado but was born of experience. Blamey had been bombed in the previous war and could tell where the bombs were going to land by watching them fall. More pertinent was the fact that the enemy planes did little damage, despite the nerve-racking noise.[7]

One time Blamey did hit the ground, lying prone next to Carlyon, because he had judged a bomb was coming close. The bomb hit a group of New Zealanders lying near a tree: the very tree that Carlyon had been attracted to, but had been compelled to move away from when Blamey moved off.[8]

* * *

On 20 April, the Greek Army surrendered in western Greece, and with that weak barrier to the German advance eliminated the evacuation plans had to be accelerated.

Winston Churchill was finally persuaded that leaving the Anzacs in a last stand would do irreparable damage to

Lieutenant Generals Blamey and Henry Maitland 'Jumbo' Wilson with Brigadier General Bernard Freyberg, in Greece, 1941. (AWM 128425)

This soldier, chatting to General Blamey in Palestine in September 1941, was taken prisoner in Crete during the fighting withdrawal from Greece but managed to escape. (AWM 009723)

Britain's relationship with Australia and New Zealand, and Wavell gained the Prime Minister's reluctant approval for the evacuation.

Plans were made for the Anzacs to defend their positions close to the beaches as they awaited the arrival of destroyers and transport ships under Royal Navy command, including Australian naval vessels. On 21 April, Blamey issued a communique praising his forces for their 'magnificent achievement in withdrawing 140 miles in four days'.[9]

Around 11.30 that evening, Wilson and Rear-Admiral Baillie-Grohman of the Royal Navy met with Blamey and advised him the evacuation would take place in four days' time. At 2 am that night, in pouring rain, Wavell and Blamey held a torchlight meeting in the back of Wavell's car. Blamey got out the road map showing the beaches he had marked up during his 'picnic' trip with Carlyon just a few weeks earlier. Carylon wrote, 'Wavell seemed astonished that Blamey had this information.'[10]

At 10 pm on 23 April, after almost the entire HQ had been sent to the beaches, a top-secret message arrived by dispatch rider, summoning Blamey to meet Wilson in Athens. There, as Carlyon reported, Wilson read out a short, sharp message from Wavell directing Blamey to be on the next plane out of Greece, and to report to GHQ in Cairo as soon as he could.[11]

Blamey objected, saying he needed to stay until he was sure the evacuation was a success, whereupon Wilson reminded Blamey that orders had to be obeyed. Wavell also ordered Mackay and Freyberg to join the flight. Mackay went but Freyberg refused.

Advised that the Royal Air Force (RAF) flying boat would leave at 3 am, Blamey made a quick decision about which six people would accompany him. He chose Mackay, Rowell, Carlyon and two other officers. Who he selected to fill the last seat would make no material difference to the fate of the Australian soldiers, but his choice would have symbolic significance. He took his son, artillery officer Major Tom Blamey, who had lately (and reluctantly) been seconded to his headquarters. The young man would much rather have taken his chances with his regiment.[12]

The evacuation ships were savaged by German aircraft as they collected the men from the beaches and steamed towards Crete and with others on to Egypt. While most ships got away, four transport ships and two destroyers were sunk, with a further loss of 500 troops as well as naval personnel.

* * *

The defeat in Greece unsurprisingly caused a great deal of finger-pointing. Sydney Rowell and another senior administrative staff officer, Brigadier William Bridgeford, would claim that Blamey acted like a coward, uncaring of his men, because he largely stayed in his headquarters throughout the campaign instead of moving around to see his commanders or raise the Diggers' morale.[13]

Other officers, including the commander of his corps of engineers, Brigadier Clive Steele, saw no problem with Blamey's behaviour. Steele had come late to a corps dinner prior to withdrawal, at which all the food and drink either needed to be consumed or left behind. Steele was grateful that Blamey had saved half a bottle of champagne for him.[14] Rowell, on the other hand, treated such frivolity with disdain. His apparently more austere, uncompromising values were one reason why he was ever willing to criticise his boss.

To the extent that Rowell's complaints about Blamey have any professional basis, they are probably rooted in their different experiences, even before the fighting withdrawal began. Blamey's outwardly relaxed demeanour during the Greek campaign can be explained by comparing that campaign with his experiences on the Western Front. During the previous war, as Chief of Staff of the Australian Corps, he'd had far greater responsibilities under far tougher conditions. It is unlikely that he considered what happened in Greece particularly taxing from a command or staff perspective. Greece was back to 'business as usual' for Blamey.

For Rowell, being a staff officer during World War II, let alone chief of staff to the Australian commander, was definitely not business as usual. He'd suddenly found himself in the deep end. Despite his apparent brilliance, Rowell's accolades until then had all been earned in peacetime. He had barely participated in World War I, spending about six months on active duty at Gallipoli and none on the Western Front. He'd then become a staff officer after the war. This was the first combat situation he'd been in with his current staff responsibilities.

In the army, and particularly in a combat situation, there is a clearly delineated chain of command. Everyone must be in their prescribed place and doing their prescribed job, otherwise the system breaks down.

Every headquarters must be at the 'right' distance from the front. The fighting men need to be at the front with their officers, usually up to the rank of captain. The higher the rank, the further back the commander. Brigadier Vasey, now 19th Brigade commander, was stationed with his men close to the front; Major General Mackay was in his HQ further back; while Lieutenant General Blamey was in *his* HQ, further back again. Each had a specific set of jobs to do. The further the HQ was from the front, the broader its set of jobs. Tasks were more tactical at the front and more strategic at the rear. There were immediate issues to deal with at the front and longer-term issues at the back. It was the job of the staff officers, rather than commanders, to do any necessary running around. The commander was best positioned in his own HQ, doing his own job. Importantly, it was where he could be found if critical, time-sensitive decisions were needed.

Blamey and his staff, from their HQ, were overseeing the battle at the front in a general sense, as well as dealing with problems of supply, manpower, transport and policy. Of course, he was also still commanding the rest of the AIF in the Middle East. He needed to work on future strategies too, which in this case included evacuation plans, and manage the greatest risk facing the AIF, which was not just the Germans but included the British command. If Blamey needed to leave his HQ to see anyone, it would be either Jumbo Wilson or Wavell – and they were even further back.

There was another very good reason why a general would remain in his HQ. On one occasion, Major General Freyberg came forward in the heat of battle to the Australian brigade HQ, seeking news of his 21st Battalion. A young Australian colonel named Chilton gently persuaded him that his presence was not helpful.[15] Tourists, even generals, can be a dangerous nuisance in the front lines during a battle. At best, they are a distraction; at worst, they might attempt to give orders that interfere with the chain of command or disrupt an ongoing action. It was Blamey's policy never to interfere with operational command mid-battle.

Rowell might have complained at the time about Blamey's tendency to stay in his HQ, but in his autobiography *Full Circle*, written 30 years later, Rowell took a much more considered view. Blamey 'could not have gone into the battle area himself without confusing another commander's authority', he noted. 'It was agreed [at a certain point] that I should go to see what was happening', he recalled, and that Blamey should not.[16]

Blamey was a hands-off leader. He wanted his officers to manage themselves; if they needed him, they could make contact with him in his HQ. According to World War I historian Charles Bean, the chief engineer of Monash's Australian Corps said of Blamey that, after real consultation to understand the essential points of any task, he 'left you to do your job'.[17] There was no micromanagement or hand-holding. There are no reports that Mackay, Vasey or any other field commander ever stated that they wanted a visit from Blamey and failed to get one.

There is also clear evidence to contradict Rowell's view that Blamey was a coward. On hearing that the Germans had broken through Greek positions, a newly arrived brigadier said Blamey's 'coolness and decisive qualities were superb'.[18] There is no reason to think Blamey was low on physical courage under fire either. Norman Carlyon reported seeing Blamey winking and smiling as he climbed out of a ditch following a bombing attack by German planes; to Carlyon's amusement, he heard a Digger saying that he wished he were safe in Athens with 'bloody old Blamey'. Blamey just smiled and walked off.[19]

Blamey did not come forward in battle not because he was a coward, and certainly not because he was uninterested in the men's welfare; rather, it was because he *was* interested in their welfare. Blamey was well aware that being seen at the front could raise the morale of his fighting men. But he also knew the costs, and judged that operational efficiency might suffer if he went forward at critical times in a battle, and that that might result in more casualties.

Rowell had complained that Blamey hid in his headquarters, but Blamey didn't just separate himself from his men during the day. Norman Carlyon was bemused when Blamey chose a village hovel for his living quarters, while the rest of his HQ lived and worked in tents about a mile away.[20] And this was very probably the root cause of Rowell's dissatisfaction.

It was uncharacteristic for Blamey to opt for discomfort and inconvenience; the most likely reason was that he was conditioning his staff to treat him as their commanding officer. In the Middle East campaign so far, Blamey had been the first among equals. Perhaps he had decided this familiarity had to end, so he put physical distance between himself and his staff. He was perhaps following Monash's example when he took over the corps headquarters in World War I. This is all conjecture, because Blamey rarely explained himself.

The important thing to note is that this physical and symbolic separation was particularly significant for Rowell. He and Blamey had shared accommodation when they first came to the Middle East, and Rowell had been one of the few people to tackle Blamey directly on private matters.

Just before the war, he had served as Director of Military Operations and Intelligence at Army Headquarters and then as staff officer to the Inspector General. As such, although he had only been a lieutenant colonel, he'd had power over Major General Blamey of the militia. The new arrangement in Greece was foreign to Rowell, and he had a lot to learn. Blamey's decision to remove himself from Rowell and the other staff forced Rowell to face the fact that he no longer had control over Blamey, and needed to act more independently.

As anyone who has been promoted from a group of 'equals' knows, the transition for both the recently elevated and those left behind can be difficult. When Blamey moved into separate quarters, Rowell had some of his special access privileges withdrawn, and he was clearly miffed. This was when he began publicly criticising Blamey for infractions such as champagne-drinking and the separation of headquarters.

In June 1941, Blamey wrote to the Chief of the General Staff, Lieutenant General Vernon Sturdee about Rowell:

> Rowell has very great ability; is quick in decision and sound in judgement. There can be no question of his personal courage, but he lacks the reserves of nervous energy over a period of long strain. I found him difficult in the last days in Greece and, as commander, had to

> exercise considerable tact. Rather a reverse of what it should be.
>
> I was a little disappointed in both him and Bridgeford over their attitude in one or two matters. They were over-impressed with the danger of the dive bomber and talked a little too freely about its effect on the men. However, a short rest fixed them both up.[21]

Blamey recognised Rowell's considerable technical command capability, but also that he was both inexperienced and highly strung. Rather than take Rowell's criticisms personally, Blamey was prepared to shrug them off – as long as he was getting a performance payoff. That he kept elevating Rowell to more senior command roles is testament both to Rowell's command capability and Blamey's willingness to promote on merit. Blamey's words about Rowell also show that he was well aware of how the stresses of war cause mental and physical fatigue to everyone from the footsoldier up.

Blamey himself was by no means immune to these stresses. As tensions rose with the evacuation in full swing, Rowell had further cause for complaint against Blamey. Wilson thought Blamey 'fought the rearguard action in Greece very well' but his 'chief of staff was Rowell – a brilliant officer who carried Blamey'.[22] In *Full Circle*, Rowell would report that Mackay came to him at one point because Blamey was in a 'rather tired and distressed state', and needed Rowell to clarify the evacuation plans.[23]

Blamey left most of the operational details to Rowell and his other commanders and there might have been times when the orders did appear strange, particularly towards the end of the evacuation. Subordinates generally don't have the full facts, nor are they subject to the colossal responsibility and uncertainty that come with more senior roles. Doubt and conflict were guaranteed as Blamey dealt with Wavell, and through him tried to influence Churchill. It is a credit to Blamey's strong character and robust dealings with the British that he achieved anything at all.

In contrast to Rowell's criticisms, Freyberg never considered anything amiss with Blamey's command; nor did Bridgeford, apart from the criticisms referred to earlier. Carlyon, too, was convinced that, even though Blamey and all his staff were working under great stress, Blamey was clear and in control the whole time: 'I was present throughout the time when those orders [about the evacuation] were prepared and issued. If Blamey's orders had been as unclear and imprecise as Rowell afterwards alleged, surely Bridgeford and the others present would have appeared puzzled and confused. That did not happen.'[24]

On the other hand, it appears that Blamey's behaviour sometimes became erratic when he was not in high-level meetings. According to Carlyon, Blamey lost control when he returned to his tent after one such meeting and discovered his raincoat was missing. He rushed back outside brandishing a pistol and grabbed the nearest Greek by the neck, but soon let him go. It was just a minute or two of explosive rage from the build-up of tension during the previous weeks.[25] This is hardly surprising, because he'd had a hellish few days since he'd pulled himself, smiling and winking, out of the ditch after the German bombing mentioned earlier. With battle-hardened Germans bearing down on his men, he was as worried about the withdrawal as all the other commanders were.

Blamey also had bigger political, strategic and logistical concerns. He had no direct control over the British, so there was no certainty that the evacuation would take place at all, let alone soon enough to avoid annihilation of the Anzac forces. He was undoubtedly worried sick. Since the withdrawal began, his bed had been wherever he could lay his head, including the back of his staff car. He'd had meetings when and where they were required; day and night had lost all meaning. The wear and tear on the man were extreme.

It is probable that Blamey was suffering from mental fatigue when he chose to evacuate his son Tom on the RAF flying boat; or perhaps, as Carlyon noted, he just didn't care a jot for public opinion.[26] Blamey, in typical fashion, never explained his action. Whatever was behind it, it was a mistake that caused him reputational damage. It was hardly a hanging offence, though, particularly when weighed against his achievements in Greece.

* * *

The Battle of Greece was an expensive failure for which Churchill and Menzies must take the blame. With no friendly air cover and a rapacious German air force, some 50,000 Allied troops had to embark by night, which required discipline and patience. By 29 April, when the evacuation was completed, 900 Allied troops were dead, 1250 wounded and 14,000 captured:

a loss of around a quarter of their strength. Australians made up 2030 of the captured, 320 of those killed and 494 of the wounded. The major cause of these losses was not the way the battle was fought, but that the Allies were in Greece at all, fighting a vastly superior force.

Without doubt, the Battle of Greece would have been far more costly had Blamey not immediately sized up the situation and made plans for a fighting withdrawal. Had he not acted promptly and vigorously, the whole force would have been either captured or killed. A lesser commander might have stood and fought the Germans as ordered, or might have had insufficient force of character to make his demands stick. As it was, the evacuation occurred just in time. It could have been an early Singapore for the Australians; instead it was another Dunkirk. The Allied force achieved wonders in managing a fighting withdrawal of some 200 kilometres with a formation of troops from three countries against a vastly stronger army. This was Blamey's work, and he must be given credit.

Blamey's efforts in limiting the effects of an inevitable defeat did not go unnoticed. Archibald Wavell described Blamey as 'probably the best soldier we had in the Middle East. Not an easy man to deal with, but a very satisfactory man to deal with. His military knowledge was unexampled and he was positive, firm and a very satisfactory commander.'[27]

These were fine words, but in the end they made little difference to Blamey or the command situation. While he was soon recognised with promotion, any claim he might have to more extensive influence over the war in the Middle East continued to be checked by the British.

7

Tragedy and Triumph

April to July 1941

When Blamey came from Greece to his new headquarters in Alexandria, Egypt, on 24 April, he found a terrible mess. The AIF forces had been fragmented by the British and spread all over the Middle Eastern theatre of operations. Officers he had left in charge had been manipulated by Wavell, and bit by bit the AIF had been broken up to meet British demands.

The worst of it was that John Lavarack, instead of striving to gain Blamey's favour, had disobeyed his direct orders and given the British his full cooperation, hiving off parts of the 7th Division to Tobruk. Blamey had already had strong words with Wavell about this matter while in Greece. This put a nail in Lavarack's professional coffin, but with so much going on, it would be some time before the nail was driven in.

There was now a substantial cabal of disaffected Australian officers with Rowell and Lavarack at its centre. Their main gripe was still the preponderance of militia officers in command positions. They met regularly and would have loved to see Blamey relieved of his command.

Aware of the resentment that Menzies's edict had caused, Blamey also knew that, over the course of the war, he would have to shuffle his command deck. Some officers would rise and others would fall based on performance, and Blamey didn't much care whether they originated from the permanent army or the militia. The permanent army officers would get their chance. By the end of the war, the highest ranks in operational command – major general and lieutenant general – would be filled nearly equally with officers originating from the permanent army and the militia.

* * *

Frederick Shedden, now Secretary of the Department of Defence Co-ordination, was with Prime Minister Menzies during his continued stay in London. On 17 April, he had penned a memorandum to Menzies expressing the view that Blamey's wartime performance had been better than Wilson's and at least as good as Wavell's, and that Menzies should press for better rank and authority for the general. Menzies agreed, and asked Field Marshal Sir John Dill, Chief of the Imperial General Staff, to visit him at Australia House. At their meeting Menzies stressed that Blamey was an excellent commander, and that there would be an outcry in Australia if 'not for the first time Australian troops have been sacrificed by incompetent Imperial Generals'.[1]

Dill was in agreement and, in a cable to Wavell, passed on Menzies's view of Blamey. He also noted that Menzies was unimpressed by Wilson's performance, particularly as Wilson 'said nothing nice about Australians and only dwelt on their indiscipline'.[2] Wavell agreed that Blamey was a fine fighting commander and ready for high command.[3]

On 23 April, London announced that Blamey would be promoted to Deputy Commander in Chief, Middle East Command. While his elevation was strongly endorsed by Wavell, in general the British weren't all that happy about it and failed to notify Blamey directly about his appointment. He first learned of his promotion by reading it in the paper on his return to Egypt.[4]

Unfortunately, it was something of a non-promotion: Blamey was not given an active command role in the theatre of operations. The decision to isolate him from setting strategy once again came down to politics. British establishment pride would be damaged if the public found out that an Australian militia officer, as Blamey was often wrongly called, had been chosen over British permanent army officers. In addition, Churchill couldn't acknowledge the key role Australians had played in fighting the war in the Middle East while most of his own forces were still at home. Still, the mistakes Churchill and his officers made in appointing top commanders ensured that painful losses would continue in the Middle East for the next 15 months.

Having experienced the 'British generals' club' during World War I, Blamey was not fooled into believing that his elevation would be particularly meaningful, nor that the British would let him command substantial numbers of British troops. To underline the relative unimportance of his post, Blamey retained the rank of lieutenant general, while Wilson was promoted to full general. Since Wilson now outranked Blamey, it was actually he who would stand in for Wavell if that were ever required.

The one considerable benefit of Blamey's ersatz elevation was that his office was now moved to Wavell's headquarters in Cairo, bringing him to the epicentre of command. While formal power eluded him, he would often exercise his considerable personal power on Wavell by walking the short distance to the commander's office and demanding action. He was now also privy to a steady stream of intelligence and high-level policy decisions, which made it harder for the British to hide their plans or spring surprise ventures on Blamey, as they had with the invasion of Greece.

Another advantage of Blamey's move to Cairo was that it further separated his headquarters from Rowell's. Rowell remained in Alexandria, feeling he could no longer work with Blamey. His unwillingness to share his HQ with Blamey would come to a head during the Pacific campaign, with dire consequences.

* * *

Blamey's first order of business after moving to Cairo was to meet with Wavell; his second was to visit the paymaster to make sure his Australian troops would get paid when they disembarked from their transports from Greece. Much of the evacuated Australian force had been landed on the poorly defended island of Crete.

Brigadier Edmund Herring, commander of the artillery during the Greek campaign, observed how impressive was the detailed care given by Blamey to the welfare of his men.[5] Unsurprisingly, though, Blamey was exhausted after getting the Allied forces clear of Greece, and by his ongoing battle with Wavell to reassemble the AIF. Norman Carlyon became concerned about Blamey's health. On 28 April, he was admitted to the 15th Scottish General Hospital in Cairo suffering dysentery. Impatient to get back to work, he discharged himself within two days – but not before complaining to the commanding officer of the hospital about its shortcomings.

With Churchill's strong support, Wavell resisted Blamey's efforts to bring the AIF back together. The Australians were the critical force in the ongoing campaign in the Western Desert and faced threats in Crete, Syria and Cyprus. A month earlier, Rommel had placed the Australian 9th Division under siege in the port of Tobruk, and while Blamey had full confidence in divisional commander Leslie Morshead, he was increasingly concerned about the condition of the men and wanted them relieved. It would require all Blamey's determination over the coming months to budge Churchill and British command on this matter.

* * *

Even before the evacuation from Greece began on 24 April, decoding of highly encrypted German signals had alerted the British to a new German interest in Crete. It seemed an invasion was imminent. Churchill, in one of his rousing addresses, had encouraged the tiny Allied force on Crete to stoutly resist the coming German attacks, but he confided to the War Cabinet that he didn't rate the defenders' chances very highly.[6] Yet he did not make alternative plans.

In total there were now 6500 Australians, 7700 New Zealanders, 18,000 Britons and 12,000 Greek and Cretan fighters on the island.[7] To his misfortune, New Zealand commander Freyberg was among them. Having refused a flight out of Greece with Blamey, Mackay and the others, Freyberg had instead landed on Crete. On 31 April, as the highest-ranking officer on the island, he was given command.

He found the island force woefully armed and equipped. It had 85 artillery pieces, one light anti-aircraft battery split between two of the three airfields, and 25 substandard tanks.

Churchill refused to send any more artillery to Crete. He played his usual duplicitous game, assuring the Australian and New Zealand Governments that equipment was available but not mentioning that he never intended to send it. The few British planes on the island were sent to Cairo, some 800 kilometres to the south-east.

Freyberg requested that about 10,000 men be evacuated because, without arms and other materiel, there was little for them to do except get up to mischief with the local population. This was yet another request ignored by Churchill, and the men were still on the island when the German invasion began.

The German high command had been unenthusiastic about invading Crete, because it interfered with their preparations for the imminent invasion of Russia. However, Luftwaffe (air force) commanders wanted to showcase their prowess and persuaded Hitler that an airborne invasion would be effective. It was a bold assertion, because this would be the first major airborne invasion in military history; nobody could predict how easy or successful it might be.

The plan was for the initial invaders to be delivered by parachute and glider; once airfields were secured, more would arrive by transport plane. With no seaborne support, the Germans would have no tanks or artillery. Their heaviest weapons would be recoilless rifles, which could launch a 6-kilogram shell over a distance of 5 kilometres.

Despite the Luftwaffe's enthusiasm, airborne invasions are extremely difficult to achieve. This one might well have failed but for a tragedy of miscommunication and command problems on the Allied side.

The first error was Churchill's choice of commander. Freyberg had the bearing of a heroic leader. He was a big, imposing man of action, and had been among the most highly decorated British Empire soldiers of World War I, having earned a Victoria Cross and three DSOs. He had just the characteristics that excited Churchill – but he also had failings that worked against the garrison on Crete. These failings were, in historian Antony Beevor's words, 'chiefly obstinacy, muddled thinking and a reluctance to criticize subordinates'.[8] All would come into play in the upcoming battle.

Even with these faults, Freyberg might have been up to the task if he had been given a clear briefing. Unfortunately, oblique communication from British intelligence collided with Freyberg's rigid thinking to set off a chain reaction that ended in calamity. It began when British intelligence attempted to hide the source of their information. They knew the invasion would be entirely airborne, but when conveying information to Freyberg, they included the possibility that there would be a conventional seaborne component too.

It is hardly surprising, therefore, that Freyberg was unable to conceive of a purely airborne invasion. He believed that historical precedents would persist and judged that the major landing force would be seaborne, supported by a minor airborne component, and made his dispositions accordingly. Instead of ensuring that all his resources were clustered around the three airfields along the 125 kilometres of tortuous rocky road on the north coast of Crete, he kept a large reserve force stationed close to the seaside capital, Chania, which he considered the most likely site for a marine landing.

British high command compounded the problem by refusing Freyberg permission to mine the airfields. The British wanted to ensure they were left operational for their own aircraft – aircraft that never came.

Brigadier George Vasey was the highest-ranking Australian officer on the island and commanded the Australians on Crete. He formed them into battalions around the easternmost airfield at Heraklion. His force was cobbled together out of the random mix of men the ocean had delivered up; it included some 1500 men who had survived the sinking of their transport ship and had arrived without equipment, in some cases even without boots.

At 8 am on 20 May 1941, waves of German planes from the north arrived over the Maleme airfield. The sky was blackened by 500 tri-motor Junkers transports and 80 troop gliders, which disgorged 22,000 paratroopers and mountain troops from the air, while 150 howling Stuka dive bombers and 280 long-range bombers rained bombs on the defenders and general population below.

The defenders put up a much stronger resistance than the Germans had expected. Many Germans were shot in their parachutes as they drifted to the ground. Those who landed were dealt with by the defenders as best they could. Despite their poor weaponry, the Allied troops were battle-hardened and organised. Germans were hunted down and machine-gunned or bayoneted. Every metre gained by the enemy was hard fought.

When the airborne attack on Heraklion came later that day, the Australians rebuffed it because they concentrated solely on the airfield. Likewise, despite being pushed back initially, the Greeks stationed around the middle airfield at Rethymno managed to beat the Germans back.

Yet because Freyberg had been so certain of a seaborne invasion, the airfield at Maleme was too weakly held, and the defending New Zealanders were forced to give ground. In the evening, the Germans gained a toehold on the airfield and held it against fierce but confused counterattacks by the defenders. Disaster was about to unfold on the western end of the island.

Sadly, three uncommitted Allied battalions remained near Chania. The situation was so finely balanced that with a little extra effort applied at the right place, the defenders would almost certainly have taken back the airfield and foiled the invasion. But on the first night of the invasion, instead of mobilising his reserves immediately, Freyberg went to bed confident the situation was under control. It wasn't. The airfield fell to the Germans and could not be recaptured.

Despite still being under heavy fire, the Germans set up an express air service on the captured airfield to bring in reinforcements. Mines on the airfield might well have prevented them from using it in this way. Aircraft shuttled onto and off the island, with just 70 seconds allowed for each plane to land, unload and take off. Some were destroyed, but the wreckage was quickly cleared away. German troops and materiel poured onto the airfield and spilled out to attack the island's defenders.

The fighting was desperate. The Allies threw everything they could at the Germans. To the latter's surprise, the locals joined in: the first concerted local resistance they had encountered during the war.

There was short-lived cheering when a lone RAF Hurricane briefly landed at one of the airfields. However, rather than heralding the arrival of Allied support, the lone aircraft was merely the pathetic remnant of a flight of six Hurricanes that had been sent as symbolic support. No more help would come from that source. The Germans owned the skies and most of the oceans all around.

The increasing German force moved east along the coast road from the captured western airfield.

* * *

On 26 May, a high-level group comprising Wavell, Blamey and Arthur Tedder, the Air Officer Commander in Chief of the RAF Middle East Command, flew to Alexandria to meet with Admiral of the Fleet Sir John Cunningham on his flagship, HMS *Warsprite*, to discuss evacuating the forces on Crete.

Also at the meeting was New Zealand's prime minister, Peter Fraser.

Wavell was gloomy about the prospects of success. Blamey was concerned but hopeful. It was agreed that the evacuation would proceed, and Wavell communicated with Freyberg to that effect.

On 29 May, Wavell and Blamey met with a liaison officer standing in for Cunningham. The officer delivered the bad news that while the rescue would proceed, it would be limited to destroyers, because the Royal Navy couldn't risk slower or bigger classes of ships. Blamey threatened that there would be serious political consequences from the Australian Government if the evacuation did not continue.

Blamey sent a coded message using Australian slang to the men on Crete,[9] urging them to fight their way to the south coast. The message was dropped by plane. Now, the defenders' only hope of salvation was to climb south, over the rugged mountain spine that dissected the island, and hope the Royal Navy would brave the conditions to get them off.

Once on the south coast, the Australian men under Vasey mounted a courageous rearguard action. Troops were evacuated over four nights, ending on 1 June. Destroyers shuttled men to cruisers, before taking a final load and heading for home. All officers with the rank of colonel or above were evacuated from Crete by air; this time Freyberg had no trouble accepting the order to leave. The navy suffered heavy damage from Stuka dive bombers, with the loss of 20 of the 54 participating warships. The Royal Navy evacuated around 10,000 Allied soldiers from Crete. More than 2000 Allied servicemen were killed. The shipping losses seriously threatened hopes of a meaningful British naval presence in the Far East if the Japanese entered the war.

The butcher's bill on Crete for the Allies was 4000 dead, with an unknown number of wounded and nearly 18,000 captured. There were around 275 Australians killed, 500 wounded and 3100 captured.

Blamey had used all his influence to get as many Australians out as he could but, as he wrote to Menzies, the result was 'very sad'.[10]

There was no way out for the local population. Because they had assisted the Allies, they were subject to more German savagery than was typical.

Freyberg gets the blame for these losses, yet the real responsibility lies with the British high command in general and with Churchill in particular. Freyberg was probably a good enough commander to have thwarted the enemy, had he been told there was to be no seaborne invasion, had he been allowed to mine the airfields and had Churchill released the artillery that was stored on the mainland. Vasey, however, believed Freyberg had botched the defence of Crete.

The German losses amounted to 6500 dead and wounded, with 370 aircraft destroyed or damaged. Far from being an operation that required limited resources, as had been touted by the German air command, it resulted in losses of aircraft and air crew that seriously hindered German operations for the rest of the war. Experienced pilots were particularly hard to replace. The Cretan engagement also delayed the invasion of Russia by four weeks, shortening the time available for the German advance before winter set in, with catastrophic results.

Hitler was shocked by the scale of the losses and, naturally enough, hid it from the Allies. The British misinterpreted the results and rushed to form airborne forces while the Germans were dismantling theirs.

Churchill, meanwhile, was sanguine about the results from Greece and Crete. The losses might have been heavy, but the hindering of German operations had brought strategic benefits for the Allies. On the downside, Churchill had paid a big price after leaving so many Allied troops on Crete when he could have taken them off in an orderly manner. He had known the parlous state of the forces on Crete, and intelligence had made it clear that an attack was coming. There had been enough time for proper preparation between the completion of the evacuation of Greece on 29 April and the first German attacks on Crete on 20 May. Even if there was a strategic reason to fight, he could have removed the 10,000 men Freyberg didn't have reason to keep on the island.

At about the same time, a drama was taking place on the high seas of the North Atlantic. The German battleship *Bismarck* and its escort sank a British battlecruiser, HMS *Hood*, on 24 May 1941. In the subsequent pursuit, RAF torpedo bombers damaged the *Bismarck*'s steering gear and the crippled ship was scuttled by its crew on 27 May. The sea battle was followed breathlessly by the press. This was an incredible piece of luck for Churchill, because it distracted the public from yet another British defeat.

The Australian Government was nowhere near as sanguine. Crete had been bad news for the Australians because Blamey and his officers had had no control over resourcing or transport. The battle had resulted in even more casualties than the Greek campaign. In total, Churchill's ill-advised forays into Greece and Crete had cost the Australian force around 600 men killed, 1000 wounded and 5000 captured.

* * *

The war had also come to Syria and Lebanon during this period. They had been French mandates since 1923, and so by 1941 they were controlled by the pro-Nazi Vichy government. Churchill was alerted in early May to the possibility of trouble in Syria, and feared it might become a base from which enemy planes could threaten British positions in the eastern Mediterranean.

On 20 May, the British Government had informed the Australian Government of its plans to invade Syria. Menzies, back in Australia after his trip to Britain, had sent a cable to Churchill on 29 May enthusiastically supporting the proposal: he feared that a build-up of enemy aircraft in the area could result in a rerun of the problems then being experienced in Crete. He did not consult Blamey. In a reply to Menzies two days later, Churchill upped the ante by claiming that Syria would soon be occupied by the Germans.

Both Wavell and Blamey were decidedly unenthusiastic about the idea of an invasion of Syria. Blamey wanted to consolidate his forces in Palestine, where the 6th Division was reforming after Greece and Crete. The only force available was two brigades of John Lavarack's 7th Division, currently in the Western Desert at Mersa Matruh.

Both commanders feared that if there were fierce resistance, more British resources would be dragged in. But with their political masters in agreement, Wavell and Blamey had no choice but to set about preparing an operation. Blamey's disquiet was increased when he learned not only that Jumbo Wilson was going to be the overall commander, but also that Wilson would remain headquartered in Jerusalem as the fighting moved towards Damascus, 270 kilometres away.

The initial force comprised the two brigades commanded by Lavarack and a brigade each of Free French and Indians. There would be no participating British national forces until mid-June, when an under-strength British division of two brigades arrived. The Australian 17th Brigade arrived at about the same time. In total, there were around 34,000 Allied troops against 25,000 predominantly Vichy French.

Given Wilson's distance from the fighting, Rowell argued strongly for local command to be given to Lavarack. Rowell confronted Blamey in Cairo and begged him to abide by his preference for the command of Australian forces by Australians and appoint Lavarack to the post. Given Blamey's ambivalence about Lavarack, it is unsurprising that initially he was noncommittal, but he soon acceded to Rowell's suggestion. Lavarack was appointed commander of the Syrian campaign on 1 June. Before the operations began, Blamey negotiated a compromise with Wavell, such that when the distances between Wilson's and Lavarack's headquarters became too great, Lavarack would take over command of local operations, while Wilson would retain theatre command.

Blamey remained anxious about the situation and the men in charge. He had no intention of abandoning Australian troops to either man, so he moved between Cairo and Syria several times. On his first Syrian visit, Blamey was on a fact-finding mission: he visited Lavarack's HQ in Nazareth, followed by Wilson's HQ 150 kilometres away in Jerusalem, then he was back with Lavarack the next day, having visited other headquarters en route.

The fighting began on 8 June. Initially, the Allies made good progress, as Churchill and Menzies had expected, but the Vichy French fought with skill and vigour. As the fighting moved away from Jerusalem, Lavarack took over field command and Rowell was given control of the HQ. When the British 6th Division arrived outside Damascus, Lavarack also took command of that division, without Wilson's ratification.

Lavarack might have had local tactical command, but he was obliged to follow Wilson's strategy. The main attack was planned to head from northern Palestine along the coast road towards Beirut, directly into the enemy's entrenched positions. Heavy Australian casualties were expected. Blamey disagreed with this strategy. He came from Cairo again, conferred with Lavarack in Nazareth, then travelled to the British division's HQ and back to Lavarack. Now with a clearer picture of the issues, Blamey immediately went back to Jerusalem by car to reprise his role in Greece – that is, to demand sensible and timely strategic decisions from a British commander.

It was close to midnight on 19 June 1941 when Blamey reached Wilson's headquarters. He barged in through security and demanded Wilson's staff rouse the sleeping general. After bluntly describing the situation to Wilson, Blamey outlined the changes he wanted. His aide-de-camp Norman Carlyon, who was within earshot, later recorded what transpired:

> Wilson listened. Then in a somewhat patronising way, indicated that he saw some merit in Blamey's view, and he would get in touch with Lavarack in the morning.
>
> Blamey was angry now. He raised his voice: 'Get on to him now immediately. Don't you know there are men out there being killed, and they include the cream of the A.I.F. I want you to get on the telephone at once to Lavarack. The morning will be too late.'
>
> It may seem strange to talk of the stocky Blamey standing over the mountainous Jumbo; but that is virtually what happened. One of the staff then got through by telephone to Lavarack's headquarters, and Wilson ordered a switch in the weight and direction of the main attack, as Blamey had recommended. The outcome was the turning-point of the campaign ... In none of the war histories that I have read is Blamey given credit for forcing a decision which ended a costly deadlock.[11]

This was indeed the turning point of the campaign. Lavarack was now in control and made good progress. Damascus fell on 24 June and the campaign effectively ended when the Allies took Beirut on 12 July.

The 36-day Syria–Lebanon campaign cost around 4700 Allied casualties, compared with 6352 (Vichy figures) or 8912 (British figures) of the enemy. Australian losses were 416 killed and 1136 wounded, giving a total of 1552.

Carlyon's words above are the only first-hand description of Blamey as he carried out his most important function as commander: making sure that a more senior foreign commander didn't use Australian soldiers casually or carelessly. Blamey was a lieutenant general standing up to a general, and thus he could have been accused of insubordination. In other heated engagements, he probably was. Nevertheless, it is clear in this instance that by using the power of his personality, assisted by ambiguous support from the Australian Government, he was able to 'command up' effectively, just as Monash had in the previous war.

8

The Rats of Tobruk

April 1941 to November 1941

The Allies might have beaten off the Italians in the Western Desert by early February 1941, but Hitler was not standing still. He had decided the fight in North Africa needed to be carried forward by someone with backbone, and on 11 January he issued Directive 22, which sent his favourite general, Erwin Rommel, and the newly constituted Afrika Korps to fight in Libya and Egypt. The first troops landed near Tripoli, Libya's capital, on 11 February 1941.

As related earlier, Rommel's sudden appearance had caught the British by surprise: they had anticipated a quiet time after beating the Italians and had sent Australian, New Zealand and British forces offshore to campaigns in Greece, Crete, Syria–Lebanon and Palestine.

The Afrika Korps was initially made up of the 15th Panzer and 5th Light Divisions. Also under Rommel's command were remnants of the Italian Motorised Corps and Italian non-motorised infantry. (For the sake of convenience, this book will use the term 'Afrika Korps' to describe all forces under Rommel, including the Italians.)

The Italians had been soundly defeated by the Allies in the previous months and were thought to be poor fighters by both sides. However, they acquitted themselves well under Rommel, showing that it wasn't the quality of the men that was the problem, but the quality of Italian command.

In fact, Rommel was technically under Italian command, with orders to defend Tripoli, but he was also under German command with a direct line to Hitler. Having an ambiguous command arrangement suited the general very well, because he could act on the orders he liked best. Rommel excelled in offensive war, believing that attack is the best form of defence and shock is the best force-multiplier. Thus, he liberally interpreted his orders to suit his tactical philosophy and aggressive character, and began to attack eastwards in the direction of Egypt.

Rommel got underway with a characteristic pell-mell rush to Egypt on 24 March 1941. As his forces sped east, he gained more support from Hitler, who liked a bit of dash from his generals. Soon Rommel had the bit between his teeth and couldn't be stopped by either Italian command or British defence.

North Africa was a hard environment to fight in. Logistics were a severe problem for all combatants, because there were few places along the coast where substantial quantities of supplies could be landed. Most had to be moved by motor vehicle along a single coast road, which stretched some 2400 kilometres from Tripoli via Benghazi and Tobruk to Cairo. As Rommel's supply lines lengthened, more fuel was guzzled by his transport trucks, leaving less available for fighting. Compounding Rommel's supply problems were the increasingly effective Allied attacks on Axis shipping and the competing demands of other theatres of war for German supplies.

For these reasons, German high command wanted Rommel to go no further than the port town of Benghazi. They surmised Rommel could sit across the coast road there, blocking Allied movement west while using relatively few resources himself. This did not suit Rommel, given his natural inclination never to take up defensive positions. With aspirations to take Cairo and maybe cut a path to the oil fields in the Middle East, he disobeyed this order and pressed on.

One of Rommel's strengths was his unorthodox attitude to supply. Where other commanders on both sides tried to ensure sufficient supply *before* an operation, Rommel was not so constrained. He set out believing that he could solve the problem as he went along. Recapturing the ports of Benghazi and Tobruk from the Allies would help, but even then, he couldn't rely on getting more than a fraction of his supply needs from across the Mediterranean. So he saved resources by demanding his men do more with less. In addition, he relied on the ever-helpful British because, luckily for him, they had a careless habit of leaving behind vast stores and copious machinery as they made their hurried retreat. Thus, they inadvertently became his second great quartermaster.

Even so, he had to run a lean, fast, bare-bones operation, which was at constant risk of running out of fuel and ammunition mid-battle, or just breaking down in the desert conditions. His army, including himself and his officers, lived on a diet of tinned meat, with little in the way of fresh fruit and vegetables. His machinery was kept moving by the midnight sweat of his mechanics as they laboured against the grinding effects of sand in the gears, on top of the normal problems associated with rapid long-distance warfare. Designed for benign European conditions and usually transported over long distances, the Panzer tanks suffered.

By 3 April, Rommel had captured Benghazi, 1000 kilometres from his starting point and nearly halfway to Cairo. In getting there, Rommel – nicknamed 'The Desert Fox' by British journalists – had played his usual tricks, racing, feinting and turning up where least expected. He wrote in his memoirs that he'd had problems getting his officers to forget their training, which had them making leisurely stops for refuelling, maintenance and restocking of ammunition.

Capturing British generals along the way gave him particular pleasure. He also noted that captured British food made a pleasant change from the monotonous German fare, and their fuel and vehicles were very helpful.

* * *

Blamey was now in Greece, as per his orders from Churchill via Wavell. As he confided to Menzies, he 'was not as sanguine [as the British] about a German counter stroke and felt that the danger had been underestimated'.[1] Back in January, he had appointed Leslie Morshead to take over command of the 9th Division from the seriously ill Major General Henry Wynter, and had promoted Morshead to major general with instructions to relieve the 6th Division in eastern Libya and continue training beyond that.

Morshead was a hard man. Official World War I historian Charles Bean described him as a small man who was the closest 'to a martinet among all the young Australian colonels, but able to distinguish the valuable from the worthless in the old army practice; insistent on punctiliousness throughout the battalion ... he had turned out a battalion which anyone acquainted with the whole force recognised, even before Messines, as one of the very best'.[2] Morshead had served at Gallipoli then, like Blamey, trained under Monash, fighting at Messines and Passchendaele. He was later gassed during the 1918 German spring offensive. Unable to find a place in the regular army after the war, he had joined the CMF.

The intervening years seemed not to have softened Morshead. His men recognised his uncompromising nature by calling him 'Ming the Merciless', after the villain in comic book *Flash Gordon*, but then changed it to just 'Ming' as a bond of mutual affection and esteem grew between the general and his men.[3]

On 5 February, Morshead left behind the 18th Brigade – 'probably the AIF's best trained and equipped and most disciplined brigade'[4] – to command the raw and inexperienced 9th Division in Palestine. With a chronic shortage of weaponry and ammunition, there was little opportunity for meaningful training. In that raw state, the division moved to Benghazi at the start of March 1941.

On arrival there, the 9th Division was chaotically organised in a configuration devised by the local British commander, Lieutenant General Sir Philip Neame. Spread out over hundreds of kilometres between Benghazi and Tobruk, they had poor cohesion, no training and no tanks or armoured cars. When

Lieutenant General Leslie Morshead in conference with Blamey next to a plane wing. (Blamey family)

Wavell arrived on 17 March, Morshead had no trouble in convincing him to allow the 9th Division to withdraw and consolidate for training. Wavell wrote that Neame's troop dispositions were 'just crazy',[5] yet typically, he didn't order his subordinate lieutenant to resolve the issue. Nor did he fire him.

Wavell's problem with Neame was resolved by the Germans on 6 April, when a patrol captured both Neame and Richard O'Connor, the British commander in Egypt. They were attempting to flee their vulnerable position in the town of Maraua in an unescorted vehicle to catch up with their headquarters in Timimi, 100 kilometres west of Tobruk. Both generals would spend the next two and half years as POWs near Florence, Italy.

Recognising the danger Rommel represented, Morshead and Wavell agreed that the Australian 9th Division would withdraw to Tobruk as a suitable place to shelter from Rommel's helter-skelter advance. Morshead begged, borrowed and stole enough transport to move his forces back to defensible positions before Rommel could overrun them. As the inexperienced Australians fell back, they were given ample protection from British artillery, machine gunners and air force. The withdrawal of the 9th Division from Timimi to Tobruk in five days from 4 April 1941 proved to be a steep learning curve for the new general. He did have some luck, though, when Rommel split his force into three weak prongs, rather than concentrating all his troops along the coast road that the Australians were using.

As the 9th Division arrived at Tobruk, they were joined by Morshead's old 18th Brigade from Palestine, along with other Australian, British, New Zealand and Indian forces. In all, Morshead had around 31,000 men under him. Of that number, 24,000 were fighting men, comprising four brigades of Australian infantry as well as some British and Indian infantry. There was also the equivalent of four regiments of artillery, two anti-tank regiments, 55 tanks and nearly 80 anti-aircraft guns. Unfortunately there was an over-supply of light weapons and an under-supply of anti-tank guns, which meant that there was insufficient firepower to stop the enemy's heavy weapons at a distance.[6]

Lavarack had taken over Australian command in the Western Desert, and it was agreed that Morshead would command within the Tobruk perimeter while Lavarack remained outside with a mobile force. On 11 April, Blamey met with Wilson and Wavell in Greece and was initially upset that the 18th Brigade had been split from the 7th Division without his approval. But he got over it soon enough; it was probably just a bit of theatre to make sure the British thought twice before interfering with his command again. Certainly Wavell was more careful and respectful of Blamey from then on.

Wavell asked if the rest of the 7th Division could join the 18th Brigade inside Tobruk. Blamey said no, claiming that four brigades were enough. Wavell then asked if Lavarack should take command of XIII Corps (Western Desert Force), which was being reactivated in order to counter Rommel's advance. Blamey declined, saying Lavarack was not suitable for high command. Wavell appointed a British officer instead. Naturally enough, when Lavarack found out, he had yet another reason to be furious with Blamey.[7]

* * *

With much of the former XIII Corps now in Greece and only a skeleton force left outside Tobruk, Rommel's troops were regrouped and encountering little difficulty as they cut across the desert en route to the Egyptian border, some 140 kilometres further east.

But Rommel was stuck with a dilemma. He had the most to gain if he chased and defeated the major part of the remaining British force, which lay between him and Cairo. Yet there were dangers in leaving an enemy force at Tobruk. He needed the port to land supplies and, more importantly, was worried that the Australians would burst out of Tobruk at his rear, putting him into a two-front battle.

Attacking Tobruk would need to become his major focus.

* * *

The Allies had begun work rehabilitating the Tobruk defences in March after they captured the port from the Italians. On his way west to take over the 9th Division, Leslie Morshead had had the good fortune to spend three days studying the layout.

He had found that the 48-kilometre perimeter of Tobruk was dotted with heavily fortified concrete bunkers, trenches, minefields and barbed wire, but it was too long for his force to hold it in depth for its whole length. Fortunately, the port was protected by a peninsula that jutted out far enough to be out of the range of German artillery.

So, drawing on his World War I experience, and undoubtedly his observations of Rommel's tactics in France, Morshead set

Brigadier Arthur 'Tubby' Allen, General Blamey and his aide-de-camp Wilmott at a surf carnival on the beach at Gaza, Palestine, July 1941. (AWM 002393)

2/13th Infantry Battalion clearing barbed wire in Tobruk, September 1941. (AWM 020780)

about turning the apparent weaknesses in Tobruk's defences into a strength.

The Diggers might have been green, but Morshead had experience from World War I and was combat-ready. While training had been rushed, a great deal of attention had been paid to the World War I technique of 'aggressive patrolling' deep beyond the perimeter to gather information. The technique emphasised stealth and the extensive use of bayonets on any enemy soldier they found asleep or awake. Such patrols unnerved the enemy and prevented it from gathering its own intelligence. As Morshead told Chester Wilmot: 'I determined we should make no-man's land our land.'[8]

Rommel's charging technique had been the modus operandi of his Ghost Division during the fall of France in June 1940, and was still his preferred tactic in North Africa. It relied heavily on the shock factor. Sooner or later someone had to catch on, and now it would be *Rommel's* turn to be shocked.

Morshead was ready for Rommel at Tobruk in 1941. Speaking to his men, he insisted: 'there'll be no Dunkirk here. If we should have to get out, we shall fight our way out. There will be no surrender and no retreat.'[9]

* * *

Rommel's basic plan was to start an attack on Tobruk in the middle of the night. He would quietly penetrate the perimeter, then advance stealthily some 8 kilometres into the centre of the Allied defences. Once well inside, the Afrika Korps would open fire, causing chaos, before aiming for the settlement and port of Tobruk. Rommel was certain this would quickly cause the collapse of the defending force as the tactic had always previously done.

So confident was Rommel that he didn't wait for the Italian plans of the defences' layout to be delivered to him, nor did he carry out proper reconnaissance. He sent out patrols to get information, but they were thwarted by shelling and machine-gun fire as soon as they got close to the perimeter, while the attempted reconnaissance alerted Morshead to the possibility of an attack and the likely point at which it would occur.

After days of feinting attacks designed to soften the defenders, the German attack proper went in on the bitterly cold night of 13–14 April. An hour before midnight, 30 German infantry busted through the wire and set up with machine guns, small field guns and a mortar. Return fire failed to budge them. The Australian post commander and six men attacked, killing 12 Germans, capturing one and driving the others off before midnight. One of the six, Infantryman Corporal Jack Edmondson, was posthumously awarded the first Victoria Cross received by an Australian in World War II.[10]

German tanks and infantry came back just after midnight and made some progress inside the perimeter through the same point of entry, but it was so dark their engineer guides became disoriented and sustained casualties as British artillery fired in the direction of their noise.

At 5.20 am, the lead tank moved forward through a narrow gap the Germans had created in another part of the perimeter. Far from being cowed, the Australian infantry were obeying orders: they had been told to stay clear of the intruders and make no attempt to stop the expected armoured column. Their job was to lie in wait for the German infantry who would follow.

Thirty-eight German tanks with trailing infantry advanced more than 1 kilometre inside the perimeter before the Australian trap snapped shut behind them. In the early light of morning, the Germans were hit with everything available – artillery, tank fire, machine guns, grenades, small arms fire and bayonets – while planes engaged in a dog fight overhead.

By 8.30 am, the battle was all over aside from the mopping up. Later in the day, Rommel ordered another attack, which was called off because insufficient forces could be assembled.

Rommel had begun his attack fully expecting to take the defenders without a fight.[11] He'd even sent over aircraft dropping flyers to say that anyone waving a white handkerchief would be treated well. Morshead had turned the tables on him. Not only didn't the defence collapse, but the RAF and anti-aircraft fire also downed four Stukas. The Australians and the British artillery had outfought Rommel. In the heat of battle, the German formations quickly became a rabble.

Rommel tried again on 16 April but failed. Twenty-six German officers and nearly 800 men were captured. The Germans then went into defensive positions, but over the next 10 days they were constantly kept off balance by the Australians' aggressive night-time patrolling, which led to the capture of approximately 1700 prisoners.

It was the first time Rommel had come up against the Australians; he observed in his papers that Australian soldiers were 'immensely big and powerful men, who without question represented an elite formation of the British Empire, a fact that was also evident in battle'.[12] German propaganda wasn't so flattering: Lord Haw-Haw, the infamous British Nazi propogandist, called the Australians at Tobruk 'rats', which the Australians repurposed as a compliment, naming themselves 'the Rats of Tobruk'.

The Diggers themselves weren't as sanguine as Rommel. One Digger wrote that 'Australians were not "born soldiers"', as many believed. He felt that many members of his 43rd Battalion of the 9th Division were embarrassed by their early ineptitude.[13] Fighting a war was something that had to be learned.

Rommel's next serious attempt at penetrating the Allies' stronghold, on 30 April, was better prepared. The Afrika Korps Panzers, infantry and dive bombers maximised their penetration efforts by concentrating their power on a particular point in the defences, and bit by bit broke into the perimeter. Clear information on the degree of penetration was hard for the Allies to obtain, and the situation was made worse by thick fog that enveloped the area the next morning. However, unaided by the element of surprise, Rommel's thrust ran out of momentum thanks to the concerted efforts of the defenders. Neither side succeeded in budging the other, so a stalemate ensued, with Rommel's forces holding part of the captured perimeter.

It might not have been a crushing victory, but the Australians had weakened Rommel by forcing him to dedicate resources to the siege that would otherwise have been used in his advance on Egypt, and by denying him a port to shorten his supply lines. Fighting Rommel to a standstill was a first for this war.

The Australians made sure that the besiegers continued to suffer by keeping up active patrols outside the boundary at night, taking prisoners for interrogation and locating concentrations of concealed enemy for the artillery to blast, often with striking accuracy.[14]

The Germans had a miserable time of it. They couldn't dig into the underlying hard limestone layer. Denied the protection of trenches or pits, they had to lie still to avoid detection during the bitterly cold nights and scorching, flyblown days. Night or day, they were unsheltered from hurricane-force winds and sandstorms. They were also at constant risk of being taken prisoner. Over 10 days in late April, patrolling harvested more than 1700 enemy prisoners.[15]

Rommel was very much a running-on-empty kind of leader, and that applied to food as much as anything else. He and his men were suffering from their bad diet. Even 25-year-olds were losing their teeth in gums that wouldn't stop bleeding.[16]

If the Germans were badly off, the besieged weren't having much fun either. While the 'Tobruk Ferry Service' – that is, the British and Australian navies – did their best to shepherd cargo ships past enemy ships and planes, shipping losses were high. Enough supplies got through to keep the defenders going, but it was very basic living. There was never enough clean water, certainly not sufficient for a proper wash. Their diet, though not as poor as the besiegers', was a meagre, monotonous mix of army biscuits and bully beef interspersed with unloved soya bean bread. Fresh fruit, vegetables and meat were seldom seen, though every now and then the tedium was relieved with parcels of chocolates, biscuits, tinned fruit and dates courtesy of the Australian Comforts Fund, an umbrella organisation that provided comfort to soldiers.

The troops were in a desert beset by intermittent sandstorms. Summer temperatures varied from below 10 degrees Celsius at night in winter to around 30 degrees during the day. Adding to the wretchedness was the constant, stress-inducing noise of shelling from outside the fortress, and worse, explosions from incoming munitions. And always and everywhere, there were flies and wind.

The soldiers out on the perimeter had it toughest. They had to be on the lookout for German machine-gun fire, and there was always the risk of walking into mines the enemy had planted.

* * *

Back in Cairo on 24 April after being ordered to evacuate from Greece, Blamey set about reuniting his scattered force. He was mindful that men in combat suffer a rapid deterioration of health and general wellbeing over and above any casualties inflicted by the enemy. He wanted the 9th Division and 18th Brigade out of Tobruk, and that fight would last for over five months.

Secret messages intercepted by the British convinced Churchill that the Afrika Korps was weak and short of supplies and could be beaten with a concerted push. In a bold move, he sent a resupply convoy through the Straits of Gibraltar, right under the Germans' noses, instead of having it sail around Africa and into the Mediterranean via the Suez Canal. The act was so audacious that the Axis forces were caught flat-footed, and the flotilla was largely untroubled by enemy ships and planes. The convoy lost only one ship and landed at Alexandria

Lady Olga Blamey presenting prizes at the Gaza Beach Surf Lifesaving Carnival, Palestine, in September 1941. General Blamey is on her right. (AWM 009904)

General Blamey and his aide-de-camp Norman Carlyon watching the AIF cricket team take on the Gezira Sporting Club in Cairo, October 1941. (AWM 020859)

on 12 May, resupplying British forces in Egypt with 238 tanks and 43 Hurricane fighter planes.[17]

Following this success, Churchill insisted that Wavell attack Rommel. While Rommel's main force was concentrated on Tobruk, a smaller group had captured the Egyptian border town of Sollum then advanced a further 20 kilometres to Halfaya Pass. In mid-May, the hastily planned Operation Brevity led to the recapture of the pass by the British, but it was back in German hands just 10 days later.

On 15 June, the British launched the more extensive Operation Battleaxe, intended to be a knock-out blow, but things did not go to plan. Thanks to Churchill's convoy, the British had more men and tanks than the Germans, but Rommel fought back in his typical unconventional way. Acting like the cavalry of old, British tanks repeatedly charged chaotically at the enemy, only to be blasted by Rommel's batteries of 88-millimetre anti-aircraft guns doing double duty as anti-tank guns. While the 88s did their deadly work, the Panzer force held back, enjoying the protection of their artillery, emerging only when a path was cleared through the incapacitated British tanks.

The two sides battled through the day on 16 June. The next day, Rommel carried out one of his characteristic surprise encircling manoeuvres. Despite having superior arms and air cover, British opposition collapsed. Most British troops escaped east towards Cairo, leaving behind 100 new tanks. Once Rommel had recovered and repaired his own damaged tanks, he found he had lost only a dozen; British tank fire had barely penetrated Panzer armour, and thus most of the damage was superficial. Rommel added to his tank collection by commandeering some abandoned British tanks.

Here was a real German victory. Morale soared even higher among his troops. Hitler was so pleased he made Rommel a full general in July 1941.

As New Zealand commander Freyberg later noted, the 'lack of success of British tactics against Germans in the spring and summer of 1941 ought to have alerted the British to the need for a complete reappraisal'. In particular, he and Blamey objected to the way the British structured their forces. 'General Blamey and myself ... were against the Brigade Group battle [used by the British]. We always moved by Brigade Groups but concentrated to fight as a Division with our guns under Divisional control.'[18] The German did likewise. If brigades are amassed to fight with their division, there is a much greater concentration of men and guns than if they act independently.

Unwilling to take advice from mere Australians and New Zealanders, or indeed to draw their own conclusions from their failed experiment, the British forces in the Western Desert would remain in their brigade groups, or 'Jock columns', for at least another year.

* * *

For the failure of Operation Battleaxe, Wavell was relieved of his position on 20 June 1941. When Wavell and his wife departed Cairo by plane, only Blamey and Carlyon were at the airport to see them off.

Wavell's replacement as Middle East commander in chief was General Claude Auchinleck; Wavell would be taking up

Auchinleck's current position as commander in chief in India. Blamey confided in a trusted officer that Auchinleck was a bully and nobody got very far trying to bully Blamey.[19] Over the coming months, Lieutenant General Sir Alan Cunningham would be appointed to lead the new Eighth Army, consisting of XIII Corps and the newly formed XXX Corps, and take the fight to Rommel.

Auchinleck took over on 5 July while Blamey was involved with the fight in Syria. Soon after this, Morshead arrived in Cairo to spend several days with Blamey. He confirmed that the Australians at Tobruk were losing their stamina and as a result would soon be unable to resist a concerted assault.[20] Separately Blamey met with Major General Burston, the Australian director of medical services for the Middle East. Burston reported that the men he had seen on leave from Tobruk were losing weight and condition, and affirmed that they would probably not hold up against a sustained attack.[21]

Blamey and Auchinleck had their first formal meeting on 13 July, and from then on Blamey kept up constant pressure on his new commander in chief to relieve the troops at Tobruk. Part of Blamey's argument was that there were plenty of rested men in forces from other nations available to replace them, and that it was time the British honoured the inter-government agreement to keep the Australian forces together. Menzies agreed with Blamey's position, and cabled Churchill urging relief of the Tobruk force.[22]

In an interchange observed by Freyberg, Auchinleck insisted that Blamey, as his deputy, must support him or be relieved. Blamey dared him to 'go ahead and do it'.[23] His bluff called, Auchinleck summoned Morshead's chief of staff, Major

Charles 'Gaffer' Lloyd, to Cairo in an attempt to browbeat him into agreeing that the men at Tobruk were fit. Again he failed. Naturally Lloyd had consulted Blamey, but his answer would have been the same anyway: the men would be ineffective in any attempt by Rommel to break the siege.[24]

The persistence of Blamey's demands of Auchinleck and Menzies's demands of Churchill finally weakened British resolve. After Auchinleck met with the Imperial General Staff in London at the end of July, he sent a telegram authorising the relief of the Australian 18th Brigade at Tobruk.

The operation to replace the brigade began in mid-August. Blamey was at the docks to see them arrive in Alexandria. Carlyon recorded that they seemed fit and tanned above the waist, but the 'majority seem to have little or no muscle in their legs. Blamey was overjoyed to see these young veterans clumping down the gangways.'[25] He quickly set about returning them to their parent 7th Division in Palestine.

It was only a partial win for Blamey, however. The 9th Division remained at Tobruk and he was forced to keep up pressure on Auchinleck and officials in Canberra.

As Auchinleck stonewalled and time dragged on without reply from Australia, Blamey became irritable. But there were big political moves underway at home. Menzies had come under severe public criticism for his handling of the war, and on 29 August 1941 he resigned as Prime Minister, to be replaced by Arthur Fadden of the Country Party.

Churchill weighed into the argument by sending a cable to Fadden on 11 September, full of his characteristic colourful language, claiming it was necessary for the Diggers at

Tobruk to stay put. This proved to be a tactical mistake on Churchill's part: Blamey's telegrams had gone unanswered, but correspondence from the British Prime Minister was too important for the Australian government to ignore. Fadden replied on 15 September, supporting Blamey's persistent and cogent arguments for the relief of the 9th Division. After Fadden's government fell on 7 October, Churchill tried again to keep the 9th Division at Tobruk by canvassing the new prime minister, John Curtin, only to receive the same answer on 16 October.

Churchill finally ordered Auchinleck to begin the Diggers' evacuation.[26] Carlyon observed that Blamey was suddenly cheerful, while it was Auchinleck's turn to become irritable. Blamey put on a dinner to celebrate.[27]

Blamey was promoted to full general on 24 September 1941, after ongoing discussions initiated by Sturdee between the governments of Britain and Australia. He was the first Australian officer to achieve this rank while on active duty.

The relief of the 9th Division was largely complete by 25 October 1941, when the British 70th Division under Major General Ronald Scobie took over in Tobruk. The toll for the 9th Division and attached troops during the siege was 832 killed, 2177 wounded and 941 taken prisoner, with a total casualty number (including prisoners) of 3950.[28] While most of the division spent several months resting in Palestine, one Australian battalion and two companies were left behind in Tobruk, after the sinking of the ship due to evacuate them.

The working atmosphere in Cairo remained tense, with the British Middle East command resentful over the recall of the 9th Division. To the increasing frustration of Churchill and

Auchinleck, Blamey continued to demand the AIF be unified under Australian control.

* * *

Back in Australia, after just 40 days as Prime Minister, Arthur Fadden had lost the confidence of the parliament. He was replaced by Labor's John Curtin on 7 October 1941.

By the end of that month, fighting in the Mediterranean region had died down. Most of the 9th Division was out of Tobruk and there were no pressing matters to keep Blamey in Cairo. Curtin ordered Blamey to return briefly to Australia to meet with him and his new cabinet.

Blamey appointed Morshead to stand in his place in Cairo and on 2 November 1941 boarded a Sunderland flying boat for home, travelling the Horseshoe Route in reverse. Blamey's flight overnighted in Bahrain, Karachi, Calcutta, Rangoon, Singapore, Darwin and Townsville, before finally arriving in Sydney on 10 November.

The overnight stops outside Australia were accompanied by lavish official dinners arranged by local British military commanders. They provided a great opportunity for Blamey to assess the situation in these far-flung outposts – and he didn't like much of what he saw. He found the situation in Singapore particularly worrying: in September, Japan had invaded French Indochina, and its new airfields and navy bases were worryingly close to the east coast of Malaya, and Singapore. After an official dinner with Lieutenant General Arthur Percival, the British army commander in Malaya, and Australian 8th Division commander

Gordon Bennett, Blamey expressed his dismay to Carlyon that these high-ranking diners seemed almost indifferent to the prospect that Japan might enter the war, and oblivious to what it might mean for them.[29]

On arrival in Australia, Blamey attended an extensive round of talks in Canberra with Curtin and his cabinet ministers, orchestrated by Blamey's old friend Frederick Shedden, Secretary of the Department of Defence Co-ordination. There were some strategic discussions, but mostly the meetings were an opportunity for Labor politicians to familiarise themselves with Blamey, gain confidence in him and overcome their prejudice towards a man they saw as a conservative opponent.

On 11 November, Blamey was welcomed to the Advisory War Council at Parliament House, where Prime Minister Curtin and former prime minister Menzies both declared that Blamey's performance since 1939 had confirmed that he was Australia's first soldier, that they knew he was doing a good job and that he enjoyed the confidence of both sides of parliament.[30]

As a result of his recent experiences in Malaya and Singapore, Blamey was certain that Japan would soon enter the war. Its longstanding military action in China and more recent annexation of French Indochina seemed to him clear indicators of this. Increasingly concerned by Japanese aggression, American president Franklin D. Roosevelt had ended shipments of scrap iron, steel and aviation fuel to Japan in mid-1940, and of oil and gasoline in August 1941, inflaming Japan's anger against the United States.

In the face of the Japanese threat, Blamey was shocked to find the Australian public carrying on with life as usual. During a press interview in Sydney, he publicly criticised Australians' complacent, fun-loving ways. His own fun-loving visit to a race meeting was criticised in turn by the press, although Carlyon would be quick to defend Blamey by writing that it was rare for the general to take a holiday and that most of the time he worked under great pressure.[31] Naturally enough, the press did not know *how much* work and pressure.

Expressing his fears to Curtin about a lack of preparation for what Blamey felt certain was the impending invasion of Singapore, Blamey requested that the 8th Division be moved out of harm's way in Singapore to the Middle East. Tragically this request was not acted on, but given that Japan would join the war a little over a month later, it probably couldn't have been because the political wheels ground slowly.

* * *

Blamey itched to get back to the reality of war. On 27 November, after only 17 days in Australia, he departed for Cairo, arriving there on 11 December 1941.

Four days earlier, Japan had bombed the US naval base at Pearl Harbor, Hawaii, then carried out a series of attacks on US and British territories across the Pacific. In consequence, the USA declared war against Japan, and joined forces with Britain and its colonial allies.

Churchill was bordering on ecstatic as the USA finally became a shooting ally. Now it really *was* a world war.

9

The Pacific War Begins

December 1941 to April 1942

At 7.55 am on Sunday, 7 December 1941, the Japanese launched a devastating surprise attack on the US Pacific Fleet at Pearl Harbor in Hawaii, using aircraft launched from aircraft carriers. Over the next seven hours, they followed up this strike with attacks on the US territories of the Philippines, Guam and Wake Island, and the British colonies of Hong Kong, Malaya and Singapore. On 8 December, the previously neutral United States declared war on Japan. Japan's two Axis partners, Germany and Italy, then declared war on the US, and the US in turn declared war on them.

After landing on the east coast of Malaya, Japanese forces had split to cascade down both coasts on 8 December 1941. (All places the Japanese attacked immediately after Pearl Harbor are on the other side of the International Date Line, hence the apparent discrepancy between the dates.) British and Indian forces in Malaya conducted a fighting withdrawal, but time and again they were beaten by an enemy that did the unexpected.

The British had seriously misjudged the Japanese. Expecting that the Malay jungle would force the Japanese to stay on the roads and slow down their advance to the pace of marching men, the British were greatly surprised to discover that the opposite was happening. The jungle was not especially dense, and it was interspersed with rubber plantations. Japanese tanks were small and could weave their way through the trees, accompanied by the troops. The Japanese also co-opted local bicycles and raced down the well-made coast roads. When they came up against fortified Allied positions, they surprised army command by moving tanks through the sparse jungle and open plantations, or commandeering boats to sail around the strong points then attacking the defenders from behind.

The Australian 8th Division, under the command of Major General Gordon Bennett, first engaged the Japanese in the southern Malayan state of Johor on 14 January. The next day, the Japanese attempted to outflank them. The Australians were pushed back, and on 27 January, all Allied forces on the Malay Peninsula were ordered to withdraw to Singapore.

* * *

Not all of the 8th Division had been deployed to Malaya, however; the 23rd Brigade had been kept in Australia, then broken up and sent to defend garrisons in the region. The 2nd Battalion became part of Lark Force, consisting of around 1400 personnel, whose role was to guard the garrison at Rabaul on the island of New Britain, northeast of New Guinea.

On 23 January, after receiving information that the Japanese fleet was approaching, Lark Force was rapidly overrun by 5000 Japanese troops and 100 aircraft. In view of the overwhelming strength of the invaders, commanding officer Lieutenant Colonel John Scanlan issued an order of 'every man for himself'. Some 400 men escaped in small boats or were picked up by larger vessels.

Around 160 Lark Force personnel made their way south along the coast of New Britain, and a few weeks later went ashore at Tol Plantation, hoping to find provisions. Discovered by the Japanese, the men were taken prisoner. Shortly thereafter, they were marched into the jungle and either shot, bayonetted or burned alive. Just six men survived with the help of locals, and joined a group of 156 civilians, soldiers and sailors rescued by HMAS *Laurabada* on 12 April 1942.

Lark Force survivors in other parts of the island were taken captive by the Japanese. In July 1942, some 845 prisoners of war, including Lark Force soldiers, were rounded up along with 209 civilians. They embarked for Hainan Island, China, on the *Montevideo Maru*. En route, the ship was torpedoed and sunk by an American submarine, the USS *Sturgeon*. All the prisoners were locked below decks and all drowned.

The remaining prisoners of war on New Britain were taken to Japan onboard the *Natuno Maru*, and would stay there until the surrender of Japan in September 1945.[1]

* * *

There were still three Australian divisions garrisoned in the Middle East, far from the action in the Pacific. Back in Cairo after his Australian visit, Blamey continued to clash with British high command over their deployment. As early as August

1941, the Australian Government had begun stripping out experienced officers from the Australian forces in the Middle East, bringing them home to deal with the urgent tasks involved in getting Australia on a war footing.[2] The very day Blamey returned to Cairo, Sydney Rowell received a cable requesting the return of several additional senior officers to Australia.

Despite the day-to-day tensions between Blamey and British command, he had been mentioned in dispatches for the eighth time on 26 December 1941 for his command in Greece. He was also appointed a Knight Commander of the Order of the Bath on 1 January 1942 and would be awarded the Greek War Cross, First Class, on 7 April. It seemed the British recognised his professionalism, but were only prepared to reward it by decoration, not with command over any substantial British forces.

* * *

On 3 January, the British Government asked Australia to send two additional divisions to fight the Japanese. They would be part of the new American–British–Dutch–Australian (ABDA) Command, covering South-East Asia and northern Australia, under General Wavell. Blamey suggested sending I Corps – the 6th and 7th Divisions – recommending Lavarack as its commander, since there was still much for Blamey himself to do in Cairo, supervising the transfer of the two divisions.

Even though Rommel remained a threat in the Middle East, there was little active war campaigning for the Australians. Blamey, still protecting the diminishing AIF and increasingly frustrating Auchinleck and the rest of the British command in Cairo, was now anxious to join the bulk of his troops in the Pacific. He cabled Curtin to that effect on 2 February. But the course of the war would soon disrupt all previous plans.

* * *

Johor – in Japanese hands following the 8th Division's defeat – was the main source of Singapore's water. The Japanese now cut off the water supply from Malaya to Singapore and attacked the island. The Allies could not defend 'fortress' Singapore, and it was surrendered on 15 February 1942.

Blamey had been right in the doubts he had held about the 'Singapore strategy' ever since his time at Quetta before World War I. He had always believed that the British could not defend Singapore from an Asian force, likely Japan, if Britain was already fighting a European and Atlantic war. This proved to be true, especially after the shipping losses suffered during the evacuations of Greece and Crete. Churchill had not sent the promised fleet, instead sending just a small force that included the battleship HMS *Prince of Wales* and battlecruiser HMS *Repulse*, both without air protection and sunk by the Japanese off Malaya on 10 December 1941.

But by far the greatest factor in the loss of Singapore was weak command by Lieutenant General Arthur Percival, the British General Officer Commanding Malaya. For months he had been repeating the old British line that to prepare for attack would be 'bad for the morale of British troops, local politicians and the native races of Malaya',[3] as he squandered the defender's advantage. Particularly egregious was his refusal, long before the Japanese invaded Malaya, to act on the advice of his chief engineer, Brigadier Ivan Simson, and build fixed defences in Johor and on the north shore of Singapore.

Usually, an attacking force needs to be considerably larger than the defending force to be successful. In the Malayan campaign, the size advantage was reversed.[4] Ironically, by the time the Japanese force had reached Singapore they had almost run out of ammunition and were considering retreating.

Of the British, Australian and Indian military force of about 140,000 across Malaya and Singapore, 130,000 were captured and 8000 killed. The Japanese also slaughtered 30,000 Chinese in Singapore and tens of thousands more in Malaya.

It would be the biggest Australian defeat of the war, with more than 1800 killed and over 15,000 taken prisoner, including most of the 8th Division. Only two-thirds of them would survive captivity in the brutal POW camps.[5] Controversially, their commander, Gordon Bennett, left Singapore on his own authority, claiming he held important information about fighting the Japanese in jungles. Around 1 am on 16 February, he and several others commandeered a small boat and, after an arduous trip via Sumatra and Java, arrived in Sydney on 1 March.[6] He was never again posted to an overseas combat command.

The campaign in Malaya and Singapore could be likened to the earlier battle for Greece. Both involved exhortations of hope and glory from Churchill, but were supported by precious little in the way of sound British military command or promised materiel. In neither theatre of war did the Allies have sufficient modern aircraft. In both, the British commanders were weak and the defenders were facing enemy forces that had not yet suffered defeat in battle.

There were two major differences, however, between the battles in the Mediterranean and those in Asia. The first was that the Axis force that invaded Greece was much better equipped and larger (by a factor of around eight to one) than the defending force, while the Japanese force that invaded Malaya and Singapore was under-equipped and half the size of the defending force. Purely in terms of force imbalance, Greece was destined to fall, while Singapore should have held out for much longer.

The second major difference between these battles is that, despite overall British command, the Allied battle in Greece was dominated by Blamey, while the battle in Singapore wasn't. Bennett was no substitute for Blamey. With Blamey, or someone of his stature, character and experience, on the Malay Peninsula to 'influence' British command, it is almost certain that the Japanese invasion could have been stalled, maybe even for long enough to evacuate most of the force.

* * *

The first convoy of the 7th Division returning from the Middle East had arrived off the island of Java on 14 February 1942, the day before Singapore fell, and just as the Japanese were preparing to invade Java. I Corps commander Lavarack had flown and was already on the island. He recommended to the Australian Government that the troops not disembark, because they were too small a force to defend Java. Nevertheless, it was Wavell who was in command, and he advised the government to land the Diggers. The government took Wavell's advice. When the Japanese invaded Java two weeks later, 36 of the 7th Division were killed and the other 2920 marched into captivity.[7] Lavarack and Wavell flew out – Lavarack becoming Acting Commander in Chief, Australian Military Forces in Australia until Blamey arrived, and Wavell returning to India.

With Singapore and Java in Japanese hands, Lieutenant General Vernon Sturdee, Chief of the General Staff, recommended to Curtin that the remainder of I Corps be brought home to Australia. On 17 February, Curtin cabled Churchill to request that the ships transporting the 6th Division and remainder of the 7th Division proceed to Australia. For several days he received no reply.

* * *

On 19 February, four days after the fall of Singapore, the Japanese launched the first of nearly 100 air raids on Australian soil, with their largest attacks focused on Darwin. The entire Australian population from the Prime Minister down was panicked by the proximity of the Japanese and terrified by the prospect of an imminent invasion. Australian home defence was desperately weak, and defended on home soil by poorly trained militia.

On 20 February, Curtin cabled Blamey: 'both the bastion of Empire defence in the south-western Pacific and the outer screen to Australia leave Australia bare ... In view of the unsatisfactory strength of our defences in Australia, the destination of the AIF should be Australia. It is desired that you arrange to return here as speedily as possible.'[8]

Curtin had still not heard from Churchill about the fate of the 6th and 7th Divisions. US President Roosevelt had weighed in on Churchill's side with the offer to send an American division, only partly trained, to Australia to replace the diverted Diggers. Late on 20 February, Curtin sent another, somewhat curt message to London.

The next day he received strongly worded cables from Churchill and Roosevelt, repeating their previous arguments. He was shocked at the interference of both powers. Australian chiefs of staff were unanimous in the view that the troops must return. Some senior officers, including Lieutenant General Sturdee, threatened to resign if the government did not heed their advice.[9] Curtin sent off a conciliatory letter to Roosevelt, but delayed responding to Churchill, agonising as he paced around the Canberra scrub in the middle of the night. Finally he sent off a carefully worded reply.

Churchill wrote back confessing that he had disregarded Curtin's original polite request, and several days earlier had diverted the leading parts of the convoy to Burma. Furious, Curtin cabled Churchill on 23 February that he would not be changing his mind, and that Churchill would be responsible for any losses to the redirected troops.

This finally achieved the desired result. The ships were turned around. The Burmese capital Rangoon fell on 8 March; had the Australians landed in Burma, they would have been killed or marched into captivity.

The only concession Curtin made to Churchill was that two brigades of the 6th Division would be landed in Ceylon (modern Sri Lanka) to help the garrison there, but he demanded that they be returned in four months. (In fact, they would not be back in Australia until August.)

Like Churchill, Curtin suffered bouts of depression followed by mania. It often sent him to bed for days, and if one came on top of a crisis, he would be utterly disabled. *Unlike* Churchill, Curtin struggled to make military decisions during the war. Historian David Day has written that Curtin was burdened by an almost debilitating worry about the troubles of other people. Regularly having to make life-and-death decisions was a terrible strain.[10]

* * *

The instructions from the Australian Government for Blamey and his small entourage were to travel home by the most expeditious route. Clearly, they couldn't take the eastern leg of the Horseshoe Route through Japanese-occupied Singapore. The solution offered by GHQ was to fly the southern leg of the Horseshoe Route to South Africa and make their way the best they could from there.

By now only the 9th Division was left in the Middle East. Its commander Leslie Morshead was promoted to lieutenant general and took Blamey's place as General Officer Commanding AIF Middle East, still under Blamey's overall command.[11] Blamey gave Morshead clear instructions to continue the task of keeping the Australians in a cohesive group and resisting the capriciousness of British command. In doing this, Morshead, like Blamey before him, would have a fight on his hands.

Blamey's flight south left at 7.30 am on 7 March 1942. Onboard were Blamey's party of five, made up of General and Lady Blamey, Blamey's aide-de-camp Carlyon, his batman, a confidential clerk, and one Corporal Farrier. The latter's role was unspecified but perhaps he was a gopher or bodyguard.

Blamey was farewelled at the airport by Australian and New Zealand officers. Auchinleck, too, appeared on the runway to see him off, and followed up this gesture with a letter expressing regret at Blamey's departure, as well as affection towards the AIF, which he had come to appreciate and value. He added that he knew how much he owed both the Diggers and Blamey. He also valued Blamey's 'shrewd and sound advice on many matters'.[12] He wished them all good luck and a speedy victory over the Japanese, and hoped that he and Blamey would meet again. Carlyon suspected the surprising sentiment expressed by Auchinleck was partly relief at Blamey's departure mixed with respect for the soldierly qualities he had exhibited.

The last leg of the flight was to Johannesburg. Blamey took a great interest in the local wildlife during that leg. He requested, through Carlyon, that the pilot fly low so he could see the elephants, brushing aside the pilot's warning that low-altitude flying would make for an extremely bumpy ride. The general was glued to the window, while everyone else, including the pilot, suffered great discomfort. After a short time, Carlyon noticed that Lady Blamey had become extremely uncomfortable and tried to get Blamey to order the plane up. He refused because he hadn't yet seen any elephants. Carlyon persisted, and to everyone's relief except Blamey's, the general relented without having seen any elephants.

From Johannesburg the party travelled by rail to Cape Town on the legendary Blue Train: a journey lasting over 27 hours. They were met by South African Field Marshal Jan Smuts and a few senior officers of the Australian Corps Headquarters, also on their return journey to Australia. The party was advised on 14 March that they would be leaving the next day on the unescorted *Queen Mary* luxury liner, which had been converted to a troopship. On embarkation they found the ship packed with US soldiers.

It was on the *Queen Mary* that Blamey heard the news on the radio that General Douglas MacArthur had been appointed Supreme Commander, South West Pacific Area. The 600 or so US officers onboard rose to cheer as one, and the Australians joined in.

Later Carlyon asked Blamey what he thought of the news. Blamey pondered briefly, then said quite cheerfully that the result couldn't be better. He noted that MacArthur 'will be so far away from his own Government that he will not receive any interference, and as for our own Government, he will take no notice of it'.[13]

* * *

By the end of March 1942, the Japanese had overtaken the Dutch East Indies and most of the islands to the east and north of Papua and New Guinea, occupying the coastal cities of Lae, Madang and Rabaul, and mopping up fragmented Australian and Dutch garrison forces as they went. Rabaul was a critical capture for the Japanese because of its sheltered deep-water harbour, and would become an important staging port.[14]

It was now very clear that Curtin needed to shift allegiances and join the American push against the Japanese to Australia's north. Australia had been dependent on Britain for well over a century. Its government and citizenry believed that, thanks to their colonial heritage as well as the sacrifices they had made during the Boer War, World War I and more recently in the Mediterranean, they would always retain British protection. But it was becoming abundantly clear that the British couldn't fight a war in both Europe and Asia; they would have to abandon their colonies in the east, including Australia and New Zealand. The USA, meanwhile, was the only Allied nation with significant military power operating in the region.

Still, old loyalties die hard. Making the decision to throw his weight behind the USA drew on all Curtin's emotional reserves.

Exploratory meetings between US and Australian officials about establishing advanced bases in Australia had occurred before Japan began its expansion, but the matter was now of grave urgency. Discussions were rapidly formalised, and the agreement integrating US and Australian forces, made by joint committees of both nations, came into effect at midnight on 18 April. With 104,000 in the AIF, 265,000 militia and only 38,000 US personnel, the home country would for some time have the largest number of men in the alliance.[15]

Clearly the Australian Government would have to give up some sovereignty to exist under their patronage. *How much* sovereignty was not yet clear.

* * *

In March, President Franklin Roosevelt had decided that US General Douglas MacArthur should be relieved of his current responsibilities commanding the defence of the Philippines and sent to Australia in an as yet undefined role.

Douglas MacArthur is to this day a controversial character, even to Americans. Given his impact on Australia's war effort in the Pacific, and his early testy relationship with Blamey, it is worthwhile reviewing his origins and record prior to arriving in Australia.

Douglas MacArthur was born on 26 January 1880, in the remote town of Little Rock, Arkansas, during the latter part of the American Indian Wars. His father was a captain, later a general. There was never any doubt that MacArthur would pursue a career in the army, and as the son of a general he would get special consideration throughout his career. He entered the West Point Military Academy, where he gained the third-highest score ever achieved. He was an aloof character with few friends, remaining so throughout his life.

His first postings were under his father's command, including the Philippines, at the time an American colony. He was a glory-seeker and disobeyed instructions, at one time going on a self-directed guerrilla raid in which he killed local 'brigands' in the unfulfilled hope of achieving military honours.

Back home in the United States, he accompanied his father on various overseas fact-finding missions, served as aide to President Theodore Roosevelt and worked in the Office of the Chief of Staff. During the US military occupation at Veracruz,

Mexico, in 1914 he again engaged in unsanctioned actions against guerrillas.

On leaving Mexico, he joined the War Department, where he headed the Bureau of Information and became the army's first press officer. There he gained the necessary skills to manipulate the press, standing him in good stead for the rest of his working life. He learned three important tricks: namely, to stress the positive and if there isn't any, invent it; to be economical with the truth; and, most important of all, to provide some theatre.

After the United States joined World War I in 1917, he fought in France, was promoted to brigadier general and briefly acted as major general. His experience as press officer served him extremely well and he gained many column inches in the US papers. By the end of the war, aged only 38, he had accumulated 13 decorations, including two from the French. As befits a true son of the army with a general for a father, he didn't suffer the ignominy of demotion to prewar ranks, but arrived home a brigadier general and remained at that level. With nothing much to do, he was appointed as the youngest-ever superintendent of West Point.

In 1922 he returned to the Philippines on rotation, and in 1925 became the army's youngest major general. Soon after this, he returned to the United States with a teenage Eurasian mistress in tow, though she didn't last because she was a potential source of scandal. He would marry that same year and divorce just seven years later.

MacArthur was made US Army Chief of Staff in 1930. He fought hard to stave off the crippling budget cuts of the austere Depression years, making many enemies. In 1932, Great War veterans converged on Washington to demand a promised bonus payment. He donned his very photogenic full-dress uniform, rode a white charger to their makeshift camp and, in full view of the media, ordered a forceful eviction in which a man was killed. The headlines were vicious but seem not to have done him any real harm.

When MacArthur's term was up, he was sent back to the Philippines as a military adviser, taking with him his reluctant but loyal chief military aide, Major Dwight D. Eisenhower. Feeding his hunger for honours, MacArthur accepted the rank of field marshal in the Philippine Army. He served the Philippine Army concurrently with his post as major general in the US Army, until he retired from the latter in 1937.

In July 1941, as war with the Japanese began to look likely, President Roosevelt recalled him to active duty, appointing him Commander of US Army Forces in the Far East. As pre-war consultant to the Philippine Government, MacArthur had deliberately overstated the preparedness of the Philippine Army. Taking off his consultant's hat and putting on his commander's hat, he was forced to come clean. Both the Philippine and US Governments were aghast when he insisted it would be well into 1942 before the army was ready. The Japanese did not allow him that time.

The Japanese assault on Pearl Harbor gave MacArthur a relatively luxurious seven hours' warning to prepare for an attack on the Philippines. When the attack occurred, many of his planes were caught parked in a neat pre-war formation on the ground. Within just a few minutes, 277 planes were destroyed, including 40 state-of-the-art B-17 bombers.

Two days later, when the Japanese onslaught arrived on land, the woefully under-equipped and under-commanded US and Philippine forces were pushed across the plains north of Manila and into the mountainous, disease-infested jungle wilderness of the Bataan Peninsula. With food for only 40,000 men and over 100,000 mouths to feed, it wasn't long before starvation set in. And all the while, US Army Chief of Staff General George C. Marshall promised relief that he had no means of delivering or intention of providing.

The Manila docks were bombed on 16 December 1941. The US Navy pulled out and MacArthur withdrew with his staff, second wife and their four-year-old son to Corregidor, a small island just off the coast of Bataan province.

MacArthur was too much of a public figure in the United States to be allowed to fall into Japanese hands. When it became clear that Bataan would fall, Roosevelt ordered him to leave for Australia to take command of all US troops there. The general was apparently reluctant to obey, but finally he, his family and some senior staff officers were evacuated on 11 March 1942.

The evacuees were spread between four torpedo boats. They eased their way through a Japanese minefield to clear the coast, and in high seas ran the gauntlet of a Japanese naval blockade. One boat was lost and another ran out of fuel. The passengers of three boats crowded onto two for the run to the southern Philippines island of Mindanao. MacArthur arrived with only the clothes he was wearing. Uniforms can be replaced, but his beloved Philippines field marshal's braided cap couldn't; luckily that survived. Despite salt stains and sun bleaching, he would wear that cap throughout the conflict in the Pacific and into the Korean War, accompanying it with a naturally bent corncob pipe to complete the signature image.

He and his family were flown to Australia in a B-17 bomber and arrived at Batchelor Airfield, 100 kilometres south of Darwin, on 18 March, a day before the first Japanese bombing of the city got underway.

The day MacArthur touched down in Australia, Lieutenant General George Brett, the head of the US Army Air Forces, telephoned Curtin to announce the general's arrival. Brett then delivered a message from President Roosevelt, which said that it would be 'highly acceptable to him and pleasing to the American people for the Australian government to nominate General MacArthur as the Supreme Commander of all Allied Forces in the South West Pacific'.[16] Curtin was surprised and pleased. It was announced the same day.[17]

After enduring the precarious journey from the Philippines, MacArthur's wife Jean insisted that the journey south be by train.[18] Just north of Adelaide, MacArthur's aide joined the train with the bad news that there were only around 30,000 Allied troops in Australia, maybe 100 planes and precious little naval support. 'God help us' was MacArthur's comment.[19]

He arrived in Adelaide with his entourage on 20 March, concluding his brief speech with 'I came through and I shall return' (to the Philippines).[20]

Arriving in Melbourne by train on 21 March 1942 to a tumultuous welcome, MacArthur reciprocated by delivering speeches of hope. With anxiety levels high after the recent Japanese attacks on Darwin, the US general's prognosis some days later that Japan would not invade northern Australia but stop at New Guinea was welcome.

* * *

While Pearl Harbor had caught the public's attention as an attack on the US homeland with the loss of highly symbolic battleships, the damage in the Philippines was also costly. Twenty-three thousand US personnel were killed or captured, along with another 100,000 Filipino soldiers. The US Government did not reveal the extent of the loss to the public, instead deflecting attention by concentrating on the US and Filipino fighters' heroic defence and MacArthur's supposedly plucky resistance. To further the deflection, Roosevelt awarded MacArthur the Congressional Medal of Honor.

Honoured or not, MacArthur was deeply shamed by his defeat and distressed at having to abandon the Philippines. He became further distressed to find that not only had Marshall exaggerated US aid to the Philippines, but also the build-up of US troops in Australia. There was little to give him hope of relieving his men on Bataan and not much hope of defending Australia either.

No matter what rhetoric the joint chiefs had put around his posting, MacArthur knew that it was intended to be a non-job. Roosevelt, with his strong navy bias, hadn't imagined the USA would have to fight with an army in the Pacific, so MacArthur's allotted role was to support the US Navy.[21] As far as the Joint Chiefs of Staff were concerned, the US Navy, not the US Army, was to do the heavy lifting in the Pacific.

That might have been the intention, but playing a bit part did not suit MacArthur at all. Having been exiled to the ends of the earth without a significant US combat force to command, MacArthur's sense of honour required him to get out from under the US Navy by regaining a US Army fighting command, as befitted an American four-star general and ex chief of staff. Consequently, everything he did had triple objectives. In no particular order of importance, his priorities were: regain a credible US Army command; beat the US Navy to the Philippines; and conquer the Japanese.

To fulfil the first two objectives, he needed to push the pace. As a result, MacArthur was always in an indecent rush to prevent the US Navy from getting ahead of him.

* * *

Blamey, still on his way home, did not yet know what role *he* would play in the war. Others like Sturdee and Lavarack had been in senior positions in Australia while he had languished in the Middle East, with much of the force he had commanded on its way home. He worked long hours at his desk and had an encyclopaedic knowledge of administrative necessities. He had also devoted much time and energy to visiting the troops, checking on training and amenities and discussing matters with senior officers.

He had managed the growth of the AIF and its maturing into an experienced organisation, stood up to his British superiors and looked to the safety and relief of his troops.[22] As an indication of how busy Blamey had been during his time in the Middle East theatre, it is useful to note that he covered some 78,000 kilometres by air, 32,000 kilometres by car and 7600 kilometres by ship.[23]

Yet he seemed to have a dangerous disregard for his own reputation. As his biographer David Horner has written, 'his leadership was hampered by tactlessness and sheer insensitivity to public relations'.[24] Blamey was widely known for frequenting brothels in Cairo and made little attempt to hide it. He was also known for drinking heavily.

One of the most serious accusations against him in the Middle East came around this time via journalist Chester Wilmot, who had begun investigations into the poor quality of movie prints that were being shown to the troops for free in AIF cinemas. The ABC correspondent was ever on the lookout for a good story. He had heard rumours that the contractor providing the films was making overly large profits. While falling short of accusing Blamey of taking kickbacks, Wilmot nevertheless believed that there were sufficient grounds to investigate the contract.

This led to a tense and inconclusive interview with Blamey, which will not have been forgotten.[25] Wilmot admitted to his father on 2 January 1943 that he had spoken with insufficient evidence about the contract.[26]

Wilmot's antipathy towards, and clashes with, Blamey would carry over into the Pacific war, when he would take up the gauntlet for rivals who undermined Blamey at any opportunity.

* * *

In stark contrast to MacArthur's theatrical entrance to Australia, there was no fanfare when Blamey arrived home on 26 March 1942. He was met in Fremantle by Major General Eric Plant, commander of the army in Western Australia. Plant was carrying a message from the Prime Minister, advising Blamey that he was to be made Commander in Chief, Australian Military Forces.

This title is somewhat misleading, in that it implies that he had command of the whole of Australia's military. In reality, he had no administrative or command responsibilities concerning the Royal Australian Navy or the Royal Australian Air Force; in the modern parlance, his position was more like 'chief of army'.

He was also given the job of Commander, Allied Land Forces, South West Pacific Area, reporting directly to MacArthur. It was a position junior to Blamey's other role, and to a certain extent was similar to the job he had been doing in the Middle East. That experience was a key reason for his appointment but there was also the fact that he had a proven record of commanding the Australian force under foreign operational control.

The two other main contenders for this role were Bennett and Lavarack. Since the start of the war, each had proven extremely tetchy for Australian politicians to manage, and in Bennett's case, there were question marks over his fitness for high command following his controversial escape from Singapore. But with Singapore's garrison fallen, the 8th Division in captivity and the Japanese cascading south, an invasion of Australia appeared a real possibility, despite MacArthur's reassurances. The Australian Government was in no mood for experimenting with untried commanders in key positions. Blamey was the only real choice for the highest Australian command position. He was by far the most experienced commander in the whole theatre of operations, and had a proven record of preserving Australian lives. He was tough but reasonable. If Curtin had heard the negative whispers about Blamey's character, he did not let them deflect him from appointing the man he felt was best for the job.

* * *

Blamey's appointment as Commander in Chief of the AMF made him the most powerful officer the Australian Army had ever had, while his position as Commander, Allied Land Forces made him a direct subordinate to MacArthur. While it was probably unintended, this wedged MacArthur between Blamey's two roles.

It is worth noting that the military takes rank very seriously, though the Australian military was probably somewhat less rigid in observing this than the US military was at the time. Blamey had been promoted to full general on 24 September 1941, three months prior to MacArthur's promotion to full general, and would remain more senior until MacArthur was promoted to five-star general in late 1944. Even without taking other factors into account, by dint of being a more senior subordinate, Blamey had to be accorded respect.

Additionally, Blamey's wartime experience far outstripped MacArthur's. The Supreme Commander had experience as chief of staff of a division and commander of a brigade in World War I, then only for a few months, and had exerted questionable command during the Battle of the Philippines.[27] Yet, as previously determined by Curtin and Roosevelt, the less experienced MacArthur was directly responsible to the two leaders, and this arrangement gave him a great deal of latitude in playing off the interests of one against the other – just as Blamey had suggested to Carlyon when he heard the news of MacArthur's appointment.

As mentioned, Blamey's new position as Commander, Allied Land Forces was similar to his role in the Middle East. Yet Blamey had asked for but had not been formally given all the powers he had exercised in that theatre of war. He could not refuse any operations or decide the direction and timing of those operations. In simple terms, MacArthur had been ceded control over the 'what', 'where' and 'when' of land operations, while Blamey retained much of the 'how' and 'who'.

However, as the man in control of the administration of the armed forces, he could resist any efforts by MacArthur to change its structure or the lines of command below him. And, by dint of his own personality, he managed to retain unity of command. It was an awkward arrangement, but Blamey mostly made it work. With Blamey running interference, MacArthur could not hive off parts of the Australian force and put them under US command. Whenever MacArthur tried and appealed to the government, Curtin refused, possibly under Blamey's influence. With unity of command, Blamey was able to ensure that the Diggers were commanded by his appointed generals, who were answerable to him and would, as he had demanded when the first AIF units left for the Middle East, look after the troops.

Blamey chafed at not having direct access to Curtin on operational matters but, to his credit, he was flexible enough to make the arrangement work while tiptoeing around the sensitivities of both Curtin and MacArthur.

The biggest concession Blamey received from Curtin in these early stages of the arrangement was that he would have direct access to the Prime Minister for policy decisions related to the army. General administrative matters were to be dealt with by the Army Minister, Frank Forde. It would seem that Forde and Blamey were temperamentally unsuited to working together so, as it transpired, Blamey had as little to do with him as possible, usually consulting Curtin in preference.

Despite this unexpected degree of access, command inevitably became an inefficient three-cornered affair, with the government seeking MacArthur's advice first and giving it priority. But it could have been much worse; the AIF could have become a puppet force operating largely at MacArthur's whim.

By controlling the 'what', 'where' and 'when' of operations, however, MacArthur was able to force the pace, which would lead to problems during the first year of operations in New Guinea, especially the dash over the Kokoda Track.

* * *

MacArthur might have been greeted as a saviour, but he was no true friend of Australia or Australians. The US conceived of Australia predominantly as a supply base for its war effort; for MacArthur himself, Australia and its defence were peripheral objectives. In 1942 and into 1943, the only substantial fighting forces available to him were Australian. He had to accept Australians, but all along, like the British before him, he wanted them completely under his command to use as he saw fit.

At the point when they began working together, not only was Blamey much more experienced than MacArthur, but the Australian Army commanders under Blamey's authority were also more experienced than their US counterparts. Most of the Australians had had significantly more experience in World War I and had also been fighting in the Middle East since early 1940. Australian officer experience could be measured in years, whereas American officers had months of experience, if they were lucky. Certainly, the terrain and climate of their new theatre of operations would take some adapting to, but the basics of command and battle remained the same.

Yet MacArthur never publicly acknowledged the greater experience of the Australian commanders. Blamey was, of course, a chief target of his barbs. The US general was happy to make use of Blamey's unsavoury reputation and sneer at him as the fat police commissioner from the militia. This smear has been so enduring that one contemporary MacArthur biographer has this to say about Blamey: 'short, fat, jovial and perennially rumpled, Blamey had a reputation for getting drunk at parties and knocking people's hats off when inebriated ... Moreover, Blamey's long spell away from active duty made him an amateur in the eyes of many American generals.'[28] This last assertion is simply laughable; the Australian general had just finished nearly two years of command in the Middle East. Unfortunately, this caricature of Blamey as the fat, drunken buffoon is not so far from the current view many Australians have of him. The only thing missing is the term 'womaniser'.

Physically, Blamey was a far cry from the tall, handsome MacArthur, who also spoke mellifluously and was adept at charming politicians. Yet this was irrelevant to his command skills, as were the many aspersions frequently cast on him.

* * *

MacArthur set up his headquarters in Melbourne, presumably because the Australian Government considered it important for him to be close to Victoria Barracks, Blamey's HQ and the army's nerve centre.

There were a number of ways in which an Allied supreme commander could set up his headquarters. He could, for example, do as General Eisenhower did in England from mid-1942 as Commanding General, European Theater of Operations, by pairing British and US officers. This way, Eisenhower and his men benefited from the experience of British officers, who, like the Australians, had been in the war longer. Eisenhower's way had the additional benefit of developing a degree of intercultural tolerance, or at least understanding. Eisenhower also gave clear indications of his intent to remain in coalition with the British.[29]

MacArthur, on the other hand, set up his HQ by totally excluding Australian officers, even after his commanding general George C. Marshall ordered otherwise. He claimed that there were no suitably experienced Australians available[30] and, given his stature and known prickliness, was not disciplined by Marshall for insubordination.

This attitude was shared by many of MacArthur's officers and even Marshall's visiting envoy General Robert C. Richardson, who reported when he visited in June and found some units under Australian command that it 'was an affront to national pride and to the dignity of the American Army'[31] to have any US forces commanded by Australians. Richardson complained about colonial officers in general, but he complained loudest about Blamey, describing him as 'a nonprofessional Australian drunk.'[32] The constant message sent back to the United States was that Australians weren't good enough to be put in command of Americans.

To protect himself from intruders, MacArthur installed his irascible long-term chief of staff, Major General Richard K. Sutherland, as gatekeeper. Sutherland was extremely loyal to MacArthur and blocked all but the most privileged from gaining access, including most US officers. The other US officer of particular note in the HQ was Major General Charles A. Willoughby, MacArthur's intelligence officer. Both men had been among those evacuated with MacArthur from Corregidor, and were favourites because of their knack for providing information and strategy opinions that MacArthur wanted to hear, rather than the things he needed to hear.

* * *

As MacArthur established his HQ in Melbourne, Blamey got to work reorganising and preparing the army for what would be its forthcoming battles in the wild tropics of New Guinea.

It was a task he approached with gusto. As Edmund Herring later observed:

> towards the end of his service in the Middle East TAB [Blamey] was showing signs of fatigue, he had trouble with one of his legs I remember. He was becoming, it appeared, a rather tired old man. But after his return to Australia he regained all his old vigour and vitality ... the task set him was no less than building a complete army with all its services, linking AIF and Militia etc etc, and he handled the whole job in the most masterly way ... Everyone privileged to work closely with him could not but be most tremendously impressed with his capacity and I was always amazed at the sureness of touch he showed in his selection of battle commanders, infantry brigade commanders, COs of battalions and so on.[33]

In his role as commander in chief, Blamey would ultimately raise an army of three-quarters of a million men, and see to it that they were fed, clothed, accommodated, armed, trained, transported, entertained and cared for in all the hundreds of ways in which troops need to be looked after.[34]

In the Middle East, the Australian Army had relied on the British supply system. Now they had to be much more self-reliant. Blamey had a strong interest in the rapidly expanding industry supplying his force, with a particular interest in munitions production and procurement. He often met with Essington Lewis, Director General of Munitions and former managing director of BHP. A powerful industrialist, Lewis was on the Defence Committee, and Blamey ensured he was exempt from the *Public Servant Act 1922*. Thus Lewis had almost unlimited authority and prodigious production skills. The factories he controlled produced a vast array of items ranging from hand grenades through to tanks, Owen guns to aeroplanes. The munitions factories alone employed 150,000 men and women.[35]

In addition, with the threat of invasion looming, Australia required a huge investment in infrastructure, especially the less developed areas that faced the enemy – the Northern Territory, northern Queensland and northern Western Australia. The sheer numbers of new recruits needing housing and provisioning meant that combat training suffered as soldiers were diverted into construction and maintenance work.

Australia was not ready for war on home soil, let alone in the jungles of New Guinea. Irrespective of this, war was on its way.

10

'Nobody in Their Right Senses Would Land There'

February to August 1942

Nineteen forty-two would be Australia's watershed year. US and Australian forces would expand and increasingly engage with the enemy as it closed in on New Guinea. The captured port of Rabaul was turned into the largest Japanese base in New Guinea, from which Japan began bombing the Papuan capital, Port Moresby, on 3 February. That same month, the Japanese made reconnaissance flights over Sydney and Melbourne in a plane launched from a submarine.

Just after midnight on 1 March, there was an Australian naval tragedy: the light cruiser HMAS *Perth* was sunk by Japanese torpedoes just west of Jakarta, while helping to defend the Dutch East Indies. Its loss must have saddened Blamey; the ship had done sterling service during the evacuation of Greece and Crete in March the previous year, under heavy German air attack. Of those onboard, 353 died, while most of the 328 who got to shore went into POW camps. Just 218 of them would survive the war.

The Japanese were progressively occupying locations in the north of New Guinea. The Salamaua–Lae area, on the Huon Peninsula in New Guinea's northeast, had been taken by 13 March. Of particular interest to MacArthur, Bataan fell on 9 April. Meanwhile, the Japanese continued moving down the island chain to the north and east of New Guinea.

In early May, the mighty Japanese Navy sent a flotilla around the eastern end of New Guinea from their large naval bases at Rabaul and Truk Atoll in the central Pacific. Their intention was to capture Port Moresby and Tulagi, the capital of the British Solomon Islands Protectorate, then other ports and airfields in the Solomon Sea and perhaps as far north and east as Nauru, Fiji, Samoa and New Caledonia. With such a huge reach, they could make passage to and from the Pacific difficult for Australia, and might also threaten sea routes between Australia and the US.

As the Japanese advance continued, the Allies had one significant advantage: codebreaking. Warned by US Navy signals intelligence, Allied naval forces quickly moved into position off the south-east tip of New Guinea in order to intercept the Japanese invasion fleet.[1] The two forces clashed in the Coral Sea between 3 and 8 May. It was a thoroughly modern fight of planes against ships, and the first battle in naval history in which opposing vessels neither sighted nor fired upon one another.

The aircraft carrier USS *Lexington* sustained damaged fuel lines and was crippled during a Japanese air attack. It was scuttled on 8 May to prevent it from being captured. The carrier USS *Yorktown* was also severely damaged by enemy aircraft but remained operational. A Japanese light carrier was destroyed and one of their two fleet carriers was damaged.

Losing their nerve, the Japanese turned back. It was a significant strategic win for the USA and Australia; they had stopped the apparently invincible Japanese for the first time, which was some compensation for the humiliation of Pearl Harbor.[2]

* * *

On 19 May, another radio signal was intercepted, revealing that Japanese forces were about to land on the north coast of Papua around the village of Buna. This seemed incredible to both Blamey and MacArthur, who responded that 'Nobody in their right senses would land there.'[3] It was clear that the Japanese planned to explore the feasibility of building bases from which to attack Port Moresby by crossing the rugged Owen Stanley Range, along the Kokoda Track.[4] Although the Kokoda Track was fairly well known, both commanders were aware of the difficulty of the terrain. Given that the Japanese would have to haul all their supplies along the track using human labour, it was highly unlikely that they would consider taking Port Moresby from that direction. Even if their men made it, they would have almost insurmountable problems in transporting the heavy artillery and ammunition they would need to mount a credible assault before they were wiped out by Australian artillery, machine guns and troops waiting on the Port Moresby side.

MacArthur had already decided that an airfield should be built at Milne Bay, on the far eastern tip of Papua, to protect seaward approaches to Port Moresby from that direction. On 14 May, he had asked Blamey to send a brigade to defend the position and protect the engineers about to begin construction. Blamey ordered the 7th Brigade to Milne Bay. Like all militia brigades, they had seen no overseas service during the war.

On 15 May, the 14th Brigade, also from the militia, was sent from Australia to Port Moresby to bolster the 30th militia Brigade, which had been sent in January. Both brigades were part of the US–Australian–Papuan New Guinea Force, formed the previous month and placed under the command of Major General Basil Morris. On hearing the news of their impending deployment, many hundreds of men of the 14th Brigade went absent without leave, and one of the ships due to take the brigade from Townsville to Port Moresby sailed nearly empty.[5] The men were rounded up and sent on a later ship.

Blamey was roundly criticised for sending militia brigades by Lieutenant General Sydney Rowell, now in command of I Corps in Queensland, and by Major General Arthur 'Tubby' Allen, commander of the corps' 7th Division. Both men thought it would have been far better to send more experienced AIF forces. MacArthur would later claim that he had asked Blamey to send his best troops and had told him the militia was not sufficiently well trained.[6] Blamey, however, reasoned that he needed his best troops for other campaigns and sent the militia instead.

In hindsight, the critics appear to be correct, but only if one takes the view that Blamey should have expected that the Australians would need to pursue the Japanese along the Kokoda Track. It is clear that at this point Blamey did not expect that route would be a major line of attack for either the

Australians or the Japanese. However, the intercepted message on 19 May indicated that a land crossing from Buna to Port Moresby was a distinct possibility.

* * *

Meanwhile, there was plenty for Blamey to do at home, balancing the demands of Australia's defence with preparation for offshore battles. He conferred with his senior commanders and paid close attention to munitions production and procurement, as well as to the multitude of details involved in managing the rapidly growing, complex military organisation. The task was made even more difficult by the need to consider how the Australian supply and organisation fitted in with US systems.

Blamey also met with Prime Minister Curtin when he was able, and otherwise with Army Minister Frank Forde. Relations between Forde and Blamey had started indifferently and got steadily worse. Many decisions, such as promotion requests, were delayed.

At the same time, Blamey invested time in building relationships with US commanders. He had frequent meetings with air commander Lieutenant General George Brett, and with Major General Richard Sutherland, MacArthur's chief of staff. He had a few private meetings with MacArthur, and on occasion joined Curtin and MacArthur at one of their regular prime minister's war conferences.

Between the end of March and early May, Blamey hardly left Melbourne and only had three Sundays off work.[7] He began to feel the need to speak directly to the troops, inspect units and confer with officers. On 13 May, he set out on a whirlwind tour of the ACT, New South Wales, Victoria and Queensland. Tens of thousands of men, either in units raised at home or returned from the Middle East, were engaged in home defence around the nation. Looking towards New Guinea, Blamey also met with Major General Morris, who flew in for a conference with Blamey and Lieutenant General Lavarack, now commanding the First Australian Army in Queensland and New South Wales. Morris then went to Canberra with Blamey to report on New Guinea.[8]

* * *

While Blamey visited his troops, the enemy was far from idle. On 20 May, and again 10 days later, Japanese planes flew over Sydney. The next night, 31 May, three Japanese midget submarines made their way into Sydney Harbour and sank a barracks ship, with the loss of 19 sailors' lives. On 7 June, shells were fired at Newcastle and Sydney from Japanese submarines, while merchant shipping was sunk along the eastern seaboard.

On the same day as these attacks were unnerving Australians, the population was cheered by news that came through from far distant Midway Atoll, about halfway between the United States and Japan. Again, the navy codebreakers had given forewarning of an impending Japanese attack, this time on the American fleet.

The five-day Battle of Midway is considered to be one of the most stunning and decisive victories in the history of naval warfare, with both fleets commanded by larger-than-life military figures – Admiral Chester Nimitz on the US side and the powerful Admiral Isoroku Yamamoto on the Japanese side. This was another naval battle in which the opposing warships did not engage directly: all the fighting was done by aircraft, operating at extreme range.

The US Navy sank four enemy aircraft carriers and a cruiser, as well as downing a large number of planes. It was a catastrophic engagement for the Japanese, because neither their ships nor the pilots of their aircraft were readily replaceable. The Japanese sank one destroyer and one aircraft carrier, the USS *Yorktown*, and just two-thirds the number of aircraft that the Americans had downed. The US ships, aircraft and pilots were easily replaced.

The balance of power was beginning to shift towards the Allies. With the Japanese Navy bested twice and the US Navy beginning to assert its rapidly increasing capability around the extremities of the Japanese advance, Australia was beginning to look safe. But news from Papua and New Guinea would soon change that.

* * *

In early June, MacArthur wrote to Blamey, advising him of mounting evidence that suggested the Japanese were searching for a route across the mountains to Port Moresby. On Monday 6 July, Blamey led a two-day conference for high-level Australian officers, with MacArthur present for the first item on the agenda. Blamey opened with a summary of the strategic situation in Papua, and the order that all formations train for 'mobile offensive operations'.

Orders were also issued for an extensive reorganisation of the parts of the army currently defending Australia. At the same time, MacArthur had become dissatisfied with the organisation of the Allied air forces. General George Brett was relieved in July 1942 and Lieutenant General George C. Kenney was ordered to Australia to take over, with the initial task of separating the Australian air force from that of the USA.[9]

That month, MacArthur moved his general headquarters north from Melbourne to Brisbane. Blamey needed to set up his own HQ in Brisbane if he and his staff were to keep in touch with key US personnel. This meant more frequent separations for Blamey from the army's primary HQ at Victoria Barracks in Melbourne. Blamey was now constantly on the move, a situation that threw up mundane yet irritating difficulties, such as fitting into the flight schedules of civilian airlines. The demands of working on confidential papers meant he also needed privacy, and after one occasion when an air hostess refused to alter the seat allocations it became clear that he would need his own air transport. Unlike some of his other requests, his application for a plane was immediately accepted by the government and he was quickly allocated an outdated but much appreciated RAAF Hudson for his personal use.[10]

* * *

Meanwhile, MacArthur's plans for an airfield to shield Port Moresby against sea attacks from the east was making

Lieutenant General Sydney Rowell, Commander of the New Guinea Force, c. September 1942. (AWM 013174)

progress. The Allies began work on an airfield at Milne Bay on 25 June 1942. On the far eastern tip of Papua, the bay was well located as a forward air base to attack Japanese shipping, as well as mount attacks on the critical enemy port at Rabaul, directly to the north. It was deep enough to provide anchorage for large ships at the end of a long, sheltered harbour, and there was enough flat land to build airfields.

Initially it could only be reached by sea. Planning and construction were carried out on the fly by the American 46th Engineer Battalion and the Australian 5th Field Regiment. Conditions were difficult: incessant rain dumped water onto the perpetually waterlogged soil, and coconut trees and jungle impeded construction; on one airfield more than 5000 coconut trees had to be cut down and taken away. Milne Bay was a festering quagmire when it came to disease: malaria was endemic and anti-malarial measures primitive and haphazard.

The inexperienced 7th Brigade, ordered to mobilise in May, arrived at Milne Bay on 11 July. The first Kittyhawks of the Royal Australian Air Force (RAAF) landed on 22 July on the first of three rough airfields.

It was not long before the Japanese recognised the threat posed by the works at Milne Bay and sent an invasion force. They also recognised the prize it would be if they captured the partially constructed airfields: they would be able to use them as a base for launching attacks on Port Moresby without having to fly over the Owen Stanley Range from Buna, and also for destroying Allied shipping in the vicinity.

In mid-July, Australian naval codebreakers intercepted Japanese communications about plans to capture Milne Bay towards the end of August. On Blamey's orders, the 18th Brigade was rushed to Milne Bay, arriving between 12 and 21 August, supported by anti-tank guns and heavy and light anti-aircraft guns.

Australian Major General Cyril Clowes took command of the Milne Bay garrison on 22 August, reporting to the head of New Guinea Force, his friend Lieutenant General Sydney Rowell. At that stage, there were around 7500 Australians and 1400 Americans at Milne Bay, of whom 4500 were infantry and 600 RAAF personnel, while the rest belonged to artillery, tank, support and engineering units.[11] Should the intelligence uncovered by the codebreakers prove correct, the Allies would be ready.

* * *

Concern was also growing about Japanese plans for an invasion of Port Moresby by land. In early June, Blamey had asked Morris to send the 300-strong Papuan Infantry Battalion to the Kokoda Track, then north to observe activity on the coast. Later that month, the 39th militia Battalion was also ordered along the track to defend the airfield at Kokoda, and the two units were grouped together as 'Maroubra Force'.[12]

Major General Morris had grave misgivings about dispatching his force along the narrow, precipitous 96-kilometre Kokoda Track. As he later said to Sydney Rowell, 'The mountains will beat the Nips and we must be careful they don't beat us.'[13]

Conditions were horrific. The track was covered in dense rainforest, which became denser as the soldiers slogged up the 2100-metre-high range through seemingly endless gorges and razorback ridges. It was hot and humid during the day and cold at night, and it rained constantly. Malaria and other tropical diseases were endemic. With no roads, and no hope that motorised transport would reach them, the soldiers had to carry most of what they needed.

The first soldiers of the 39th Battalion began their trek over the Owen Stanley Range on 8 July, arriving at the village of Kokoda on the north side of the range a week later. On 21 July, the Japanese began an invasion at the coastal villages of Buna, Sananada and Gona, establishing beachheads to facilitate the later landing of troops and supplies. Advance parties of troops began moving inland. Their first contact with Maroubra Force occurred at Awala, between Kokoda and Gona, when the overwhelmed Australians and Papuans were forced back towards Kokoda.[14]

Transport planes landed small numbers of troops to reinforce the Australians. It wasn't enough. The Japanese threatened encirclement.

The US Navy had their own war objectives in the Pacific, Atlantic and Mediterranean; in the Pacific, they were preparing to land their marine forces on Guadalcanal, north of New Guinea. Merchant ships were being sunk at a catastrophic rate and shipping of all sorts was in short supply everywhere. MacArthur was denied seaborne transport to mount an amphibious attack anywhere along the Papuan north-east coast. Without US Navy transport, his only option was to attack the Japanese overland, starting from Port Moresby.

Lack of supply caused substantial problems when the Diggers came up against fresh Japanese troops, who were being supplied along a much easier route from the beaches on the north coast. The Australians fought valiantly for Kokoda and its airfield from 28 to 29 July but, without reinforcements, supplies and transport, the challenge was too great.

MacArthur ordered the remaining troops of the 39th Battalion, along with the rest of the 30th Brigade – the 49th and 53rd Battalions – to march from Port Moresby across the Owen Stanley Range in support of the troops already there. The plan was for them to attack Kokoda on 8 August, but this second attack was likewise unsuccessful.

By mid-August, worn down and exhausted, the Australians had been forced back into the mountains at Isurava, about 5 kilometres uphill through steep jungle. The 39th Battalion's new commanding officer, Lieutenant Colonel Ralph Honner, arrived on 16 August and described his young warriors as coming to a standstill for want of sleep, food and shelter and worn out by arduous fighting and gruelling movement.[15]

By now Allied aircraft from Port Moresby and Milne Bay were flying missions to sink Japanese convoys heading with reinforcements to the beachheads at Buna, Sanananda and Gona, and attacking airfields that the enemy was trying to construct. They also attempted, with limited success, to assist the Australian soldiers by strafing Japanese troops along the track and dropping supplies, but it was almost impossible to see targets or drop zones in the heavy jungle. Too often, the result was that food, weapons and ammunition meant for the Diggers ended up with the Japanese.[16]

* * *

It was now clear that more experienced forces were needed to attack the Japanese along the Kokoda Track. Curtin, with MacArthur's prompting, demanded the return of the 9th Division from the Middle East. Blamey, however, argued that the division should stay put, because it had been promised for the seminal Second Battle of El Alamein.

On 12 August, Lieutenant General Sydney Rowell arrived in Port Moresby to take over command from Major General Morris. Morris, who had never expected or wanted the role of general officer commanding, was happy to take care of the administration of Port Moresby, and Rowell's I Corps headquarters were amalgamated with New Guinea Force.

Among those joining him in Port Moresby was Major General Arthur 'Tubby' Allen. As mentioned, Allen's veteran 7th Division, having returned from the Middle East in mid-March, had been doing defensive duties in Australia with the rest of I Corps.

The 7th Division's 21st Brigade, under Brigadier Arnold Potts, arrived in Port Moresby on 8 August. The first of his three battalions, the 14th, began the struggle up the track on 16 August, the 16th took to the track the next day, while the 27th was left in Port Moresby in reserve.

Rowell's immediate concern was to get supplies to the Diggers along the track. Like Morris before him, he was not in favour of fighting across the Owen Stanley Range. Responding to journalist Osmar White on the subject, he said, '[I'm] willing to pull back and let the enemy have the rough stuff if he wants it. I'm willing to present the Jap with the supply headache I've got. But there are those who think otherwise. We need victory in the Pacific, and a lot of poor bastards have got to get killed to provide it.'[17]

Both Blamey and MacArthur continued to believe that the threat to Port Moresby from the Japanese on the Kokoda Track was slight. Nevertheless, cognisant of the poor supply situation, Blamey repeatedly asked MacArthur to increase the number of aircraft dropping supplies to his men on the track. MacArthur refused. Despite this rebuff, some supplies were getting through using local labour. Initially around 600 Papuans laboured up the track with supplies and back down carrying the wounded on makeshift stretchers made of poles and blankets. By the end of October, the number of local porters working on Kokoda Track would grow by 1000.[18]

* * *

Meanwhile, the forces stationed at Milne Bay prepared for imminent Japanese attack. New American air commander Lieutenant General George C. Kenney ordered pre-emptive strikes against Japanese airfields at Buna on 24 and 25 August, which reduced the number of Japanese fighters in the area to six.[19]

As the invaders amassed at Goodenough Island, about 100 kilometres north of Milne Bay, Allied aircraft destroyed two of their landing barges, killing 350 Japanese. They partly destroyed other landing craft and supplies when the Japanese invasion force got to Milne Bay.

The Japanese pressed on, and on 25 August landed 2000 members of their elite Special Naval Landing Forces in the bay, along with light tanks. Yet the defenders had two pieces of luck. The first was that the Japanese landings took place 3 kilometres further away from the airfields than intended, and the second was that Japanese jungle training was as inadequate as that of the Allies at this time.

The fighting was at close quarters, and vicious. The Australians learned the hard way about Japanese ruthlessness, and were soon bayoneting all 'corpses', because the Japanese had a nasty habit of playing dead then hopping up to kill the passing soldiers. During daylight hours, RAAF Kittyhawks strafed Japanese positions, forcing the Japanese to attack when the sun went down. The battle see-sawed, with the Australians pushing the Japanese back by day and the Japanese advancing again at night. At any one time, 82 Allied soldiers out of 1000 were infected by malaria, dwarfing the number of battle casualties.

All through the battle for Milne Bay, MacArthur exhorted precipitous action from his headquarters in Brisbane, either directly or through Blamey in Port Moresby. The fighting was so tough and the conditions so difficult that exhortations to go faster didn't make much difference, except to add to Clowes's frustration levels.

The Japanese made headway in heavy fighting against the Allied force until they met elements of the AIF that had been held in reserve. They had underestimated the strength of the Allied defence. The Allies eventually gained the upper hand and began pushing the Japanese back.

In their wake, the Japanese left behind evidence of war crimes. All 36 captured Allied troops had been executed; some had even been mutilated. Fifty-nine of the local population had also been murdered, and there was evidence that a number of the women had been sexually assaulted prior to being killed.[20]

These Japanese atrocities hardened the attitude of the Australians and Americans. From then on, they dedicated themselves to killing Japanese soldiers as a kind of retaliation.[21]

The outnumbered Japanese finally gave up the fight and were evacuated on the night of 5 September, abandoning any comrades who didn't make it to their boat. These were swallowed up by the jungle and never seen again.

While a relatively small engagement, the Battle of Milne Bay is highly significant: it was the first land battle lost by the Japanese since they started their rampage at Pearl Harbor on 7 December 1941. It cost the Australians 161 dead and 212 wounded, and the Americans 14 dead.[22] It is believed that more than 700 Japanese were killed.[23] Thus, there was a ratio of four dead Japanese to every one dead Ally.

This much-needed victory showed that the seemingly unstoppable Japanese could not only be defeated but also driven off.

11

Retreat to Victory

September to November 1942

While the Allies at Milne Bay were gaining the upper hand, on the Kokoda Track, the Maroubra Force was still in retreat. On 26 August, the day after the Milne Bay invasion, the Japanese Kokoda Track commander, Major General Tomitaro Horii, landed some 13,500 troops at Buna, with a plan to build a base and airstrip there to support the advance over the track to Port Moresby.

Along the track, Japanese attacks on the Australian position at Isurava became more intense until, on 27 August, the Japanese brought up a mountain gun. 'The enemy came on in waves over a short stretch of open ground, regardless of casualties,' Ralph Honner would recount. 'They were met with Bren-gun and Tommy-gun, with bayonet and grenade; but still they came, too close with the buffet of fist and boot and rifle-butt ... [It was] vicious fighting, man to man and hand to hand.'[1]

The 39th Battalion managed to hold on until they were joined by the 14th Battalion of the 21st Brigade under Brigadier Arnold Potts, but despite personal acts of courage, Isurava couldn't be held. Short of supplies and in constant threat of being outflanked, the Maroubra Force began a fighting withdrawal that would be a feature of the rest of the campaign.[2]

* * *

Suddenly MacArthur's mood changed. He had experienced this kind of threat before when the Japanese invaded the Philippines, and that had turned into a defender's rout.

After a lifetime of honing his manner to suit his audience, MacArthur could put on a good show in meetings and during speeches, but behind the scenes, the fact that the Japanese seemed to be gaining the upper hand, even in modest force, seemed to knock him off course. The same was true of his chief of staff, Major General Richard K. Sutherland, and chief of intelligence, Brigadier General Charles Willoughby. Each time the progress slowed – as it often did in the extremely difficult Owen Stanley Range – all three were suddenly chorusing 'The Australians won't fight,' despite not having laid their eyes on the Kokoda Track since they remained at base in Brisbane.

Blamey is often criticised for not managing expectations, but he had a huge perception problem to deal with. A fighting withdrawal looks like defeat to all but those initiated in military tactics. MacArthur knew this intellectually, but as his growing panic suggested, he feared the proximity of even this small band of Japanese troops.

As criticism of withdrawals along the track became more strident from MacArthur's GHQ, Blamey remained relatively calm. He and his officers had experienced plenty of battle reversals in both wars, and his reaction was almost always to hurry slowly and thoughtfully. Rowell's concern was subdued and controlled, and he remained sure that Port Moresby was not under threat of falling to the Japanese.[3] Unfortunately, at least in the short term, neither Blamey nor his officers would be given the opportunity to hurry slowly. MacArthur began to shoot off criticisms to Rowell via Major General George Vasey, now Deputy Chief of the General Staff, in the Brisbane headquarters. Rowell was not a man to roll with the punches, and he became increasingly testy, even as Vasey explained to him that the mood at MacArthur's headquarters in Brisbane was bordering on hysterical.

To MacArthur's alarm, the Japanese continued to land reinforcements at Buna, including battle-hardened veterans from the Chinese campaign, causing MacArthur to complain to General George Marshall, the US Army Chief of Staff in Washington, on 6 September that 'The Australians have proved themselves unable to match the enemy in jungle fighting. Aggressive leadership is lacking.'[4]

It was not how the enemy saw them. According to one Japanese soldier later interviewed by historian Peter Williams, the Australians were tenacious: 'I was a veteran of China, but I'd never encountered such hard fighting before … [they] … didn't run, they fought … [they] knew our tactics and used them against us … [they] had excellent weapons, like the Bren gun. It was better than our light machine gun and I saw to it that, after Isurava, all my company was using captured Bren guns.'[5]

As Blamey and the other Australian commanders knew, it was a matter of supply. At that point, the Australians had little in the way of support. That would be the Japanese soldiers' problem in the future. Yet MacArthur continued to deny Blamey's requests for increased air supply to the troops.

On 8 September, clearly under pressure, Rowell told Vasey that he intended to relieve the current Maroubra Force commander, Brigadier Potts, who it was deemed needed a rest after the severe strain of battle.[6] Command was handed over to Brigadier Selwyn Porter two days later.

With unease about the fighting withdrawal increasing, Army Minister Forde asked Blamey to visit Papua and fix the problem. On 11 September, Curtin confidentially briefed the press, telling them there was 'now official worry about the position there' and that, according to Macarthur, 'the Allied forces' – meaning the Australians – 'had been out-generalled and out-manoeuvred'.[7] Blamey had personally told Curtin of the dire supply situation, but the Prime Minister was invested in MacArthur as commander.

The same day, Blamey met with MacArthur, then flew to Port Moresby the next day, as per Forde's request. There he met Rowell and Allen, and after discussion the three Australians agreed they were happy with progress. That evening he addressed the press to praise the success of the troops. Blamey assured Rowell and Allen that Port Moresby was 'in no danger and I think we shall find that the Japs will be beaten by their own advance with its attendant problems of supply ... It will be a Japanese advance to disaster, an Australian retreat to victory.'[8]

This confidence was certainly not reflected at GHQ. MacArthur's newly appointed air commander, Lieutenant General George Kenney, went so far as to claim that Rowell was defeatist, despite not having met the man.[9]

General Blamey (hands on hips, front row) addressing an AIF artillery unit in Papua. Major General Allen is to his right, holding a cigarette. October 1942. (AWM 013366)

Blamey also came face to face with his nemesis, journalist Chester Wilmot, in Papua, and the two men had another rough exchange. Wilmot questioned the choice of khaki uniforms for the Australians rather than jungle greens. Blamey's response was that the khaki uniforms had been designed for the jungles of India and that the jungles in Papua were no different. Wilmot then offered to bring him several thousand men who had fought in Papua and thought otherwise.[10] Wilmot had written a piece about the issue, and it had so impressed Rowell that he had sent it to HQ in Brisbane, asking that it be issued to all troops. Though Blamey vetoed distribution of the paper, jungle-green uniforms were soon adopted.

By 13 September, Blamey was with Rowell at New Guinea Force headquarters in Port Moresby, where they discussed the issue of Brigadier Potts. They both agreed that he had substantial experience and should be reinstated as 21st Brigade commander.

Meanwhile, the 25th Brigade of the 7th Division had been summoned from defence duty on the beaches of the Sunshine Coast. They arrived in Port Moresby in early September and were committed to the Kokoda Track campaign to reinforce the struggling 21st Brigade at Ioribaiwa, just 13 kilometres from the start of the track at Owers' Corner. On 17 September, under heavy attack, they both withdrew to Imita Ridge, a mere 60 kilometres from Port Moresby.

That same day, having returned to Canberra, Blamey was grilled by the Advisory War Council, comprised of members of both major political parties. Since nothing short of immediate victory against the Japanese was apparently going to satisfy them; his explanations of the manoeuvres in progress and his assertion that the Japanese would be defeated by a lack of supplies only made the council nervous.

That night, MacArthur spoke to Curtin by phone, voicing his concern that the Australians were withdrawing despite outnumbering the Japanese. The cause of MacArthur's disquiet was the 21st and 25th Brigades' withdrawal.

MacArthur also demanded that Curtin post Blamey to Port Moresby 'to take personal command, not only to energise the situation, but to save himself, because, in the event of the situation in New Guinea becoming really serious, it would be difficult for General Blamey to meet his responsibility to the Australian public'.[11] Curtin immediately rang Blamey and ordered him to Port Moresby.

MacArthur was clearly orchestrating a campaign to undermine Blamey's position. Was he trying to deflect responsibility for perceived failures on the Kokoda Track, or was this part of his plan to gain full control of the Australian Army? Either way, it seemed to be working.

* * *

Ironically, what MacArthur did not know was that the Japanese forward troops on the Kokoda Track had in fact been ordered to go on the defensive because they could no longer be supplied.[12]

Despite exhortations from MacArthur to advance while battling disease, hunger, fatigue, rain, precipitous muddy terrain and the Japanese, the Australians had continued their fighting withdrawal. The Japanese were just as exhausted as they mounted the final ridge, from where they could see the lights of Port Moresby, just 30 kilometres away. Having stretched their supply line well beyond its ability to provide, they were out of food and ammunition. They could go no further. As Blamey had predicted, they had advanced to defeat.

The land and sea battle that had been raging at Guadalcanal in the Solomons through much of August was also not going well for the Japanese, and they needed reinforcements. On 8 September, Lieutenant General Tomitaro Horii, the Japanese commander on the Kokoda Track, was sent a signal to withdraw to Kokoda. A similar signal was sent several days later. It is unclear whether he received the signals because he continued his drive towards Ioribaiwa. On 14 September, Horii cancelled the offensive. The Japanese began withdrawing two days later.[13]

It was not until 28 September that Australian patrols discovered that the Japanese advanced position overlooking Port Moresby had been vacated. But the Japanese did not withdraw fast, nor did they make it easy for the pursuing Australians. They were pursued tentatively by the 25th Brigade, soon to be joined by the 16th.

* * *

The enemy might have been in retreat, but Blamey's position was still under threat. Now that he was to be stationed in Port Moresby, any military reversal would be blamed on him and could lead to his removal.[14]

Blamey should not have been ordered to Papua. Rowell had the situation in hand, and Blamey's work required him to be in mainland Australia, in as close proximity to MacArthur as he could be. With no telephone and fragile radio communications, Papua was a dreadfully inefficient place for a commander in chief to work from. Any face-to-face contact with officers based in his HQ in Brisbane or the main army nerve centre in Melbourne required them to travel to him, making their jobs less efficient too. Not only did the move serve no military purpose, but it soon caused considerable disruption in the chain of command.

With more to do in Australia than Papua, Blamey had dawdled until, according to a story told by Chester Wilmot, Curtin rang and threatened him with the words: 'If you value your position, you will not remain in Brisbane another day.'[15] Thus provoked, he arrived in Papua on 23 September. He was greeted by an exceedingly disgruntled Rowell, who took Blamey's presence as a direct vote of no confidence in his command.

Blamey obviously valued Rowell's command abilities; after all, he had promoted him to lieutenant general. But, as Blamey had observed in Greece, he believed Rowell lacked 'the reserves of nervous energy over a period of long strain'.[16] The day before Blamey arrived, Rowell had confided to his friend Major General Cyril Clowes: 'He cannot influence the local situation in any way, but he will get the kudos and it will be said, rather pityingly, that he came here to hold my hand and bolster me up. Shades of Greece in April 41!'[17]

Blamey tried to sugar-coat the situation by stressing that it was only temporary and cosmetic. He was technically the commander of the New Guinea Force while he was based in

Port Moresby, but Blamey assured Rowell that as far as the chain of command went, Rowell would remain in command of operations in Papua while Blamey got on with other things, such as the continuing administrative load of managing the Australian Army's business everywhere.

Part of Rowell's problem was that Blamey, under MacArthur's orders, was violating unwritten military protocols. Merely by his presence, the army's commander in chief appeared to be removing personal command in the field from Rowell. The government was unaware of the discord this would cause, having, as Carlyon noted, been urged on by MacArthur, who certainly knew the problems this could create.[18]

Crucially, Blamey was too proud to explain to Rowell that his problems were political and that he needed Rowell's help. Yet such an admission might actually have been palatable to Rowell.

As it transpired, Blamey couldn't help himself. He did interfere with Rowell's command, just as MacArthur had interfered with his. After a discussion with the two Australians about the dispersal of air forces on the Owen Stanley Range, US air commander Kenney wrote in his diary: 'Blamey is really in charge. Rowell is not even consulted. He is just hanging around either waiting for Blamey to go home or send *him* home.'[19]

Blamey tried, but failed, to work out their differences to his satisfaction during three late-night discussions in Port Moresby. Rowell, having a dogmatic, tetchy nature and a fixed attitude to army command structures, petulantly refused to cooperate. As he himself put it in another letter to Clowes: 'We've had three first class brawls. I would never have believed a senior

D Company, 30th Battalion, slogging uphill through deep mud after a battle at Isurava on the Kokoda Track, Papua, c. September 1942. (AWM 013288)

The 14th Field Regiment struggling to get a 25-pounder gun into position uphill through jungle on the Kokoda Track, Papua, c. September 1942. (AWM 026850)

officer would have taken what I said to him.'[20]

On 28 September, just five days after Blamey's arrival in Papua, Rowell was dismissed. Blamey finished his termination report: 'Rowell is competent but of a temperament that harbours imaginary grievances ... [It is essential] to have a commander of cheerful temperament and one who is prepared to cooperate to the limit.'[21] To Curtin, Blamey said that 'the personal animus displayed towards me was most unexpected'.[22]

Thirty years after the event, Rowell somewhat disingenuously wrote in *Full Circle* that maybe he should have said, 'Very good sir, what you say goes.'[23] If he had wanted to keep his job, then that was the only possible response. The reality was that Rowell had been insubordinate towards his superior officer, despite being given three opportunities to explain himself. His dismissal was an entirely reasonable response.

The affair demonstrated a chronic lack of flexibility on Rowell's part. He had dug in his toes on principle, to the detriment of the Papuan campaign. There was no legal, administrative or moral issue at stake in temporarily sharing an HQ with Blamey, nor was there any threat to the situation on the battlefield. Rowell just thought it made him look like he was not up to doing his own job.

Blamey suggested that Rowell be demoted to his substantive rank of colonel, and prevented him from taking a meaningful role in the military anywhere under his command. To many this seems harsh, but Blamey could not have a dissatisfied former senior officer making mischief in a critical position.

Rowell did not suffer too long, however. Curtin agreed with Sturdee, the Chief of the General Staff, that Rowell should be reinstated to major general, and sent him to a non-job in the Middle East. In 1944 Rowell negotiated with his old staff college lecturer, General Sir Alan Brooke, Chief of the Imperial General Staff, to become the Director of Tactical Investigation: the first Dominion officer appointed to such a post. He stayed there for the remainder of the war.

His mostly negative post-war reflections on Blamey are frequently cited. But given the circumstances of his dismissal by Blamey, can they be trusted?

* * *

Edmund Herring took command of New Guinea Force in Rowell's stead on 1 October.[24] Since returning from the Middle East with the 6th Division, he had been involved in the defence of Australia, and was now a lieutenant general.

Before leaving for Port Moresby he met with MacArthur who, mindful of the row between Rowell and Blamey, impressed upon him that it was his duty as a soldier to get on with the officer above him. Herring assured MacArthur that he would, and that he had found Blamey to be a good man to serve under in the Middle East.

Later, Blamey told Herring that he wouldn't interfere because of his responsibilities elsewhere. This time he was true to his word. He made himself available to give advice, and often made suggestions, but mostly resisted any urges to interfere. There was never any doubt that Blamey was the man in control. When Herring went forward during the later campaign at the Japanese beachheads, he sent lengthy detailed reports on the progress of fighting to Blamey, who responded with advice if he thought it useful.

It was lucky that Herring could work with this arrangement, because MacArthur made Blamey stay in Papua for nearly four more months.

* * *

After word came through about the Japanese withdrawal, Blamey's force might have hunkered down at the southern end of the Kokoda Track near Port Moresby in the knowledge that the enemy was too weak to dent their defences, let alone threaten Australia. But this was not to be. MacArthur, finally enthusiastic about the campaign, had decided to go on the attack.[25] On 1 October, he issued an order to Blamey for the New Guinea Force to advance over the Owen Stanley Range in pursuit of the retreating Japanese.

The next day, MacArthur came to Port Moresby from Brisbane. On 3 October, he, Blamey, Herring and Army Minister Frank Forde met Australian reinforcements from the 16th Brigade of the 7th Division at Owers' Corner as they were about to head up the track. MacArthur told them the Western world would be watching them. He wished them the best of luck but told them not to stop.[26] It was clear that his primary interest was in good press, and also that he had an expectation there would be no withdrawal – fighting or otherwise. Having made this lightning visit to the track, he returned to Brisbane the next morning.

On 6 October, MacArthur again prompted Curtin to demand the rapid return of the 9th Division from the Middle

General Blamey discussing food with men from a militia unit in Papua, October 1942. (AWM 013372)

A tea break for the commanders during an inspection of forward areas in Papua, October 1942. Left to right: Major General Arthur Allen, Australian Minister for the Army Frank Forde, US General Douglas MacArthur and General Blamey. (AWM 150836)

East. This time the US Joint Chiefs weighed into the discussion and indicated that they wanted the division to stay in the Middle East, supporting Blamey's recommendation. Roosevelt even promised a replacement American division, the 32nd; Curtin acquiesced on the proviso that the 9th Division was returned to Australia in early 1943.

Given the fact that Australia was no longer in obvious danger, Blamey had grave misgivings about chasing the Japanese to the beachheads. The supply situation on the track was already very unreliable and difficult, and would be worse on the beachheads until there was suitable shipping available. A new campaign would also mean bringing in yet more inadequately trained troops. Lieutenant Colonel Frank Sublet, a company commander on the Kokoda Track, later wrote that the men had received 'training quite irrelevant to the conditions of warfare into which they were thrown ... and were greatly outnumbered by an enemy which was trained and experienced in the conditions'.[27] Blamey knew that, for an army at war, learning on the job is very dangerous. It always comes at a cost in men's lives.[28]

Taking into account Blamey's doubts, the question must be asked: why chase the Japanese along the Kokoda Track at all? It is clear that, as on many previous occasions, the decision was political, not military. MacArthur wanted it. Why would MacArthur want the Australians to battle across the Kokoda Track onto the more open area of the beachheads without solving the supply situation? Shipping was still not available to transport the heavy supplies and weaponry they would need to beat a dug-in enemy, as the Japanese would certainly be, without sustaining excessive casualties. Planes and porters were not the answer. The only likely reason for the rush was that the US Navy was winning at Guadalcanal and MacArthur wanted to beat them to victory. He also needed a win to impress the American Joint Chiefs Admiral Ernest J. King and General George C. Marshall so that they would give him more resources.

Some days after MacArthur's visit, Blamey suggested that the Prime Minister visit Papua. Most likely, he hoped to gain Curtin's support in delaying the army's pursuit of the Japanese until the supply situation changed. MacArthur advised Curtin that a trip to Port Moresby would be foolishly dangerous, so Curtin declined. Blamey then asked to return to Australia for consultation, but that request was also blocked. The subtext was clear: the Australian Government was only going to take strategic advice from MacArthur.

Blamey was in exile. With Curtin no longer listening to him, his hold on command was fragile, and becoming increasingly so.

Sending his men out without proper training and supply, to fight a campaign he saw as unnecessary, violated every principle that he had fought for and amply demonstrated in the Middle East. In December 1941, he had refused Auchinleck when he was asked to release a division before it was properly trained and equipped.[29] The British had had to wait until he was ready. This was the Blamey way.

With every route for government intervention blocked, Blamey had no choice but to push his underprepared, undersupplied soldiers over the Kokoda Track.

12
Courting Controversy
November to December 1942

Progress to the beachheads was slow. In attacking via this route, the Allies had the Japanese problem in reverse: every step they took lengthened their difficult, fragile supply line. Yet MacArthur wanted progress, even though the men on the Kokoda Track couldn't carry enough supplies to feed themselves, let alone successfully fight a battle. They needed tanks, but most of all they needed artillery, the ammunition to fire it and the machinery to move it. They needed tents, bedding, hospital facilities, clean water, nutritious food and medicines. Air transport could help, but that had load limits, and there were many days when the planes couldn't fly over the Owen Stanley Range because of foul weather.

By mid-October, the 16th Brigade had reinforced the 25th Brigade as it pursued the Japanese towards the beachheads. Between 11 and 28 October, skilful Japanese defence held up the Australian advance with heavy fighting at Eora Creek and Templeton's Crossing, three-quarters of the way to Kokoda.

It took a week for the 25th Brigade to clear Templeton's Crossing, at a cost of 50 Australian deaths and 133 wounded.

As always in that fetid environment, the toll in sicknesses was higher. There were 730 sickness-related evacuations by mid-October.

The Japanese manned a deadly rearguard at Eora Creek and the 16th Brigade suffered between around 300 killed or wounded in nine days.

* * *

As the campaign continued, Blamey, feeling increasingly cut off from both Brisbane and Canberra, and weighed down by MacArthur's pressing need for speed, would do several things that dog his reputation to this day.

The first of them concerned Brigadier Arnold Potts, who had been commander of the 21st Brigade during the fighting withdrawal on the Kokoda Track until he had been relieved by Rowell on 10 September; he had then been restored to his position by Blamey and Rowell three days later.

By 22 October, Blamey had changed his mind again. He rang Potts at his base and told him: 'Change of climate for you, Potts. You go to Darwin. Your successor, Dougherty, will meet you tomorrow and take over.'[1]

In fact, it had been Herring, Rowell's replacement, who wanted the change of commander, and Blamey had taken on the responsibility of informing Potts. 'Neither of us was looking for anyone's head on a charger,' Herring later claimed. 'We had a war and a very tough war to win, and it was our job to call in the best man we could.'[2] For Herring, that 'best man' was Brigadier Ivan Dougherty, who had served under Herring previously.

It would appear that Potts hadn't done anything wrong at all. The successful fighting withdrawal along the Kokoda Track by his brigade under heavy Japanese attack would in time be considered 'masterful'.[3] Potts would be reinstated to field command in New Guinea in April 1944 by Major General Stanley Savige. In its official history, the 14th Battalion of the 21st Brigade would express regret but no rancour at losing the 'lion-hearted' Potts, then noted that Brigadier Ivan Dougherty was 'a very happy choice'.[4]

At any rate, the 21st Division would soon have an entirely different reason to feel ill-treated by Blamey – but first he would relieve another senior officer, in circumstances even more controversial than the removal of Potts.

* * *

In early October, under orders to advance as rapidly as possible, Major General 'Tubby' Allen, commander of the 7th Division, had begun complaining that he was not being given enough supplies. On 8 October, he went up the track to see conditions for himself.

Allen was an exemplary commander, much loved by his men, but with an irritable manner and prone to be difficult with his superiors. As he ascended, a string of increasingly prickly messages was sent back and forth between Allen and HQ about the difficulties of the terrain and the supply situation.

MacArthur was feeling under pressure from Washington to produce results and he penned a message to Blamey demanding progress. The Australians had been fighting on the Kokoda

Track with a view to minimising casualties, as Blamey had commanded. Now, Blamey was being pressed by a general who had little battle experience and a lot of ego. 'General MacArthur considers extremely light casualties indicate no serious effort to displace enemy,' Blamey telegraphed Allen, without comment.[5] Allen responded snappily that casualties were no measure of success.

On top of continued complaints from MacArthur that the advance was too slow, Blamey received a scathing report from Army Minister Forde about the progress of the Kokoda campaign. Something had to give. Blamey relieved Allen on 27 October, replacing him with Major General Vasey.

As Commander in Chief, Blamey had to satisfy multiple objectives and end up with a result that was at least as good but preferably better for the Diggers than their current situation. He also needed to keep MacArthur onside. The troops believed this was the main reason for Allen's dismissal, and they did not like it.[6] Yet placating MacArthur was in fact a desirable outcome, because the general controlled many things. If Blamey had behaved towards MacArthur as Rowell had towards him, MacArthur would have become uncooperative.

Almost certainly, Blamey interpreted Allen's increasingly snappy behaviour and public comments on tactics as outward signs of battle fatigue or stress. Perhaps he feared Allen was heading for a breakdown. He may also have asked himself if Allen was still the best commander for the job. When it came to the availability of capable generals, Blamey was spoiled for choice. Vasey was proven in combat and he was fresh, fit and a lot lighter than 'Tubby' Allen, which would have helped in moving up and down the precipitous Owen Stanley Range. Blamey was dedicated to merit-based promotion – it saved lives and got the job done quicker and better. And he certainly wasn't sentimental when he came to moving people on. As he once said to a friend, the commander in chief needs to be able to have breakfast with a friend and shoot him by lunchtime.[7]

Should Allen have been relieved? This is unanswerable from the outside, but Blamey apparently felt it was necessary. Operationally it paid off. The consensus is that the dynamic Vasey was a fortunate choice of replacement.[8] The men of the 14th Battalion certainly thought so: in their official history, published in 1948, they report being inspected in May 1943 by their own 'beloved' general, George Vasey.[9]

* * *

It is interesting to note the comments made by US General Robert L. Eichelberger regarding the relief of senior officers. Eichelberger arrived in Australia in late August 1942 as commander of US I Corps. He wrote a sympathetic letter to Herring in 1959 about comments by historian Dudley McCarthy in the official Australian war history:

> It is a funny thing about historians. If a general relieves a subordinate at any time he is immediately attacked. Whereas in our football game, if you have a better player for a particular play, you always play him, and everyone expects you to do this. I have little doubt that the same is true of your ball game. War historians never seem to give

> generals the credit for having thought that X might be better than Y for the next phase of operations.[10]

Blamey's dismissal of high-ranking officers has led to the claim that he was a bully. This is a somewhat overstated accusation, since he wasn't actually responsible for many dismissals over the entire course of the war. The allegation mainly relates to ill-feeling towards Blamey during the Kokoda Track campaign, and perhaps sympathy can be extended to the officers he dismissed.

But in the end, subordinates have to work with their senior officer. There is no evidence that Blamey ever dismissed officers capriciously; rather, he did so to ensure the continued efficient and effective running of the army. In addressing the press in 1945, Blamey said: 'I think you people have been unkind to me ... you have charged me with getting rid of generals ... We have only removed one in the field during this war.'[11]

This statement is perhaps a bit self-serving. It is technically true that Rowell was the only general that was got rid of by being removed from within Blamey's area of command. Allen and Potts were (technically) relieved and went to serve in the army back in Australia.

On another occasion, Blamey reflected: 'the most marked feature that has developed with the Second AIF has been the harmonious and cordial cooperation amongst high officers. In a period of six years only four cases of difficulty have arisen, and I think it marvellous, in the complexity of human life, that this number should be so small.'[12] In any event, Blamey did not have the final say as to what happened to individual generals.

On occasion he was overruled by the government and simply had to obey.

When he did relieve officers, he acted quickly. This was the case for Allen, who was dismissed by message. Some have suggested that Blamey should have observed peacetime etiquette, and that he or another senior officer should have climbed up the track to relieve Allen or, at a minimum, recalled him to base to dismiss him face to face. However, it was not peacetime, and any delay was likely to have cost lives. The troops felt ill-will towards Blamey for this, but a commander in chief has to weather this kind of storm because he is not in a position to explain.

* * *

On 1 November, ABC correspondent Chester Wilmot was once again called to front Blamey. Wilmot was an avid supporter of Rowell, Allen and Potts, and Blamey considered Wilmot's criticisms of the way he was managing the war subversive.[13]

For the final time, Blamey withdrew Wilmot's accreditation. He could no longer work as a correspondent in any of the Australian Army's area of operations.[14] Wilmot departed for the UK. He covered much of the rest of the European war including D-Day for the BBC, and went on to have a distinguished career as a BBC broadcaster and military historian. He died in a plane crash in January 1954.

* * *

The 25th Brigade under Major General Vasey entered Kokoda on 2 November to find it empty. On receiving the news, MacArthur sent his hearty congratulations to Blamey, with a message that these fine troops should feel pride and satisfaction at this splendid accomplishment, in which he fully shared.

Keeping a blanket censorship ban on the news until he and other Americans were in Port Moresby to take the credit, MacArthur arrived on 6 November when the risks from enemy attacks were minimal. He commandeered Government House for his forward HQ, then made an announcement that implied US forces had rolled the Japanese back, whereas in reality US ground forces had not yet been engaged along the track. Blamey was strongly rebuffed when he asked that his presence be announced.

There would be two more vicious engagements during the second week in November at Oivi and Gorari, just north-east of Kokoda, but on 16 November, after the Australians crossed the Kumusi River, some kilometres further up the track, the campaign was finally considered finished.[15]

* * *

On 9 November, during the final days of fighting, Blamey addressed the soldiers of Potts's previous command, the 21st Brigade, at the Koitaki cricket ground near the start of the Kokoda Track. The men had marched the 37 minutes from their barracks at Sogeri, an hour's drive from Port Moresby, under the orders of General Blamey. They assembled in the hot sun waiting for the general, who arrived 45 minutes late.

The men were expecting the same thing from the most senior Australian commander as two other brigades had recently received: congratulations for their tough fighting on the Kokoda Track.[16] But what Blamey said has perhaps caused the most lasting blemish on his career.

According to his normally sympathetic aide-de-camp, Norman Carlyon:

> [Blamey] told the men that they had been defeated, that he had been defeated and Australia had been defeated. He said that this was simply not good enough. Every soldier here had to remember that he was worth three Japanese. In future he expected no further retirements, but advance at all costs. He concluded with a remark that I think was particularly ill-chosen and unfair. Some others who heard it have claimed that it was not offensive.
>
> 'Remember,' he said, 'it is not the man with the gun that gets shot; it's the rabbit that is running away.'
>
> In view of the overall tone of this speech, the rank and file assumed they were being described as rabbits. It amazed me that Blamey should deal so insensitively with the men of such a well-proved brigade.[17]

Many later reports would detail the men's bitterness at Blamey's remarks. Brigade member Stanley Bisset would recall that Blamey 'just misguidedly and, you know, without knowledge and without being briefed correctly beforehand, he just told us that we'd been defeated by inferior troops with inferior numbers, and that the soldiers that run, they get shot like rabbits and, you know, it was just something that's made everyone in mutinous rage. And I was very upset and I could hear rustling going on in the troops and the troops had they … there was … it was incredible that, you know, somebody hadn't really shot him at that particular stage, because it was so unjust.'[18]

Blamey followed up his speech to the troops by calling the officers into a briefing at the ground where, according to Bisset, he went on with 'the same theme'.[19] Company commander Frank Sublet felt that 'This was regrettable in as much as it harmed himself as well as the 21st Brigade'; the men assumed he was criticising some of their actions during the fighting withdrawal much earlier in the campaign.[20]

It may well be that Blamey recognised the damage quickly. Captain Robert Porter, Blamey's assistant, observed that in 'the staff car later Gen. Blamey was strangely quiet. He was on the point of weeping.'[21]

Brigade commander Ivan Dougherty, who had replaced Potts just 17 days earlier, wrote:

> It never entered my head as I stood there on parade that the general had any idea he was being offensive, or that he intended to be so … but the brigade gave to what he said the interpretation that 'they ran like rabbits' … Following his address to the whole brigade [General Blamey] addressed the officers separately. He was direct with them and said that a few officers in the brigade had failed. This caused bitterness. But after both addresses Blamey told me that he thought highly of the brigade, and repeated to me

> what he had told the whole brigade – that I, as their new brigade commander, would be very proud of them.[22]

Whatever Blamey's intentions, the incident would be a stain on his reputation. In the short term, he would lose the respect of the 21st Brigade.[23] In the long term, he would lose the public relations battle, because he never spoke up in his own defence – nor did many others.

The 21st Brigade was made up of three battalions. Each battalion was present on that fateful day at Koitaki. Yet the histories of the 14th, 16th and 27th Battalions, respectively published in 1948, 1959 and 1960, don't mention the incident at all. In fact, the history of the 14th Battalion refers to Blamey with warmth, speaking of a lecture 'of considerable interest' given in October 1942 by Blamey, who was fascinated by the local flora and fauna.[24]

Raymond Paull's *Retreat from Kokoda* was published in 1958. Paull interviewed an assortment of ex-Diggers but also drew heavily on sources written by those who had reason to dislike Blamey, particularly Rowell, Allen and Potts. It is not impossible that the story has become embellished as it has been handed down verbally over the years. Nevertheless, since Paull's book, the dominant narrative has been an entirely negative one.

While writing this book, this author discussed Blamey with many people. Their most common first response, and often their only response, was that 'Blamey is that bastard who insulted the men on the Kokoda Track.'

But should so much of Blamey's reputation hang on this single mistake? The contention of this book is that the answer

the out-of-character address Blamey gave the 21st Battalion at Koitaki.

* * *

The Kokoda Track campaign had lasted from 21 July to 16 November 1942. Of the around 30,000 Australian troops who fought in Papua and New Guinea to that time, according to MacCarthy's official history, a total of 607 Australians died on the Kokoda Track and 1015 were wounded, giving a total of 1622 battle casualties. Two to three times the number of battle casualties, or somewhere between 3000 and 5000, were hospitalised with sickness. The numbers are difficult to determine precisely.

The Japanese had landed around 13,500 troops, of which 10,000 were in the fighting group.[28] There were approximately 2050 Japanese casualties,[29] meaning that the Japanese lost around 25 per cent more men than the Australians.

* * *

With the winding down of the Kokoda campaign, at last there *was* sufficient time to reflect and improve. The sudden arrival of the enemy in Papua had resulted in a rush of activity to get troops and equipment to the front. Many of the troops underwent training in Queensland but there had been serious doubts about its applicability to Papua.[30]

When the Australians first landed in Papua, training was the responsibility of each brigade or division.[31] When the 7th Division arrived in August 1942, the process of learning how to fight in the jungle accelerated but fell well short of being systematised. The 7th was an experienced division and the men naturally thought they would be able to handle any conditions they found themselves in. Flushed with victory from their fighting in Lebanon and Syria, they strode up the track full of confidence.

A few days of battling the mountainous Owen Stanley jungle changed their minds. Targeting mortar or artillery fire had been relatively straightforward in the Middle Eastern desert, but was a completely different proposition in precipitous, nearly impenetrable jungle in pouring rain. Plus, the big guns and their ammunition were also incredibly difficult to move around on the track without machinery. Rifles were cumbersome in the thick vegetation. Unit command was exceedingly difficult because officers could not see their own men in the jungle if they were more than a few metres away. Without roads, vehicles could not be used, thus evacuations were difficult and men died of wounds and sickness that they should have survived.

Realising just what they were faced with, the Australians began to develop methods of dealing with jungle warfare in earnest.[32] There were many problems and the hunt for solutions was constant. Thompson submachine guns proved too unreliable, as they clogged with mud, so a substitute was found: the Australian designed and manufactured Owen guns, which would fire under extreme conditions.

During most of the battles along the Kokoda Track and at the beachheads, the learning process was largely trial and error.[33] Yet this was not a simple lab situation; the outcome of trial and error in war is too often death or wounding. Luckily there was a sense of urgency, which meant that experiences were collated, assessed and rapidly passed on to others.

In November 1942, recognising the need for better training, Blamey ordered the establishment of the Jungle Training Centre at Canungra in Queensland. It would admit its first trainees at the start of December. The big advantage of the centre was that it collected and evaluated solutions, then developed training and techniques specific to the myriad issues the soldiers in the jungles faced. Separate training manuals were produced for infantry, engineering, signals, medical and artillery corps, and progressively updated as more information came to hand from the soldiers and others on the front lines. By the end of the year, mechanisms had been put in place to feed the information back to those in the field.[34] Less than six months after the Japanese landed at the beachheads in Papua, systemised training was well underway.

It was recognised that not all groups could get to the training centre, so by the end of 1942 two training teams had been set up to visit units recently returned from battle and review their experiences, so these could be included in the manuals. They would also circulate around the battle areas, running seminars and developing practical exercises.[35]

By April 1943, when the 9th Division returned from the Middle East and went into training at Canungra, silhouette targets operated by remote control jumped out of the bushes. Soldiers fired live ammunition at them or not, depending on whether they mimicked friend or foe.[36]

By the end of the war, the centre was turning out 4000 graduates a month. By then there were 40 schools catering for different types of soldiers and officers, delivering a total of 96,000 different courses, each lasting between a few weeks and four months.[37] The courses were so demanding that real war was reckoned to be less trying, except that in real war the targets fired back.

In stark contrast to the Australians, who fought better as the war went on, the Japanese suffered from almost a complete absence of innovation.[38] Japanese command eschewed customised training, believing that the enemy, despite its material strength, would be beaten by the spiritual might of Japanese forces.[39] Without information transfer, training, logistics, medical and weapons improvements, and other innovations, Japanese 'spirit' could not keep pace with Australian adaptation.

* * *

The other major challenge the Australians faced was disease.

In December 1942, after malaria infection rates far outstripped casualties at Milne Bay, Blamey's chief medical officer, General Burston, sent Lieutenant Colonel Edward Ford to investigate. Ford was a doctor specialising in tropical medicine, and a sometime academic at the Sydney University School of Public Health and Tropical Medicine.[40]

Ford made a thorough investigation, then reported back to Blamey in his command tent outside Port Moresby during a rainstorm. Ford recommended three actions: anti-malarial earthworks must be carried out to improve drainage; the new anti-malarial medicines needed to be brought into Papua in quantity; and the men must adopt measures to prevent malaria, including sleeping under a net and covering up bare skin after dark, as well as taking the anti-malarial medicines.

Blamey sent 1000 Papuan labourers to Milne Bay to dig drains. Sufficient quantity of anti-malarial medications were brought in, but there was resistance to taking them because a rumour had circulated among the men that the quinine they contained caused impotence. Finally an article came out in the army newspaper, reputedly written by Blamey, saying that quinine wouldn't make you impotent but repeated attacks of malaria would.

At Milne Bay in December 1942, there were 82 cases of malaria per week per 1000 troops; by May 1944, in the upper Ramu, there was only 0.9 cases per 1000 troops.[41]

The environment, almost as much as the enemy, had delivered some hard lessons to the Australians. Under Blamey's direction, the challenges were met head-on with systemic improvements to health and jungle fighting. The investment in those innovations would dramatically reduce the sickness and fatality rates of the Diggers in the coming battles.

13
On the Ascendant

October 1942 to January 1943

While clearing the Kokoda Track had been a triumph, it was actually just the end of stage one. This was a victory in itself, but the job wouldn't be finished until stage two – removing the Japanese from the beachheads of Gona, Sanananda and Buna – was over. The early battles in Papua had proven tough, and, as Blamey had predicted, things were about to get tougher as MacArthur pushed the Diggers into heavily fortified enemy positions.

In October, while the 25th Brigade of the 7th Division under George Vasey continued to pursue the now retreating Japanese from Kokoda towards the north coast of the island, the very green 126th and 128th Regiments of the US 32nd Division, commanded by Major General Edwin F. Harding, were sent to Buna via air, sea and land routes.

Despite having been frustrated in taking Port Moresby, the Japanese intended to stay in Papua. They had plenty of supplies and had reinforced the beachheads with more men. They had commandeered the only dry ground available close to the beach and built an impressive set of interlocking weapon pits, bunkers and trenches backing onto the sea. The heavily disguised defences were covered with tough, fibrous coconut palm trunks and other vegetation. Swamps channelled the attacking Allies along a small number of land bridges that lined up with the Japanese bunkers. Any approaching enemy would be raked by machine-gun fire. The Japanese had constructed a defensive masterpiece.[1]

At least the odds were favourable for the Allies in terms of manpower: there were now 12,000 Japanese to the Allies' 20,000. Yet conditions were as miserable as anywhere else in the New Guinea theatre. The Allies were now fighting on flat, swampy ground, covered in a jungle of coconut palms and razor-sharp, head-high kunai grass. There was no relief from the rainfall, and malaria and other tropical diseases were such a problem that at one time two out of three men were sick. At this point, anti-malarial medications were not yet readily available.

The lack of maps was another serious issue, but dwarfing all other problems the Allies faced was the difficulty of supply. Heavy items – particularly tanks, artillery and artillery shells in quantity – could not be transported into the region by plane. With no roads over or around the Owen Stanley Range, sea transport was the only option.

Requests were made to the US Navy, but it was concentrating on winning its first major battle in the area at Guadalcanal and had no shipping to spare.

Back in May, at the start of the New Guinea campaign, MacArthur had recognised that shallow-draught shipping could go where deep-draught ships couldn't. In the months since, his team had recruited all the shallow-draught vessels around Australia they could lay their hands on. The small vessels did sterling service transporting light loads, hauling barges and charting the treacherous coastline. In something of a breakthrough for sea transport, the US 128th Infantry Regiment was put ashore by vessels belonging to the US Army Small Ships Section. But small ships were entirely inadequate for transporting heavy equipment.[2]

The Allies tried to land tanks by barge, but the barge sank. Another barge bearing the first two 25-pounder artillery pieces bound for the front was destroyed by the enemy. Later, Bren gun carriers were brought up from Milne Bay, but they proved to be useless because they had insufficient armour nor enough firepower. They could not substitute for the tanks that should have been there.

Without tanks and other heavy weapons, the Japanese defences would be exceedingly tough and dangerous to penetrate, or even reach.

Meanwhile, construction of two airfields was underway close to the settlement of Popondetta, about 40 kilometres inland from the beachheads. Both opened on 21 November 1942. With these strips completed, the zone was ready for the mixed air force of US and Australian personnel and planes commanded by Lieutenant General George C. Kenney – when the highly variable weather over the Owen Stanley Range permitted.

Kenney had proclaimed that his force would do the job of the artillery in the forthcoming battle for Gona, Sanananda and Buna. Despite load constraints and fickle weather, it would prove extremely valuable in conducting reconnaissance, hauling supplies, moving troops, destroying Japanese transports and evacuating the sick and wounded. But it manifestly failed as an artillery substitute, because bombing from planes was wildly inaccurate.

* * *

Major General Harding led the first engagement with the Japanese at Buna on 19 November. The US soldiers attacked en masse in the pouring rain and were cut to ribbons. On 21 November, they received a direct order from MacArthur to keep attacking, regardless of losses. This time they were supported by air bombardment, but with no better result. In addition to losses at the hands of the Japanese defenders, they suffered many fatalities from 'friendly fire'. They tried again the next day, but the supporting air bombardment arrived at the wrong time and place. When it came, ordnance was again dropped on the attacking US troops. Thanks to the beliefs of air commander Kenney, inaccurate air attacks and deaths by friendly air fire were to be a feature of this battlefront.

With only ten 25-pound artillery pieces, four mountain guns, one 105-millimetre howitzer and few artillery shells getting through, the forces had to struggle on with frontal infantry attacks on strong Japanese defences using only small arms, mortars and unreliable air ordnance. With insufficient heavy weaponry and MacArthur pressing them to use the wrong tactics at speed, deaths and casualties skyrocketed. After a week at Buna, US forces were failing. With soaring

General Blamey farewelling reinforcements for the Buna area, Papua, c. December 1942. They were the first Australian troops to be flown into action. (AWM 013818)

A 2/6th Armoured Regiment M3 Stuart light tank supporting infantry during the assault on Buna, c, January 1943. (AWM 014008)

casualty rates, their officers were having trouble motivating the GIs to fight.

* * *

MacArthur relocated his HQ to Port Moresby and was apprised of conditions around the beachheads by his loyal chief of staff, Major General Richard Sutherland, who visited the coast for a conference on 30 November. Sutherland reported that the Japanese positions could be easily taken – despite all the evidence to the contrary. Hearing this, MacArthur was keen to take the beachheads as rapidly as possible.

But as reports of the reality on the ground came through to Port Moresby, it was Blamey's turn to make MacArthur eat crow. According to Kenney, at a meeting between Blamey and MacArthur, the Supreme Commander suggested bringing in another US division. 'Blamey frankly said that he would rather put in more Australians, as he knew they would fight … I think it was a bitter pill for General MacArthur to swallow.'[3] Nevertheless, Macarthur agreed to use the Australian 21st Brigade instead of the US 41st Division. After enduring months of humiliation, Blamey must have been gratified to hear MacArthur acknowledging that an Australian brigade was better than a US division three times its size.

The under-strength 21st Brigade had been the recipient of Blamey's ill-advised speech at Koitaki, and had since been reforming after its brutal ordeal on the Kokoda Track. It was flown to the beachheads from Port Moresby in late November to assist the similarly under-strength 25th Brigade, which had already pursued the Japanese to the coast. The 25th had launched an attack on Gona on 22 November, and again two days later with reinforcements from the 21st and air bombardment, and both times failed to make much headway. Attacks were launched again on 6 December with disappointing results. Yet the Japanese *were* being worn down. Finally, an attack two days later shattered their resistance and they were decimated as they attempted to break out. The positions at Gona were finally cleared with vicious hand-to-hand combat the next day at the cost of 750 Australian casualties.

Things were not going so well for US forces at Buna. Desperately concerned about local US command, MacArthur ordered US I Corps commander General Eichelberger to travel north from Rockhampton to Port Moresby to take charge of US forces at the beachheads, with the dramatic command that 'If you don't take Buna I want to hear that you are buried there.'[4]

Eichelberger had previously expressed concerns about the preparedness of his forces, telling Generals MacArthur and Sutherland that the green 32nd Division was not sufficiently prepared to beat battle-hardened Japanese. This had already proven to be true.

Eichelberger arrived at the beachheads on 1 December and immediately replaced scores of officers, including Harding, and then, after goading by MacArthur, proceeded to push the division into more futile and failed attacks on the Japanese. Part of the problem, Eichelberger observed, was that the so-called intelligence reports made by MacArthur's chief of staff Sutherland had grossly underestimated the Japanese strength, a problem that was exacerbated by the fact that no US intelligence officers had come forward to observe the incredibly difficult fighting conditions, and the impenetrability and near-invisibility of Japanese dug-in positions.

Eichelberger later described the men on the front lines as half-starved. '[The 32nd] were riddled with malaria, dengue fever, tropical dysentery, and were covered with jungle ulcers ... Every member – I repeat, every member – of that company was running a fever. Yet to evacuate all those with fever at Buna would have meant immediate victory for the enemy, I had to encourage most of those troops back into combat.'[5]

According to the official medical history of the campaign, Allied losses from tropical disease were 4.8 times that of battle casualties.[6] Of the 37,360 cases of disease, malaria accounted for three-quarters. No Japanese figures exist but their suffering was likely even more extreme.

Like all US commanders, Eichelberger had less experience than the Australian commanders from brigade level up. He realised that he had a great deal to learn and deliberately developed good relations with them. As Eichelberger recalled later, he soon found Blamey to be 'a very fair commander and I would have taken his judgment at any time above the three characters who were behind me in the command chain – I refer to MacArthur, Krueger and Sutherland'.[7]

Even so, Eichelberger had thought it curious that troops of his American I Corps were under Australian control with Blamey as Commander Allied Land Forces and Herring as General Officer Commanding New Guinea Force, as soon as they landed in New Guinea. Yet he raised no objections.

Tolerance of Australians put him out of step with MacArthur and his cabal.[8]

Eichelberger worked closely with Herring, then when the 18th Australian Brigade was put under him, he allowed Australian Brigadier George Wootten to command US troops. He admired the Australians, later writing that 'when the going is tough, in a brawl or a battle, there is no better fighting partner than the man from Down Under ... The 7th Division and the 18th Brigade, which came in later [11 December], were crack outfits.'[9]

With daily increasing evidence of the US forces' poor performance, Blamey became emboldened. On 4 December, he wrote to Curtin: 'I am afraid the bulk of the fighting will fall on our troops in spite of the greater number of the 32nd US Division. [The US forces] ... will not attain any high standard of training or war spirit for many months to come ... My faith in the Militia is growing, but my faith in the Americans has sunk to zero.'[10]

After MacArthur's constant boasting of the capability of the American infantry, Blamey's revelation about the inadequacies of the American force came as a surprise to Curtin.

* * *

On 11 December, the supply situation changed dramatically for the better when the first large coastal trader arrived at Oro Bay, 24 kilometres south of Buna. It was part of Operation Lilliput, whose objective was to supply the Allies with a regular large tonnage transport service between Milne and Oro Bays.

General Blamey and Lieutenant General Robert L. Eichelberger scrutinise a Japanese bunker near Buna, c. January 1943. (AWM 014091)

General Blamey and Lieutenant General Eichelberger follow the path of the advancing Allied force as road workers make repairs near Buna, c. January 1943. (AWM 014097)

The first ship delivered four Stuart light tanks, artillery, ammunition and other supplies, along with the 18th Brigade, commanded by Brigadier George Wootten. Operation Lilliput would ultimately deliver 60,000 tons of cargo to the supply-starved forces at the beachheads, as well as nearly 4000 troops. The quantum improvement in supply would radically change the course of the battle for the Allies.

Under Wootten, Australian (18th Brigade) and US (32nd Division) infantry, tanks and artillery were finally able to make progress around the Buna airstrip. On 1 January 1943, the surviving Japanese tried to escape to Sananada. As Wootten's 2/9th battalion's history proudly noted, success at Buna was due to the tough discipline of the men and the capability of the command, factors that had been missing previously.[11] Still, for all the pride the battalion had in the win, it was a relatively 'inefficient' battle, even with the addition of tanks and artillery, because troops were forced to attack along very dangerous lines into extremely strong fortifications.

To take Buna, the 18th Brigade suffered 863 casualties, the 32nd Division around 2000 casualties and the Japanese 1390 deaths.[12] Three US generals were wounded at Buna, leaving only Eichelberger. He considered the fatality rate to be equivalent to the heaviest losses in American Civil War battles.

MacArthur was still in a constant state of high hysteria as he shot off irrational demands for immediate success.[13] By 26 December, Blamey must have been feeling even more confident of support from Curtin when he chastised the Supreme Commander for unexpectedly moving Allied infantry units about during one of Wootten's actions under Eichelberger without Wootten's knowledge. An unexpected move like this could jeopardise the whole operation and result in many more casualties. Addressing MacArthur as Commander in Chief, he wrote:

> I regret ... that you should have personally taken control of a single phase of the action ... but I thought I made it clear that I did not concur in the command of the action being taken out of my hands ... nothing is more contrary to sound principles of command than that the Commander-in-Chief or the Commander, Allied Land Forces, should take over the personal direction of a portion of the battle.[14]

Naturally MacArthur didn't agree, but Blamey ignored his rambling response, which ended with the disingenuous remark that his verbal discussions were advisory only. The positive result for Blamey was that, while MacArthur continued to keep a tight rein on his own commanders, he stopped interfering with Blamey's.

From then on, Blamey was able to take much more direct action. One of his first acts was to send Herring back to Port Moresby for a short rest and bring Deputy Chief of the General Staff Major General Frank Berryman to the beachheads until Herring returned. Berryman had become Chief of Staff of New Guinea Force on 11 December, when the force was divided between a rear headquarters under Blamey and an advanced headquarters under Herring. As Blamey became more confident of his standing, he placed more trust in his officers than he ever had before. Berryman, Herring and Wootten, in particular, were fully apprised of the difficult command situation. Inserting the affable Berryman revitalised the team without offending anybody.[15] Increasingly, Blamey came to rely on Berryman both for his intelligence and for his good nature, which aided in communicating with and gaining cooperation from the various commanders of both nations.

Blamey made his first visit to the beachheads front between 5 and 7 January 1943. Blamey's biographer David Horner criticises him for not having visited earlier but, in Blamey's defence, it is possible that it was only at that point that he felt he had enough control over MacArthur and his senior officers to be able to leave Port Moresby. With the force now reinforced by artillery and tanks, and his work on all the other vexatious issues well underway, he could afford to spare a couple of days to boost his troops' morale, as well as actually seeing conditions for himself. MacArthur never visited at all.

Unlike MacArthur, Blamey was also getting reliable information from his commanders at the front. This is clear from his rebuke to MacArthur prior to his visit when he had pointed out that the fighting fronts were a mere 500 metres wide,[16] whereas MacArthur thought they were equal to those of the Western Front.

Blamey arrived by plane and stayed with Herring, now back at the front. One of the officers he met there was Brigadier Ivan Dougherty, commander of the 21st Brigade, whose troops Blamey had so offended on the Koitaki cricket field two months previously. There seemed to be no obvious fallout from the incident; rather, discussions ranged over their differing opinions as to whether the tanks could manage the ground conditions around Sananada. Blamey said, 'Let's go see,' and proceeded to organise an unescorted visit well forward of the front line. Vasey, who was also at the meeting, considered it quite a mad thing to do. Vasey worried about Blamey's safety as he roamed around the beachheads ahead of the forward Australian soldiers.[17]

The following day, Blamey set off in a jeep with Eichelberger, inspecting captured Japanese defences. On seeing the defences on Buna, Blamey said that 'a miracle had been performed'.[18]

As Blamey and Eichelberger moved about, one of air commander Kenney's fighters roared in with machine guns chattering. Blamey saw first-hand the inaccuracy of Kenney's flying 'artillery' and the deadly effect the strafing runs had on US forces. The pilots thought they were firing at a target three miles away, and the soldiers got so annoyed they fired back at the planes, Eichelberger later noted. Five or 10 minutes later, another 'friendly' plane came over with guns ablaze and wounded three infantrymen.[19]

* * *

The Japanese survivors from Buna withdrew north to Sananda, so Herring now concentrated his efforts there. Vasey's 7th Division was sent in, supported by a regiment from the 41st US Infantry Division, along with tanks and artillery. The Allied attack began on 12 January against newly reinforced positions. A Japanese anti-tank gun knocked out two of the three tanks and the assault was halted. Unknown to the Allies, their efforts had exhausted Japanese anti-tank ammunition and cut off further supplies.

On 8 January, Blamey advised Herring that Eichelberger would take over command from Herring on the north coast of Papua. Eichelberger was the only foreign general to directly command an Australian formation during the war; Blamey and the other Australian commanders, including Vasey, trusted him, but further, Eichelberger was more or less under Blamey's operational control.

Four days later, Eichelberger ordered an attack on Sananda with all the power they had.

A Japanese breakout from the beachheads was planned for late January 1943 but individual commanders chose to withdraw their troops early. Some were lucky to be picked up by Japanese barges up the coast beyond the Allied perimeter, while the remainder had to walk to Lae, some 250 kilometres away. Many soldiers were too sick to retreat or were wounded. One Japanese soldier described seeing many of his comrades who were too weak to walk being shot dead after begging for an end to their misery.[20]

As the Japanese began to evacuate by sea, the Allies advanced cautiously against fading resistance, and after days of difficult and dangerous bunker-busting, finally eliminated the enemy on 22 January.

* * *

The beachheads campaign had resulted in 1261 Australian Army dead and 2210 wounded, for a total of 3471 casualties. The US Army suffered 734 deaths in action and 2037 wounded in action, with 8259 evacuated sick, for their whole Papuan engagement, which included 14 dead at Milne Bay.[21] That the Australian totals are greater than the US totals is reflective of the much greater role the Australians played. MacArthur put the number of Japanese dead at 7000, with 3000 dying in action and the remainder dying of illness.[22] The ratio of Japanese to Allied deaths (which totalled 1995) is 1.5 if only battle deaths are included, but 3.5 times if medical deaths are included. In this case, the Japanese medical deaths can be legitimately considered as battle deaths because they were achieved under siege conditions as a result of Allied action, therefore the true ratio of Japanese to Allied battle deaths is 3.5.

These are grim figures indeed, reflecting the extraordinary difficulty of busting the Japanese positions at the beachheads. This was a particularly vicious battle, a tropical version of the worst battles of World War I, featuring exposed infantry attacking an enemy with extremely strong defences, with both sides hampered by too little artillery, ammunition and tanks. Worse, it was carried out in too much of a hurry, as demanded by MacArthur.

Could it have been run better? If Blamey had been given a free hand, he certainly could have done so. Simply slowing down the pace would have helped considerably. Many men would have been saved if the Japanese had been put under siege while the Allies built up their forces and supplies, particularly heavy weapons, before attacking. But then, that was the story of the whole New Guinea campaign.

The Japanese were always in a much more difficult position. They were lesser in number than the Allies. They were irregularly supplied, if at all, and were starving.[23] They were

Major General George Vasey and Lieutenant General Edmund Herring visit Brigadier George Wootten at the Sanananda front, c. February 1943. (AWM 014308)

also fighting with equipment that was inferior both in quality and quantity.

* * *

The Papuan campaign had taught the Australian Army some bitter lessons. It had been unprepared for combat in Papua, and while it had adapted rapidly, it had lost too many men. Hampered by inadequate supply lines, commanders had been forced to improvise. Those at every level in the army's hierarchy had been required to learn on the job. The men fighting in the jungle had to develop specific skills to keep themselves and their compatriots alive and winning. Those skills were of less value to officers, although they had to be prepared to encourage and abet those whom they commanded.

The entire campaign – from the time the Diggers first encountered the Japanese in July to the conclusion at the beachheads on 22 January 1943 – had been expensive for the Allies, but even more so for the Japanese.

For the whole campaign from Kokoda to the beachheads, the total Australian Army deaths were 2134, with 3632 wounded in action, totalling casualties of 5766. Adding the US Army casualties brings the total Allied army dead to 2868. The total of Japanese dead was 13,600, 15 per cent of them from the navy, which fought on land as well as at sea. Japanese battle deaths were 1800, and deaths because of illness 300, partly as a result of the blocking of medical supplies and evacuations by the Allies. In terms of total deaths, the Allies had a 4.74 times advantage.[24]

Having won the battles of Milne Bay and Kokoda Track, the beachheads battle was the third won by the Allies since the start of the war against Japan. It was completed before the US Navy won their first land engagement at the Battle of Guadalcanal on 9 February. The Australians under Blamey had proved they could fight and win.

* * *

In mid-January, MacArthur decided to return to his main HQ in Brisbane and advised Blamey that he could return at a time of his choosing. Given Blamey should not have been commanding from New Guinea, he left almost immediately on 13 January, before the beachheads campaign had ended. He had been cut off for too long from the political decision-makers and, more importantly, did not want MacArthur to have unsupervised access to Curtin. His work was on mainland Australia, where it had been accumulating during his forced absence.

The exile to New Guinea had been tough on Blamey. According to one of his backroom advisors, Colonel Alfred Conlon: 'It was pathetic to see how out of touch he was. Poor old bugger didn't have a clue who was up who in Canberra.' His job was made even harder by being 'hated by a number of ALP ministers ... He was also distrusted by several conservative politicians. There were some gaping holes in the C-in-C's armour.'[25]

By ordering Blamey to New Guinea, the Australian Government had inadvertently hampered his effectiveness. Blamey had not been needed on the front line and had

had plenty of work that would have best been done on the Australian mainland. That included reorganising the Australian Army, furthering jungle training and ensuring that ordnance manufacture and supply ran smoothly.

McCarthy concludes his official history of the first year of fighting in the Pacific with praise for individual soldiers, and for the way superb leadership had emerged at all levels. But he reserves special praise for Blamey:

> At the very peak of leadership development was General Blamey himself. His capability was demonstrated almost daily by a knowledge unparalleled in Australia of how an army should be formed and put to work; by his exercise of the vital field command at the same time as he kept within his grasp a vastly detailed control of the Australian Army as a whole; by his sagacity and strength in meeting the rapidly changing demands of a difficult political situation; by his ability speedily to encompass the requirements of the new war and plan far ahead of the events of the day as he controlled them; by his generally unappreciated humanity.[26]

14
The High Point of Australian Military Operations

January 1943 to April 1944

The winds of change were blowing through high command. General MacArthur had been humiliated by the poor showing of the US Army compared with the Diggers. But he realised he needed the Australians, at least until he had enough US troops with experience under their belts.

Without fanfare, the power balance was shifting. The coming year would be the sweet spot of the Australian–American alliance in the South West Pacific Area.

On 14 January 1943, the day after he left Port Moresby, Blamey arrived in Canberra to report to Curtin and Shedden. They discussed the Pacific campaign and Curtin's concerns about the number of men required to compensate for the substantial losses. Casualties in battle were one – unavoidable – part of war, but non-battle casualties, due particularly to malaria and other diseases, were proving a significant drain on manpower. There was not much that could be done, however, until practical solutions could be found and implemented.

Without the additional resources required to move assaults along more quickly, it was necessary to use the slow approach of holding and starving out the enemy.[1]

Australia was struggling to maintain an adequate number of personnel for MacArthur's offensive efforts, in addition to the numbers required for home defence and the production of war materiel and equipment. There was also a great need for workers in food production, given that Australia was providing food for MacArthur's expanding army.

Another matter that came up in the meeting with Curtin was the so-called 'Battle of Brisbane'. Over two days in November 1942, resentment over the large numbers of US soldiers in the city had reached the point of pitched battle between Australian soldiers and civilians and US forces, which had left one Australian dead and many injured on both sides. Blamey's response was to propose removing the officer in charge of the Australian soldiers involved, who, in his view, had not handled the riots appropriately. He later suggested to MacArthur that there should be some outward display of cooperation between the forces, including lectures to be presented by both Australian and US force members. MacArthur dismissed the idea, perhaps due to a lack of concern for promoting Australian interests.[2]

On 18 January, Blamey flew to Melbourne and delivered a radio broadcast to the nation about the battles in Papua. He praised MacArthur, his team, and the Australian officers and men, concluding by saying that the Japanese to this point had been beaten by the superior quality of Allied troops.[3] But while Blamey was publicly paying tribute to MacArthur and his force's efforts, MacArthur himself was playing a two-faced game with the goal of achieving absolute power over Allied forces in the South West Pacific Area. He did not particularly care whether this meant gaining total control over Australian forces, or removing them from active fighting so that his own troops could do the fighting and claim the victories.

MacArthur complained to Defence Co-ordination Secretary Shedden in a meeting that the Australians in the Papua campaign had been slow 'in exploiting advantages',[4] and that Blamey didn't have the full support of the army, perhaps alluding to the removals of Rowell and other commanders. His major gambit was to suggest that 9th Division's commander Leslie Morshead should take command of the expeditionary (offensive) forces and Blamey should focus on his position as Commander, Allied Land Forces, thereby curbing Blamey's role with the aim of expanding his own.[5]

Blamey's political standing was now slightly stronger than it had been when he was exiled to New Guinea. Curtin – if not Army Minister Frank Forde – was giving him a hearing and had even acknowledged that he (Curtin) had affected Blamey's administrative capacity by sending him to Port Moresby on MacArthur's advice. Blamey clearly felt relaxed enough to take a week's leave on 31 January to Wonboyn Lake in south-east New South Wales to indulge in his favourite recreation, fishing.[6]

Even so, his position remained shaky. At MacArthur's suggestion, Curtin approached Morshead on 1 March to ask him if he would be willing to take over the role of commander in chief. Morshead rejected the proposition out of hand and later telegrammed Curtin that it 'would be a national calamity if [Blamey] were to become a casualty'.[7] Morshead's widow later elaborated by saying that her husband felt he was better suited to serving as a field officer, and as such did not want to be involved in the politics or the heavy administration load of Blamey's position. Vasey was also approached and similarly declined the offer.[8] Despite this, Blamey was soon to be recognised for his service during the Papuan campaign, being appointed a Knight Grand Cross of the Military Division of the British Empire (GBE) on 28 May 1943. This was an exceptional honour, and Blamey is one of only 10 Australian men and women ever to have received it.

Meanwhile, one of Blamey's first orders of business after his week off had been to organise, rest and train the Australian forces for the next phase of the war. The 7th Division was withdrawn from Papua to rest, rebuild and train, safe from the risk of tropical infections. They were joined in training on the Atherton Tableland by the 6th Division, and by the 9th Division when it returned from the Middle East. The latter division had acquitted itself exceptionally well in October and November 1942 during the Second Battle of El Alamein, in which the Afrika Korps was finally defeated. Eighth Army commander Bernard Law Montgomery would later reflect: 'The more I think back the more I realise that winning was only made possible by the bravery of the 9th Australian Division in holding the road against counter-attacks and slowly pushing forward despite increasing casualties.'[9] When they returned to Australia early in 1943, the 9th were greeted with welcome-home parades in every Australian capital city.

Fishing was Blamey's favourite recreation, 1943. (Blamey family)

Soon after this, Blamey announced that Morshead would lead II Corps, consisting of the 6th, 7th and 9th Divisions. For the time being it would continue to be based in Australia. The New Guinea Force, still stationed in New Guinea under acting commander Lieutenant General Iven Mackay, would include the previously home-based 3rd, 5th and 11th Divisions. Herring took over command of the New Guinea Force after returning from leave in May 1943.

* * *

US Army forces continued to pour into the Pacific – including, between February and April 1943, the Sixth American Army under General Walter Krueger. With the increased presence of US forces, the Australians were being pushed into the background. MacArthur was increasingly taking over the role of Commander, Allied Land Forces, and leaving Blamey with his other role of Commander in Chief, Australian Military Forces, an administrative rather than operational position. MacArthur did not consult any government on these command changes, and Blamey raised no objections, believing that it was ultimately the only arrangement that Washington would accept. The advantage was that he would no longer need to be so vigilant in protecting Australian forces from being subsumed under MacArthur's command.

On 1 April, Forde wrote to Blamey, expressing concern that highly placed officers considered money to be of no consequence and were resenting being accountable. Blamey replied that he was not aware of such officers but told Forde bluntly that there 'is nothing so costly as a lost battle and nothing so disastrous as a lost war'.[10]

On 26 April, MacArthur advised Curtin that the joint chiefs had set three objectives for the South West Pacific Area. These were to establish airfields on two adjacent islands, Kiriwina and Woodlark, south of New Britain, then occupy West New Britain; to capture the coast of New Guinea's Huon Peninsula from Salamaua north-west to Lae, then Finschhafen and Madang; and to take the Solomon Islands, including Bougainville. The latter task was given to US Vice Admiral William 'Bull' Halsey Jr, who at the time was assigned to MacArthur. The Supreme Commander reshuffled the objectives, giving US General Walter Krueger the relatively minor task of establishing airfields on Kiriwina and Woodlark islands, and occupying West New Britain with the yet-to-be-formed US Alamo Force. Blamey and the Australians and some US Army soldiers were to capture locations up the New Guinea coast. The overall plan was named Operation Cartwheel.

This was an extraordinary switch for MacArthur. After denigrating the Australians throughout the previous year, and with the option of using a senior US commander to spearhead the campaign on the coast, which was to include the retaking of Lae, he instead assigned the most significant operation to Blamey and the Diggers, while his most senior general was given only a minor role. It clearly demonstrated that he had greater confidence in the fighting capability of Australian forces than in his own troops at this point in time.

With this obvious stamp of approval from the boss, trust and goodwill flowed down through both national organisations in a way that hadn't previously been in evidence. The grumblings of US officers were silenced. Cooperation seemed to be bursting out all over. MacArthur's and Blamey's senior staff were now working well together, as was also happening with senior naval and air commanders. The cooperation got better further from GHQ and closer to the battlefront.[11] It even extended to MacArthur, who uncharacteristically limited himself to an 'acceptable' level of interference between a supreme commander and his ground-force commanders, rather than the persistent day-to-day interruptions he had been prone to deliver during the previous campaigns.

The Cartwheel operation, as envisaged and set in motion by the joint chiefs back in April, was a big one. As former director of the Australian War Memorial Dr Brendan Nelson has noted, it was the largest military operation ever conducted by the combined Australian forces of army, navy and air, and certainly much bigger than any of the operations on the Western Front in World War I.[12]

The Japanese had originally used Lae, in the Huon Peninsula, as a base to launch their Kokoda campaign. Following that defeat, they had retreated to establish a major supply base there with a substantial garrison in Salamaua, about 50 kilometres south. They were also patrolling around the inland settlement of Wau, about 50 kilometres south-west of Salamaua, where Australia's 3rd Division had been sent in January.

It was also where Blamey had ordered the upgrade of what would become the infamous Bulldog Track. Casting around for a land route to help the Allies reach the north coast of Papua in force, he had become aware of an old gold mining track from Wau that, if developed, would give access to Lae and Salamaua. Like just about every activity in Papua, it was an exceptionally difficult task.[13]

Blamey had already predicted the joint chiefs' decision that Lae should be taken and had begun devising a beautifully simple plan: an Allied force coming over the Bulldog Track from Wau would feint towards Salamaua to draw off the Japanese from Lae. With the main Allied attack appearing to be coming from Salamaua, the Allies would then aim their largest thrust at Lae. This would be a coordinated amphibious and airborne invasion of the other side of Lae from Salamaua to quickly take the weakened positions at Lae. With the main Japanese supply port of Lae taken, the Japanese outside Lae would be marooned in near-impenetrable jungle with few supplies or reinforcements, and could then be picked off, if disease and lack of food didn't take them first. The biggest potential complication would be the length of time it took to solve transport problems, because the operation would require a large number of men, along with heavy machinery and copious supplies.

Planning had begun in June 1942 with a broad-brush set of strategic objectives ordered by the joint chiefs, the carriage of which was assigned to Blamey by MacArthur on 6 May 1943. It would be a large-scale operation, but a routine exercise for the military, because they knew in advance what elements should go into it – men, machines, weapons and supplies – and how to get these to the job. As for any major operation, Blamey's HQ saw to the high-level objectives, timing and resourcing, and left the divisions to do their own detailed planning while he and his staff kept a keen eye on feasibility, cost and progress.

With the essential concept developed, Blamey handed the detailed planning over to Major General Frank Berryman, who had a talent for getting on with the Americans. Herring joined him as lead planner. Their preparation was thorough, to the point of creating a large-scale model of the Lae–Salamaua area, which became integral to the planning. Blamey met with both men as he moved around to check progress and iron out any issues, but certainly did not micromanage.[14]

Blamey's broad plan was for the 3rd Australian Division under his old friend Major General Stanley Savige to advance overland from their base at Wau to Salamaua. They were to attack Salamaua but not take it immediately. With Japanese attention deflected south to Salamaua, the 9th Division would mount an amphibious landing on the eastern side of Lae for what was expected to be an unopposed landing.

The 9th Division would be supported by the 162nd US Regiment; transported by ships into Nassau Bay, some 20 kilometres south of Salamaua; and marched into position east of Lae. Nassau Bay would be used as a supply base for the operations. More US forces would also be involved, with the US 503rd Parachute Infantry Regiment assigned to capture Nadzab Airfield, inland from Lae. Once the airport was secured, the 7th Division would be flown into Nadzab.

The plan to take Nadzab Airfield was Vasey's contribution. He was unhappy with the original intention to land his 7th Division at Wau and march 90 kilometres through extremely rough jungle to Lae. All the divisional commanders and their senior staff were consulted and alterations made to the plan according to their input.

Blamey had an evolving secret 'weapon' in his armoury that wasn't actually a weapon at all. Since the attack on Pearl Harbor, the incredible industrial might of America had rapidly geared up to produce large amounts of war materiel of all kinds. Of particular impact in this battle were large landing craft and cargo planes to deliver parachutists. For the first time in the Pacific war, Blamey had sufficient transport to deliver divisions and regiments, along with thousands of tons of materiel and machinery, at near-perfectly timed short intervals anywhere he wanted. This made rapid mass movement possible. It was an Allied advantage the Japanese in New Guinea had not faced before. Should they detect a hard-slog overland Allied invasion heading towards Lae, they would have expected to have time to get back from Salamaua. Instead, they would be totally blindsided when the Allies landed in force behind their lines in two locations in short succession.

A key element of Blamey's plan was for the Japanese to believe Salamaua was the Allies' first military objective.[15] MacArthur, demonstrating a basic lack of understanding of the plan and an unquenchable thirst for speed, visited Herring in Brisbane on 5 July, asking that Salamaua be taken as soon as possible, well before the planned invasion of Lae. Herring demurred and passed the matter on to Blamey, who could not get a clear commitment from MacArthur to stick to the plan until they met in conference on 28 July. On several further occasions, Blamey needed to hold the line against both MacArthur and Kenney, insisting that a quick victory at Salamaua would jeopardise the greater prize of an easy capture of Lae.[16]

Another cause of anxiety for MacArthur during the planning process was that Blamey's HQ couldn't answer all his questions because they weren't aware of the detail of each division's plans until late in the process. MacArthur and his planner, Lieutenant Stephen J. Chamberlin, were used to a top-down planning and unable to understand the less centralised Australian planning method.

On 15 August, Blamey flew to Port Moresby to take control, and on 20 August, he officially took command of the New Guinea Force, with Herring taking over I Corps. With planning to take Lae virtually complete, on 4 September, MacArthur ordered Blamey to prepare plans for the next stage of the operations from Finschhafen, east of Lae, to Madang, about 300 kilometres north-west. This future operation could be compromised if West New Britain, just across a narrow strait from Finschhafen, was not also taken.

* * *

While these plans were evolving, US air commander Kenney was not about to be outdone in extravagant planning, and his target was the airfields at Wewak to the north-west, where the Japanese had a large number of aircraft that could be used in a counterattack. Kenney knew they were beyond the range of his bombers, so he devised an ingenious plan to use decoy targets to deceive the Japanese while he established new airfields within striking range of Wewak. In typically aggressive style, he sent

US airborne engineers to set up an airfield at Marilinan, some 30 kilometres west of Lae. In two weeks, they cut a strip out of the jungle to take transport planes, and in late July, less than a month later, US fighter planes began arriving.

Troops then built the decoy airfield with dummy planes 85 kilometres north-west of the first airfield in a way that would attract the attention of Japanese aviators. On 14 August, the decoy airfield was spotted by the Japanese and attacked the following day. The attack was met by US fighters and sent off. The Japanese then concentrated more than 250 planes at their own airfield at Wewak to meet the apparent threat.

On 17 August, the Americans hit the airfield at Wewak with planes from the actual base. The Japanese lost over 100 planes, along with air and ground crew. The outcome was not decisive but it gave the Allies equal air power.

* * *

Meanwhile, the 3rd Division had been engaging the Japanese around Wau since January, in a grinding campaign on foot in typically difficult terrain between Wau and Salamaua. The Australian artillery was flown in and, while extraordinarily difficult to move and target, it provided both practical and psychological aid to the infantry against the outgunned enemy.

Local labour was vital to moving all supplies, including guns and ammunition. The items were broken down into manageable bits and carried by individual Papuan porters. The Australians' practical learning about jungle warfare had been collated since 1942, and its incorporation into training programs meant the Diggers had become skilled jungle fighters, able to locate isolated Japanese positions from subtle clues, and attack from all sides with combined arms. The infantry would go in under machine-gun and mortar fire and, where possible, call in air and artillery support. Aggressive patrolling was the order of the day. As they got closer to Japanese positions, Bren gunners would fire on the pillboxes to keep the enemies' heads down while Owen gunners attacked from the flank. Once they were close enough, the Diggers would lob grenades into the pillboxes, which became death traps for the enemy.[17]

It wasn't all one way, though. One slight advantage the Japanese had over the Allies was that they were trained in night fighting while the Australians weren't.[18]

On 19 August, after seven months of hostilities around Wau, Blamey sent Berryman forward from Port Moresby to clarify the situation, because reports from 3rd Division commander Savige had been sketchy. As a permanent officer, Berryman had nursed resentment towards Savige, and had had a low opinion of the militia man's ability since the beginning of the war. By this time, however, both officers were major generals with considerable command experience. Berryman admitted in his diary that he had misjudged Savige and was positive about Savige in his reports.[19] It was a belated acknowledgment that Blamey had judged wisely in his choice of officers. Blamey had promoted both men on merit, and both major generals would end the war at the even higher rank of lieutenant general.

Nevertheless, on 23 August, despite Savige's desire to keep fighting, Blamey ordered him and his division out of the field.

It was only about two weeks before the attack on Lae, but this was Blamey looking after the men at all levels. Fatigue sets in if they are in combat too long, and when that happens casualties rise. Relieving his men was what he had fought long and hard for, and eventually achieved, when the Australian 9th Division was fighting the Afrika Korps at Tobruk. Now, with the luxury of more control over the AIF, more divisions and more shipping, he was able to move divisions out of battle to recuperate in rear areas, while other divisions took over the fight. The rest areas were most often in Australia. Savige and his tired 3rd Division were relieved by the 5th Division, led by Major General Edward Milford.

The fighting from Wau to Salamaua had been extremely tough and caused as much misery as on the Kokoda Track. Again disease – chiefly malaria – and anti-malarial medication took a heavy toll.[20] The death toll was 707 Australians to an estimated 2770 Japanese. But artillery, close air support, training and experience, as well as freedom from MacArthur's exhortations for speed, made a difference.

* * *

Australian Army engineers, helped by local labour, were hewing the Bulldog Track towards the north coast from Wau out of precipitous jungle. Blamey had ordered it to be widened into a road suitable for supporting the activities of a mechanised army. It had to be able to take supply trucks, troop carriers, artillery and heavy vehicles. During the peak construction phase in 1943, more than 3000 local porters were employed.

General Blamey briefs journalists on operations around Lae using a scale model, 13 September 1943. (AWM 056892)

Australian troops disembarking from American Landing Ships onto Red Beach, east of Lae, prior to their assault on Lae, 1943. (AWM 306542)

Bulldozers were brought in, but the sodden soil and steep grades meant a great deal of the work still had to be done with picks and shovels. By late August it was finally ready for use.

The Diggers had a tough fight getting over the track to Salamaua, but Blamey's magnet was effective in attracting and holding Japanese attention. Fighting close to but deliberately not at Salamaua kept up until the landings at Lae were underway in the first week of September. The Japanese had reinforced Salamaua at the expense of Lae – held now by only 2000 troops, mainly service personnel and those manning fixed artillery and anti-aircraft guns. They were utterly wrongfooted when the main attacks began.

The invasion of Lae began on 4 September, with the Australians' first major amphibious landing since Gallipoli. The 9th Division, under Major General George Wootten, landed on the side of Lae away from Salamaua. At the last minute, the amphibious craft expected for use had been upgraded by the US Navy to larger landing ships. This gave the men a smoother journey, but there had been no time for landing training in the new vessels. Fortunately that did not cause major problems.[21]

In all there were 106 landing craft of various sizes in service, which delivered a mix of machinery – road graders, tractors and wire mesh needed to make roads over swamp and sand. Power saws were unloaded so palm trees could be felled and placed as foundations for roads. Then came jeeps, trucks and artillery. There were some encounters during the advance to Lae from Japanese air and land forces, but overall losses were light.

The shock of the seaborne invasion was compounded when US paratroopers made a successful combat drop to the enemy's rear at Nadzab Airfield the next day. This was the only time in the Pacific war that a whole parachute regiment was dropped in one lift. While US fighters circled for protection, 81 Dakota transport planes disgorged their load over three landing zones in the incredibly short time of four and a half minutes.

Once the paratroopers took Nadzab, the airfield was pressed into immediate service to ferry in the 7th Division, under Major General George Vasey, complete with artillery and supplies. The rapidity of the invasion ensured breakdown in Japanese coordination and general confusion so Allied losses around Nadzab were light. Vasey's greatest losses occurred before leaving Port Moresby, when a B-24 Liberator crashed into trucks carrying infantry. Sixty men were killed and 92 others injured.

By the time the Japanese commander realised that their base at Lae was under threat, it was too late. Men were rushed back to Lae only to arrive exhausted, and certainly with no time to organise a proper defence. The Diggers, on the other hand, had been well and truly briefed, trained and supplied before embarking on their mission. Now engaged on two fronts, one from the seaward landings and the other from soldiers arriving from Nadzab airfield, Japanese resistance at Lae collapsed.

When news of the attack at Lae spread to Salamaua, the Japanese position there collapsed. Salamaua was abandoned by the Japanese then occupied by the Allies on 11 September. Lae had also been abandoned and was occupied by the Allies five days later.

The operation had been so successful and so fast that there hadn't even been time to bring the Bulldog Track into full operation – just as it was finally able to take three-ton trucks. Work on making the track a road over the full length to Lae had started when there was no certainty that shipping would be available. The track had delivered the Allies to Salamaua, but its terrain was so terrible and sea transport had improved so much that it soon fell into disuse.

As the Japanese garrisoned at Salamaua made their escape into the jungle, their orders were captured and passed up the chain of command to Vasey then Berryman, who was with Blamey in Port Moresby. They both agreed on the specific actions that should be taken to block the Japanese exodus and relayed instructions to Herring at the front.

Herring was deeply affronted by such direct instructions, and delayed acting on them. In the absence of any instructions, his subordinates, Vasey and Wootten, acted on their own initiatives. Vasey blocked one of the paths out of the area around Lae, while Wootten concentrated his activity on Lae, leaving an exit path for the Japanese. As a result, it is believed that around 6500 Japanese escaped into the surrounding jungle, while 1500 were killed and, most unusually, 2000 were taken prisoner and interned in Australia.[22] The Allies' experience of the Japanese to that point was that they would fight to the death.

The battle for Lae had been an outstanding success, particularly as it was the first coordinated large-scale land, sea and air operation in the region. It was also a triumph of US–Australian cooperation, with the critical sea and air services provided by the Americans, and the bulk of the artillery and infantry engagement carried out by the Australians.

The battle in the Lae–Salamaua area lasted just 12 days. The losses for the 7th and 9th Divisions were 115 Allies killed with another 574 wounded or missing, giving a total of 689 casualties. The low Allied casualty rates at Lae were helped by the fact that this time the Japanese didn't stand and fight to the last man.

The Lae–Salamaua campaign was such a quick and thorough victory that Blamey was able to cancel a number of scheduled follow-on forces. Noting the campaign's great strategic value, rapid success and low casualties, historian Peter Dean has declared it one of the most successful in Australia's military history. Strangely, it is also one of the least known.[23] Here is a paradox of military history: a memorable battle requires large-scale death, suffering and heroism. It is particularly poignant if high-level planning is poor. Taking Lae featured little of this – almost everything went right – so it is largely forgotten.

In reality, though, the battle for Lae and Salamaua would not be over until Herring's blunder had been rectified and the escaped Japanese garrison neutralised. But with Lae secured and the escaped Japanese now untethered in the Huon Peninsula, the campaign split. Vasey's 7th Division went in an almost straight line inland from Lae, north-west along the Markham and Ramu Valleys. George Wootten's 9th Division, keeping near the coast, set off due east from Lae to take Finschhafen, at the eastern tip of the Huon Peninsula. Once Wootten's men rounded the far eastern tip of the peninsula, their path would closely parallel that of Vasey's 7th Division, though the two forces would be separated by about

75 kilometres of the extremely rugged Finisterre Range. At the end of their trek through the Markham and Ramu Valleys, Vasey's force would swing towards the coast and the two would converge at Madang.

The campaign on the Huon Peninsula was far from over, and the advance to Madang would see some of the fiercest fighting yet.

15

Consolidating the Win

September 1943 to April 1944

Command of both campaigns converging on Madang was in the hands of two of Blamey's trusted senior commanders. Lieutenant General Iven Mackay had again taken over as head of New Guinea Force, with Berryman as Chief of Staff. With little to keep him in the area, on 22 September 1943, Blamey followed MacArthur south to Australia. He needed to stay close to the key decision-makers and his key staff officers as he grappled with the constant issue of the size and composition of Australian forces and how they interconnected with US forces.

It was becoming clear that the land forces of each nation were decoupling as more US troops became available, and Blamey would soon be Commander, Allied Land Forces, South West Pacific Area in name only. This was not of great concern. Blamey had expected it. And it had its advantages, in that MacArthur would lose interest in the day-to-day operation of the Australian Army, even if he maintained its strategic direction.

* * *

Historian Lachlan Grant has suggested that Finisterre was the toughest challenge for the approximately 17,000 veterans of Vasey's 7th Division, who had already experienced the rigours of North Africa, the Middle East and Papua.[1] Blamey's orders to Vasey were to capture the airfields at Kaiapit and Dumpu, respectively 130 and 200 kilometres' march along large open plains of kunai grass up the Markham Valley north-east from Lae, to prevent any Japanese from advancing down the valley to Lae. Speed was critical: they needed to get there before the 12,000 Japanese of the Eighteenth Army arrived from further north and west.

An Australian commando squadron attached to the 7th Division was flown into an airfield near Kaiapit and quickly linked up with a Papuan infantry battalion advancing up the valley. On 19 September, elements of both the commandos and Papuans advanced on Kaiapit village, occupied by the Japanese. They had decided against reconnaissance in case it alerted the enemy. They engaged the defenders without warning and drove them off. Several Japanese counterattacks came that night, and they too were beaten off. Kaiapit was captured the next morning, with 14 Australians killed and 23 wounded, compared with at least 200 Japanese killed. This action is now considered to be one of the most successful commando operations of the war.

Vasey tended to move around in a small, unarmed spotter plane. As the name suggests, these were reconnaissance planes and Vasey certainly used them for this purpose, but in addition he could rapidly move around between groups of his force or travel back to Lae for meetings. Once the coast was clear following the capture of Kaiapit, Vasey landed on the village's rough airstrip, and transport planes were soon ferrying in soldiers and supplies. Documents found at Kaiapit indicated that the Japanese had planned for one of their divisions to advance down the valley with a battalion of field artillery, intending to retake Nadzab and Lae. The Diggers' rapid advance up the valley meant the Japanese plan was stillborn.

American air commander General Kenney was so delighted that the threat to Nadzab Airfield had been eliminated that he offered to fly in a planeload of anything the company wanted. In due course, a load of sweets, cigarettes and reading matter appeared.[2]

Vasey held his forces at Kaiapit while he waited for supplies to build up. In the interim, aggressive patrolling by the Australians – which involved making contact with the enemy and engaging in close fighting – persuaded the Japanese that the Australians were too tough to mess with. They withdrew beyond Dumpu Airfield, the next Australian objective.

The advance to Dumpu Airfield, some 60 kilometres further up the valley, was therefore unopposed, and the march through open swathes of kunai grass was relatively easy. The Australians arrived at their destination in early October. Because they had achieved their objective of blocking a Japanese advance to Lae via the Markham and Ramu Valleys, Blamey called a halt to their progress.

Vasey made the decision not to sit tight at Dumpu but ordered his men to carry out aggressive patrolling. He feared the effects on morale of an extended period in static defence, and wanted to provide a diversion to draw the enemy away from other

Australian operations, particularly the 9th Division's campaign on the other side of the Finisterre Ranges.[3]

The 7th Division patrolling was hellishly dangerous. The Diggers had frequent sudden-death encounters as they stumbled across nests of Japanese defenders in the rugged jungle leading to razor-backed Shaggy Ridge beyond Dumpu, and in several other difficult-to-take locations. It was difficult, dangerous fighting, with any false move likely to end in fatalities. Attacks were made along ridges barely wide enough to take one person, and with sheer drops on either side into dug-in Japanese positions. By sheer grit, the Australians slowly progressed towards Shaggy Ridge, supported by field artillery sited at the bottom of the ridge, as well as air attacks.

Early in October, there had been some changes in command. Herring had been relieved and was sent to train I Corps in Australia. He was replaced by Leslie Morshead commanding II Corps. Morshead also assumed the role of head of New Guinea Force the following month, replacing Mackay. Morshead refused Vasey's request for reinforcements at Shaggy Ridge to support what he considered to be a non-strategic campaign.

Blamey, meanwhile, had changed his mode of operation and begun making short visits to Australian HQs by air around the South West Pacific Area. This allowed him to check in on his commanders and their men, and gauge their condition. On 19 December, he made a lightning visit to Shaggy Ridge to discuss operations with Vasey. Vasey later recalled that Blamey didn't say much but seemed pleased, and that the bottle of whisky they cracked might have had something to do with this.[4]

The following day, Blamey flew across the Finisterre Range to the 9th Division, where he addressed several war correspondents and told them that the Japanese were now on the run.

While Vasey pressed on with attacks along Shaggy Ridge, he was getting testy about the sheer number of 'tourists' coming forward to get a taste of battle. 'These visitors are a curse! We've had 280 of them – 16 Generals and 1 Admiral – cheap tour of the world – a lot of them being able to say they've been to the war.'[5] He specifically exempted from his ire necessary visits from American and Australian pilots, and British officers who were there to learn about jungle fighting. One of the officers even took over command of a company when the Australian leader went off sick with dysentery.[6]

In January, four 25-pounder guns were delivered to augment the eight already on-site, along with 13,000 artillery shells.[7] It is probably not just a coincidence that this delivery followed close on Blamey's discussions with Vasey during his lightning visit.

The guns were directed by artillery officers high up on Shaggy Ridge, who ordered that rounds be aimed into the trees, splintering the wood into deadly shrapnel. With no line of sight from the valley floor and precious little visibility in the jungle or anywhere on the slopes, artillery officers were forced to lie terrifyingly close to the Japanese positions on the ridge and the exploding shells they were firing.

The Japanese only had one mountain gun, but it too was lethal. Its shells splintered the treetops so close to the Diggers' dug-in positions that there was no gap between the sound of the firing gun and the explosion of the round in the trees overhead. Planes flew many sorties to strafe Japanese positions and eventually the mountain gun was silenced.

The Japanese were finally worn down by the sheer determination of the Diggers on the ridges. Shaggy Ridge and other ridges around it were finally taken on 31 January 1944. The 15th Brigade led the division in the advance across the ranges to the coast. It was tough going, hindered by enemy rearguard action, rain and the difficult terrain. On 17 April, a patrol from the 7th Division met a US patrol on the north coast. A week later, parts of the Australian division entered the deep-water port at Madang.

The seven-month campaign had cost over 200 Diggers' lives and wounded 460, while most of the 7th Division's average strength of around 13,600 was evacuated sick, mainly as a result of malaria and other tropical diseases. The Japanese losses are unknown.

Vasey was a popular and capable commander. He was often up front and visible, sharing a cigarette and a chat with his men or circling in his plane close to the action, shouting encouragement and directions. Sadly, he would die in a plane crash 13 months later, on 5 March 1945 – not in a little reconnaissance plane on a dangerous close-in operation but a Lockheed Hudson as it tried to land at Cairns airport during a cyclone.

* * *

The campaign to take Finschhafen, led by George Wootten's 9th Division with the addition of the 4th Brigade, had also been progressing. The basic plan for their campaign had some similarities to the one used to take Lae. The campaign would begin with a seaborne invasion on the far side of Finschhafen. Japanese attention would be deflected to this assault while Allied forces advanced up the coast from Lae. The enemy would be caught off guard when they were attacked on the opposite side of town.

MacArthur had insisted that the operation begin as soon as possible, because the town overlooked the strategic straits between the New Guinea mainland and New Britain and was a focal point for Japanese barges operating along the coast from Madang. There had been a lack of coordination between MacArthur's HQ and Blamey's commanders. Consequently there were shortcuts in planning, particularly in intelligence assessments. As a result, the planners had no idea how many Japanese defenders there would be or what the landing areas were like.

The 20th Brigade of the 9th Division embarked on the seaborne leg to Finschhafen on the evening of 21 September 1943, while the 22nd Battalion marched from a starting point outside Lae. Arriving blind, the armada delivering the 20th Brigade had a difficult run to its landing beach, 10 kilometres north of Finschhafen. It was later described by Captain Maxwell Worthley of the 20th Brigade as an 'ungodly balls up'.[8] Landing craft went to the wrong places and bellied on sandbars. Some men were dropped too far from shore and had to wade in under fire. Despite the problems, the force was ashore by 6 am and a beachhead was established.

Finschhafen occupied a strategic position guarding the Bismark Sea. If the Japanese lost it to the Allies, their shipping

Above: A Matilda tank barged to Finschhafen increases the power of the assault force, c. January 1944. (AWM 016490)

Left: General Blamey climbs a ridge en route to inspect forward elements of the 7th Australian Division in the Ramu Valley, New Guinea, 18 December 1943. Officers with him include Major Generals Vasey and Berryman. (AWM 062651)

from Rabaul to the New Guinea mainland would be jeopardised and they would be unable to supply, reinforce or evacuate their thousands of men still in New Guinea. While they had recognised the importance of Finschhafen and anticipated an invasion there from June, they had not been able to get reinforcements in place and their defending garrison was weak. They were helped, however, by the typically rough jungle-covered terrain that separated the Allies' landing spot from the town.

The 20th Battalion made slow progress as it fought towards town, but meanwhile, as hoped, the 22nd Battalion was able to march up the coast from Lae with little opposition. With Japanese attention focused north, the 22nd Battalion arrived in Finschhafen unopposed on 2 October and the town fell. The defending Japanese were sandwiched between the two Australian forces and fought ferociously in rough jungle.

It had been decided during the planning stage that the Australian positions at Finschhafen would be reinforced by the remaining elements of the 9th Division using US Navy transports. But this had not been agreed to by MacArthur's HQ. Herring tried and failed to make any headway with MacArthur's men, then Mackay became involved and also had little luck. The Australian situation at Finschhafen soon became critical, with supplies running short and casualties building up on the beaches.

When he was notified of the situation, Blamey joined the fray. Even then, the transport situation took five days to resolve. US Navy ships were not under MacArthur's control and access to them was denied. Fortunately, the US Army Engineer Boat and Shore Regiment *did* come under MacArthur's control and it was pressed into service. With the problem solved, the transportation of the rest of the 9th Division could begin. Thanks to the delays, it was not completed until 15 October.

In the meantime, elements of the 20th Japanese Division had trudged forlornly overland from the jungles north of Lae to Finschhafen, determined to join the fighting. Starving, bedraggled, malaria-infected and without artillery, the Japanese made bunched, uncoordinated, unsophisticated attacks on the rear of the Australians, causing considerable anxiety but little damage.

After suffering an estimated 50 per cent casualty rate, the Japanese called off their attack on 24 October. Finschhafen was secured and a large combined-arms force built up to protect the town and surrounds.

* * *

The lack of coordination regarding the landing arrangements for the battle highlighted a problem for Blamey. He needed someone who could get on with the Americans. While Morshead had been brought in as Commander of the New Guinea Force and II Corps, his relationships with the Americans were not fruitful. Berryman had taken over Morshead's II Corps in an acting role, made permanent in January 1944. Berryman was a good choice because he had a happy knack of getting along with the Americans.

On 17 November 1943, Wootten's 9th Division began its advance from Finschhafen along the coast towards Madang. The going was rough, but the Australians soon adapted their combined-arms experience, learned in the Middle East, to coordinate artillery, armour, engineers and infantry into a winning formula for jungle warfare.[9] They prepared by rehearsing the plan using earth models and combined-arms training. It helped that they were hugging the coast and could be supplied with heavy equipment and other materiel at regular intervals by sea.

As head of II Corps, Berryman, now promoted to lieutenant general, was under pressure to quickly take the whole of the north coast of the Huon Peninsula prior to the US Army's invasion of West New Britain, a short distance away across the sea. The Japanese, on the other hand, had been given the task of holding up the 9th Division so that West New Britain could be reinforced.[10] While Berryman was more aggressive than Wootten, it mattered little, because the pace was ultimately determined by the formidable terrain, the rainfall, the enemy and a shared purpose of minimising Australian casualties.[11]

Japanese logistics had broken down by 5 December, while the Japanese forces were 10 kilometres beyond Finschhafen. With most of their artillery captured, their infantry at half-strength and two-thirds of their men sick with malaria, the Japanese began a desperate withdrawal along the coast towards Madang. They used two paths: one on the coast with rearguard protection, and the other moving parallel to it, 10 kilometres inland. Both tracks were through dense jungle.

After the Americans went ashore at West New Britain on 15 December, Japanese command saw no point in holding the New Guinea coast facing that part of the island and ordered a withdrawal to Sio, some 85 kilometres further up the coast from Finschhafen.

The inexperienced 4th Brigade was brought to the front from Australia and was given the spearhead role in the advance. The troops proved too green and Wootten pulled them off operations for more training on 5 December. When they went back into action, they were supplied with experienced teams of officers and men to improve the all-important on-the-job learning. Blamey, Berryman and Wootten came forward on 21 December and reinforced their orders to avoid unnecessary casualties by using tanks and artillery. In the new year, Berryman wrote to Blamey confirming the battle casualties had been kept very low, but because of the foul conditions a plague of dengue fever was sweeping through the force.[12]

Australian advances towards Sio were initially slow, but they picked up tempo as methods became streamlined and everyone got used to working together. The Japanese were outclassed both in tactics and machinery. They had little artillery left, and what they had needed to be transported and set up manually. They also had no engineers to build roadblocks to impede Australian progress. The Australians, on the other hand, continuously improved their systems, even as their force strength dwindled to around half due to malaria and other diseases, which had more impact on force strength than did the Japanese.

The 9th Division was nearly worn down by the time it occupied Sio on 15 January 1944. By then, the 20th Japanese Division was virtually destroyed as a fighting force. At Sio, Wootten's men handed over operations to Milford's 5th

Division and the 20th Brigade, and headed south to Australia for a well-earned rest, recuperation and refit.

So far the campaign had been pursued without the benefit of breaking the codes used by the Japanese army (although they had broken the Japanese naval codes). This was about to change dramatically in January 1944 when, on the way to Sio, Australian engineers pinged what they thought was a mine but turned out to be a buried steel trunk packed with the entire code library for the Japanese 20th Division. It had clearly been too heavy for their ailing porters to continue hauling along as the Japanese retreated. This treasure trove was sent to MacArthur's codebreakers and used to decode over 36,000 Japanese signals in the following March alone. The Japanese never realised that it had been found.[13]

As 4300 Japanese shambled on from Sio towards Saidor, 150 kilometres north-west, they were joined by a 6500-strong remnant of the Japanese 51st Division. US forces were holding Saidor, but instead of blocking the Japanese retreat, they were content to watch the Japanese pass in front of their defences without even firing artillery, leaving the necessary job of dealing with the Japanese to others. The Australian and US forces met at Saidor on 10 February, while the Japanese headed further west to Madang. The Japanese were followed into Madang by the 8th and 15th Infantry Brigades of the 5th Division on 24 to 25 April. Resistance was virtually non-existent. The Japanese fled from the town, heading for Wewak, where they would fight the Australians in 1945. According to Australian War Memorial historian David Dexter, there were around 1200 Japanese deaths on the track from Sio to Saidor.[14]

* * *

Beginning with Blamey's 'magnet' for taking Lae, the campaign from Wau through Lae to Madang had cost around 1231 Australian lives and wounded 2867, giving a total casualty figure of 4098, while the Japanese had lost around 35,000.[15]

The number of Japanese deaths included a large but unknown number who died of starvation and disease as a direct result of being cut off from supplies and services when force-marched through the fetid, disease-ridden jungle. While technically not causing battlefield deaths, cutting off supplies and services to an army is a legitimate act of war. In effect, Blamey implemented a 'green siege' by using the nearly impenetrable jungle to block movement of men and supplies. This tactic benefited from being part of a coordinated Allied effort to starve the Japanese of everything. Allied losses were probably lower than they might otherwise have been because of the Japanese decision not to stand and fight to the end, but to march to 'safety' through horrific jungle conditions while chronically under-provisioned.

While relatively well fed, the Australians had had their own problems with disease. In the three months from November 1942 to January 1943, disease invalided over three times the number of men as battle casualties did, and malaria accounted for nearly 90 per cent of cases.

* * *

The campaign from Wau to Madang featured the key tactics Blamey had used before: thoroughly brief and train officers and men; do as much as possible to confuse the enemy and strike fast while they are off-centre; have overwhelming supply and use machines as much as possible; and orchestrate everything while leaving enough leeway for the inevitable variations to be coped with by trusted commanders using on-the-spot initiative.

As a result, the campaign from Salamaua–Lae through to Madang was spectacularly efficient; 28.4 Japanese dead for each Ally. As Dr Brendan Nelson, former director of the Australian War Memorial, has said, 'That Australian casualties remained so relatively low says something of their leadership, professionalism and conduct of Australia's forces during the campaign.'[16]

MacArthur obviously paid close attention and modelled many of his later campaigns on this formula. He even managed to curb his innate enthusiasm for attacking the enemy head-on. The successes in New Guinea were MacArthur's springboard to beat the US Navy in conquering the Japanese further north. By following the Australian method, he reaped the benefits of a change in efficiency.

As historian Peter Dean has written, victory by the Australians (with help from US servicemen) 'reaped enormous strategic advantages for the SWPA [South West Pacific Area] and was achieved with an extraordinarily minimal loss of life. It represents the high point of Australian military operations during the Second World War.'[17] It is no wonder that the Australians under Blamey were considered the best jungle fighters in the world.

16
Fighting for a Place at the International Table

March 1944 to September 1945

After such a stellar performance in the Salamaua–Lae through to Madang campaign (referred to in the official war histories as part of 'the New Guinea Offensives' of 25 January 1942 to 15 August 1945), what followed was a letdown for both Blamey and the Diggers.

In June 1943, MacArthur had advised Curtin that the threat to Australia had been removed. Consequently, there was no need to maintain as much armed force in the country. Issues of manpower and how many Australian divisions to maintain, as well as the direction and control of the military, hung over the government and Blamey. Australia might no longer be under direct threat, but its forces were at the disposal of the United States and Britain, and it had a stake in future operations. Curtin was also adamant that Australia should remain fighting in the war until the end to retain some political standing with the Americans and bolster Australia's influence over the South West Pacific Area when the war finished.[1]

In October 1943, as Australians were fighting their way towards Madang in New Guinea, the War Cabinet met to discuss a paper prepared by Defence Co-ordination Secretary Frederick Shedden. In attendance were Prime Minister Curtin, Shedden and other assorted ministers, as well as Blamey and Chief of the General Staff Lieutenant General John Northcote, who were present for the first part of the meeting.

After a five-hour session, the War Cabinet's critical decisions were that:

> (a) It is of vital importance to the future of Australia and her status at the peace table in regard to the settlement in the Pacific that her military effort should be concentrated as far as possible in the Pacific and that it should be on a scale to guarantee her an effective voice in the peace settlement.
>
> (b) If necessary, the extent of this effort should be maintained at the expense of commitments in other theatres.[2]

The upshot was that Australia would keep six divisions in the South West Pacific Area, and reduce armed services numbers in Australia by 20,000 and numbers in war-related industries by 10,000. Blamey supported the need for an Australian presence in the South West Pacific Area but advised that it should not fall below three divisions.

Yet no decision was thus far forthcoming from the United States or Britain as to what Australia's future role would be. The two nations met to discuss the matter in Cairo in November

1943, but it wasn't until March 1944 that Churchill finally communicated the outcomes to the Australian Government. The meeting had failed to outline any definite role for Australian forces, though Churchill did convey the news that the British intended to set up a base in Australia and eventually send ships and troops to fight in the South West Pacific Area.

MacArthur, too, made no public declaration of Australia's role in his campaigning. On a visit to Australia in March 1944, Captain Alan Hillgarth, chief of intelligence for the British Eastern Fleet, discussed the future disposition of forces with MacArthur. His impression was that MacArthur intended to attack the Philippines and would avoid using Australian troops, but was 'reluctant to relinquish control over the AIF – probably the finest jungle fighters in the world – in case he *has* to use them'. He noted that Blamey was 'regarded as a great general and the best man available for land fighting against the Japanese', but there was no role defined for him either.[3] It seemed Blamey and the AIF were to be MacArthur's insurance, kept in reserve in case he needed them, but until that time they were to make themselves useful in remote places and not steal any glory.

In an attempt to achieve some meaningful involvement for Australia, Curtin, Blamey and Shedden set sail for the United States on 5 April 1944. They travelled aboard the USS *Lurline* with more than 400 wounded Allied personnel, along with 40 Australian war wives. Blamey smuggled a case of whisky aboard the dry ship and, with nothing much else to do, partied in his room with a few select passengers.[4] Curtin, previously an alcoholic and now a teetotaller, was miffed by Blamey's behaviour. This might have led to an 'estrangement' between them, as Blamey's biographer David Horner claims, but there is no evidence that Blamey ever had a close personal relationship with Curtin. Whatever the outcome on a personal level, the professional relationship continued.

On arrival in the United States, Curtin met President Roosevelt for informal talks, but generally laid low. He had decided to wait until after he had attended the inaugural Commonwealth prime ministers' conference in London before entering into formal discussions with the Americans. That conference was scheduled to begin on 1 May. Blamey, on the other hand, mingled widely with his professional peers. Despite his reputation in some US quarters for being a drunken buffoon, he was received warmly by the US Joint Chiefs of Staff, who appreciated his vast knowledge of operations in the South West Pacific Area. He also played a daily round of golf and went out to the theatre.[5]

The contingent left for Britain by flying boat on 28 April. A bed was made up for Curtin, but he was too tense to use it because he hated flying. As he sat gripping the arms of his seat, Blamey took the opportunity to sleep like a baby in Curtin's bed.

The hope of getting a clear outcome from the British was stillborn. Discussions with Churchill and the British service chiefs exposed the usual differences between Churchill's wishes and those of the military. As Curtin and Blamey would find out, British intentions in the Pacific had many permutations, but since Australia was only a bit player, and an ex-colony to boot, the two leaders were just going to have to wait until the decision was handed down from someone on high.

Nevertheless, Churchill made mention of a possible joint British–Australian offensive into the Dutch East Indies, based out of Darwin. It dovetailed with ideas Blamey had already entertained for a campaign that he imagined he might lead. But while Curtin agreed that the British should establish an Australian base, he was unwilling to agree to anything without the oversight of MacArthur and the British and US Combined Chiefs of Staff.[6]

Away from the formal discussions, Churchill held a reception at 10 Downing Street, during which Blamey found himself alone with the British Prime Minister in his den. The two men shared some time together over a bottle of whisky, demonstrating that there were no residual hard feelings from their game of political brinksmanship during the Middle East and Greek campaigns. This was no formal meeting with expected outcomes, but probably just two hardened old warriors enjoying each other's company and swapping yarns over their favourite drink.

While in London, Blamey also went to a series of high-level meetings with Curtin. At one of these, with British Chief of Staff Field Marshal Sir Alan Brooke, Blamey was so unwell he was thought to be drunk. Rowell, now working in the British War Office, undoubtedly coloured Brooke's opinion. Notwithstanding this, Brooke wrote in his diary that he found Blamey easy to get along with, but he considered both Blamey and Curtin to be totally under MacArthur's influence and fixed in their attitude to Australia's command arrangements.[7]

On 15 May, Blamey attended the investiture at which the King dubbed him three times for the three knighthoods he had achieved but had not been available to receive in person. He also did the rounds of the military. The next day, he met General Bernard Montgomery, but this was not a meeting of minds, likely because Montgomery, never a great conversationalist, was only interested in his own war. He had no interest in the war in the Pacific.

Blamey also visited British VIII Corps, which was preparing to spearhead the invasion of Normandy, and addressed by name the 13 Australian officers attached to British units. He arranged to be part of the invasion fleet as General Eisenhower's guest, but this option was scotched by Curtin's decision that being in London during the invasion would be too dangerous.

Another meeting of note was with Howard Florey, the Australian involved in the discovery of penicillin, then based at Oxford University. Given the toll that disease and injury had been taking on the men's health in the jungle conditions of Papua and New Guinea, Blamey had a special interest in new treatments. On a personal note, Blamey visited his nearly 100-year-old aunt Bessie Cardell at her house in Cornwall. Almost blind, she was nevertheless alert and delighted that her famous nephew had taken the time to visit for a cup of tea.[8]

* * *

Blamey, Shedden and Curtin flew to Canada on 29 May, and from there returned to the United States. Curtin gained understandings from Roosevelt and the Joint Chiefs of Staff assuring him of Australia's continuing involvement in the war, many of which disappeared into thin air, because MacArthur was able to independently manipulate both him and the US joint chiefs.

With no major campaigns in progress for the AIF, Blamey continued to enjoy himself in Washington and later in New York, attending shows and dinners, drinking and socialising. He met Walt Disney and took home a signed cartoon frame. Shedden noted disparagingly in his diary that Blamey had twice smuggled a female guest into their hotel.[9] His socialising and drinking could perhaps be forgiven as a legitimate means of establishing relationships with key players; less can be said in defence of his womanising. Overall, it was not wise, and his behaviour antagonised both Curtin and Shedden.

To everyone's relief, Blamey parted company with the Prime Minister's party in San Francisco and flew home using US military planes. He stopped off to talk to US commanders along the way, including a meeting on 14 June with Admiral Chester Nimitz, Commander in Chief, Pacific Ocean Areas, and General Robert C. Richardson, now Nimitz's land force commander. This gave Blamey a clear idea of the strategic situation. The Americans were still deciding whether to invade Formosa (modern-day Taiwan) under Nimitz or the Philippines under MacArthur. It was evident that there would be no role for Australian soldiers unless they accompanied MacArthur or the British managed to bring a force into the fray.

On 15 June, Blamey visited the American jungle training centre in Hawaii then set off for home via Canton Island, the Ellice Islands (now Tuvalu) and Guadalcanal. Next stop was Port Moresby to confer with Major General Morris, Commander of the Australian New Guinea Administrative

General Blamey with Elsie Curtin and Prime Minister John Curtin on board the USS *Lurline*, en route to the United States from Sydney, 1944. (NLA 3583643)

General Blamey and US Fleet Admiral Chester Nimitz meet in Hawaii, 14 June 1944. (Blamey family)

Unit, on 17 June, then on to Lae for discussions with Stan Savige, now in command of New Guinea Force.

Blamey arrived at the Atherton Tablelands on 19 June 1944, where he was met by Lady Blamey, General Sturdee and Lieutenant General Berryman, now back in Australia commanding I Corps (previously II Corps). He visited the 6th and 9th Divisions, and was pleased with the recovery they were making after the New Guinea campaign.

On 22 June, Blamey met with MacArthur and let slip the possibility of British involvement in the Pacific war. MacArthur claimed he had no knowledge of any such plan and was disturbed by the notion. His ignorance was unlikely. In any event, Blamey seemed committed to British involvement in the coming months – he had even had his staff consider how a British force would be accommodated. This turned out to be a bit of a fantasy on Blamey's part. The British weren't coming. Despite being Australia's most senior officer, ultimately Blamey couldn't direct grand strategy; that was up to Curtin and MacArthur. As always, when it came to major operations, Blamey would have to do as ordered. MacArthur was able to use this to his own advantage, telling Curtin and the Combined Chiefs of Staff that Blamey was unwilling to commit Australian troops to the Philippines invasion. Blamey had given him additional ammunition by suggesting that Australian troop numbers could take some time to rebuild after the men's recuperation.

Curtin and Shedden arrived from the USA at the Brisbane docks on 26 June, where they were met by Blamey and Acting Prime Minister Frank Forde. The next day, Blamey flew to Melbourne and received a guard of honour at the airport. He was greeted by the press and several senior officers, and gave a speech praising the unity among the Allied countries, and affirming that Australian soldiers still had a part to play.[10]

What that part would be was being determined by Curtin and MacArthur. Shedden had written ahead to MacArthur, requesting a meeting. He specifically asked that Blamey not attend.

Meeting with Curtin and Shedden, MacArthur claimed that he had intended to use the Australian divisions in his pursuit of the Japanese into Asia and the Philippines. But if they were not up to strength, as Blamey had suggested, then that plan would have to be put aside. In a later meeting with Shedden, MacArthur again tried to undermine Blamey, accusing him of disloyalty and trying to carve out a more ambitious role for himself.[11]

Blamey had suggested his troops would be ready in time for the planned Philippines assault in November. MacArthur remained coy on whether the Australians would be used. One proposal he put to Curtin was for two Australian divisions to fight as part of a US corps, thus bringing the Australians under his control. Blamey refused this arrangement, saying he would only agree if Australians were also given command of US forces at the same level. Curtin agreed. In response, MacArthur complained to Churchill's representative in Australia that Blamey was becoming difficult to work with and more interested with fighting alongside the British. In reality, it irked him that Blamey was under his orders yet could also act independently.

* * *

Uncertainty continued about the future role of Australian troops. On 30 September, MacArthur – with Curtin's agreement – gave Blamey the unavoidable instruction for Australians to relieve US forces garrisoned in New Guinea and Bougainville, prior to the US advance to the Philippines, to 'mop up' in those theatres, and also carry out an invasion of Borneo.

The foundation for Australia's war strategy in the last two years of the war was set by the War Cabinet on 1 October 1943. Blamey advised that Australia needed to keep a sufficient presence of at least three divisions to show enough strength to have a say in deciding future outcomes.[12] The upshot was that from 1944 the troops were fighting for political objectives; if they hadn't fought, it wouldn't have made any difference to the outcome of the war.

Arguments have raged ever since about the necessity of the Borneo operation and of the risk to Australian lives. If Australian troops had been committed to the Philippines assault under US command, it is possible that their casualty rates would have soared. MacArthur's biographer D. Clayton James has noted that it would have been 'the most tragic blood bath of the Pacific War' if MacArthur had been able to use Australia's 6th Division – against Blamey's advice – in a plan he had conceived to invade Java.[13] Prompted by both Blamey and Shedden, Curtin wrote to MacArthur, saying that it would be publicly unacceptable for the troops not to be active at all, and that retiring from any engagement would deny Australia any post-war say.[14]

The best Blamey could do was to make operations as efficient and effective as possible, while waiting to hear what

MacArthur wanted to do with the remaining Australian divisions, including involvement in the Philippines invasion, which MacArthur had not completely ruled out.

* * *

The order to relieve the US troops of their garrison duty came in July 1944. Defensive duties may sound safe, but as Blamey was well aware, if defence lasts long enough, casualty rates can exceed those of offence. Australian soldiers don't like sitting still; they get bored and troublesome. They lose condition. Morale plummets. Added to all this were the high rates of disease in the tropics and the cost of idle manpower. As Blamey knew, it wouldn't be long before the bill for Diggers sitting idle in the tropics became astronomical.

His frustrations soon increased. When the US Sixth Army invaded the Philippine island of Leyte on 20 October 1944, MacArthur used Australian naval units but left the ground forces and the RAAF almost completely behind.

He would never return to New Guinea or Australia.

17

'Mopping Up'

November 1944 to 2 September 1945

Despite the derogatory term 'mopping up', the campaigns that the Australians now embarked on would be among the longest and toughest they would fight in the war. The Papuan campaign had resulted in more casualties – as was to be expected from the haste with which it was run, as well as the woeful supply situation. But the next highest number of casualties occurred in these final campaigns.

They were carried out in particularly difficult conditions: in isolated jungle full of stinking swamps; subject to torrential downpours, dangerous flash flooding and horrible diseases; and against an enemy that was losing yet was still fanatically willing to fight to the death.

In all cases, MacArthur specified which locations were to be held, while Blamey had control of what was done by whom. The American and Australian infantries were now operating independently.

* * *

Following its defeat on the Huon Peninsula in 1943, the Japanese Eighteenth Army had continued its forced march north-west through Madang, past Wewak and on towards Aitape, near the border with the Dutch East Indies. The Japanese arrived at the Aitape Airfield, about 32 kilometres to the east of the settlement, in early July. US forces had taken Aitape on 22 April and been tasked with protecting the airfield.

From 10 July to 25 August 1944, the retreating Japanese made repeated attacks on the airfield. Hunkered down in their defensive perimeter, the Americans were given the gift of an easy if gory victory as the Japanese made desperate, fanatical charges at the wire of the garrison. Japanese losses in this battle – 8000 – were the second highest of the war after the beachheads. By comparison, US losses were a mere 440 killed and 2560 wounded.

The Japanese survivors fell back towards Wewak, 180 kilometres to the east, while the Americans remained in defensive positions at Aitape.[1] That left about 35,000 Japanese soldiers wandering in the jungle, weak with malnutrition and disease. Abandoned by their country, they had to support themselves as best as they could. They were desperately low on ammunition, and refused to waste any shooting wild game. Rather, they chose to dig in at specific locations and grow food. Still fanatically loyal to their emperor, they remained extremely dangerous despite their weakened state.

The 6th Division, under Major General Jack Stevens, steamed into Aitape in mid-October 1944 to relieve the Americans. The departing force was unable to provide information about Japanese numbers, movements or positions, because it had remained in a defensive position the whole time. To rectify this, Stevens ordered vigorous patrols to locate Japanese positions and provide estimations of their condition, as well as maintain an offensive spirit. This was the same approach as Vasey had used the previous year in the Ramu Valley, and as Morshead had used when he commanded the troops at Tobruk.[2]

Stevens split his patrolling force into two. One group of commandos went inland and travelled east behind the Torricelli Ranges, while the other moved along the coast in the same direction towards Wewak. The rate of progress was constrained on both routes due to lack of supplies. While it was safer for Allied shipping now that the Japanese no longer had an effective air force or navy, much of the Diggers' food and equipment had been diverted to support MacArthur's preparations for retaking the Philippines.

Supply to the troops on the inland route suffered the most, because they had to bush-bash their way through, and their meagre supplies had to be carried in by porters from airfield drops along the way. Equipped with a bulldozer, the brigade on the coast road was able to keep moving through a concerted road- and bridge-making effort, but was hampered overall by a lack of earthmoving equipment. A total of 118 bridges with a cumulative span of 2.7 kilometres were built across the numerous streams and rivers – always at risk, with the torrential rain, of washing away and needing to be replaced.[3]

* * *

With US forces making rapid progress in their invasion of the Philippines, MacArthur had moved his HQ to Leyte. He had not yet decided on how the remaining Australian troops should be deployed. On the Atherton Tablelands, Morshead – back in Australia since May 1944 – was waiting impatiently to learn the new assignment for I Corps. Similarly, Berryman, now in charge of a forward headquarters in Hollandia in the Dutch East Indies, was also frustrated with the lack of direction.

The only way for Blamey to solve the deployment mystery was to consult MacArthur himself. So on 29 November, he began his journey to Leyte. En route he called in on Major General Jack Stevens at Aitape for discussions, and that same evening arrived at Hollandia to stay with Berryman while he waited for permission from MacArthur to go to Leyte. The Americans had used Hollandia as a base for their advance on the Philippines and Berryman had been stationed there since September 1944.[4]

Bringing Berryman with him, Blamey arrived for his meeting with MacArthur on 5 December. Little was achieved. All that Blamey could get was an understanding that MacArthur wanted to keep I Corps in reserve in the tropics in case the resistance was strong during the upcoming invasion of Luzon, the main island of the Philippines.

In the meantime, the mopping up had to go on.

* * *

The Japanese had occupied Aitape and most coastal towns since their initial advances in 1942. Recently they had been joined by the remnant of the Japanese army from the Salamaua–Lae campaign. Japanese troops in the area were thought to number between 30,000 and 35,000. With increasing dominance of sea and air, the Allies had cut them off from external support. They were chronically short of everything including ammunition, food and medicine.

On 2 January 1945, the forward patrols of Australian 6th Division, commanded by Major General Jack Stevens, on the coast route from Aitape heading towards Wewak began to encounter pockets of the enemy offering stiff resistance. They attacked the positions, and as the Japanese moved east, they kept up the pressure, trying to prevent the enemy from heading up into the hills. Being close to the coast meant there was some supporting naval fire available.

As always, the apparent caution of the Australians nonplussed the Japanese. One soldier interviewed long after the war by historian Peter Williams observed that the Australians were agonisingly slow because they hid in holes while their artillery did all the work. In the same situation the Japanese would have charged, but without artillery they couldn't do much. When the Australian attack eventually came, their Arisaka rifles were no match for the Australians' Bren guns and submachine guns – nor for flamethrowers, which were increasingly used as a substitute for grenades and small arms.[5] Not only did the flamethrowers reduce the risk of injury or death to the Australians, but they also had a strong psychological effect on the Japanese, who would often run out of position, screaming, before the flamethrowers were even in range.[6]

Under the constant Australian barrage, the Japanese repeatedly fell back in disarray before finally regrouping to make a stand at Tokuku Pass, two-thirds of the way to Wewak in late March.

Meanwhile, the commando group on the inland side of the Torricelli mountains was having a much harder time of it. Twice the commandos were surrounded by the Japanese, and twice they fought their way out after days under siege. Worn out by the effort of fighting in the tough jungle conditions, the men were relieved by an infantry battalion in late March. Their supply situation improved briefly after they captured successive airfields, but deteriorated as they moved on. By late April, they were still only halfway to Wewak.

Morale became a major problem. As well as having to deal with a malaria epidemic, the Diggers were not being given proper credit for the difficulties they faced, or the success they achieved. One war correspondent wrote in a letter, 'Everyone insists on calling this "mopping up" and that annoys me ... These boys are mopping up tens upon tens of thousands of Japs, and getting neither praise nor any publicity for it ... but it is the filthiest, most tedious and sustained heroism that any war can produce anywhere.'[7]

* * *

On 27 April 1945, the brigade on the coast route finally arrived outside Wewak and was ordered to attack. The assault was supported by air and sea bombardment, artillery, Matilda tanks and flamethrowers. As it got underway, 11 Australians

Defeated by ankle-deep mud, General Blamey's jeep is towed up a hill by a bulldozer in the Wewak area, New Guinea, 14 June 1945. (AWM 093121)

General Blamey checks a jungle road constructed by Australian engineers while on a trip to inspect troops in combat zones, New Britain, c. April 1945. (AWM 018319)

were killed by 'friendly fire' from US P-38 Lightning fighters. Many Japanese followed their country's orders not to surrender and fought to the bitter end, and those who were not killed were chased into the mountains.

The Australian force advancing via the inland route was by now directly parallel with the coast road to Wewak, but not able to close the gap through 40 kilometres of rough, jungle-covered mountains. As a result, the remnant Japanese force would remain active until the war ended.[8]

Australian cautious heroism – and skill – are supported by the numbers. Japanese losses for this campaign were around 7200 killed and 14,600 dead from malnutrition and disease. Australian losses were 587 killed and 1141 wounded. Tropical diseases caused great problems, with 6200 Australians admitted to medical units with malaria and 11,300 admitted for other diseases.[9]

* * *

Situated 450 kilometres east of New Britain, the 250-kilometre-long and 60-kilometre-wide island of Bougainville was typical of the terrain of New Guinea: precipitous rainforest-covered mountains; constant rain; and slippery, muddy ground crossed by violently flooding streams. The island had been invaded in November 1943 by 144,000 US infantry and marines against a Japanese force of up to 65,000. The Americans mainly stayed garrisoned around two airbases, but still claimed 9890 Japanese fatalities. By November 1944, there were two US infantry regiments garrisoned at Torokina on the middle of Bougainville's west coast, facing mainland New Guinea. Impenetrable jungle began right outside the garrison's security fence.[10]

The Japanese troops who remained on the island were organised into four widely dispersed enclaves: the largest at Buin, at the south-east end of the island; the next largest at Buka, on an island at the north-west end; and two smaller settlements at Numa Numa and Kieta, on the coast opposite Torokina. Conditions were primitive but, abiding by an unspoken agreement with the Americans to live and let live, the Japanese survivors had established gardens for food.

Lieutenant General Stanley Savige, commander of New Guinea Force, began the handover from the US garrison in late November 1944. The 3rd Division and an additional brigade were stationed on Bougainville itself, while the 23rd Brigade, under Brigadier Arnold Potts, was sent to islands close by.[11]

On 7 November, following an exchange with Sturdee about orders given, Blamey said that any action by Australians to clear the island of the remaining Japanese troops 'must be of a gradual nature' to 'locate the enemy and continually harass him, and ultimately, prepare plans to destroy him'. The most important part of this limited offensive would be to keep Australian casualties to a minimum.[12]

Progress was slow but steady. Savige set about cutting his men's teeth in jungle warfare by sending them over the mountain range in the centre of the island to an area known to be weakly held by the enemy, where they could engage the enemy without too much risk. Once the centre of the island was secure, he sent a battalion north-west, travelling both on foot and in landing craft, to capture Buka. His instructions were to be cautious and to avoid costly head-on assaults. The Japanese put up a skilful, aggressive and stubborn defence from fortified positions on nearby Tsimba Ridge, with support from 75-millimetre mountain guns operating from an elaborate honeycombed trench system. Their camouflage was excellent and their snipers took a toll on the Australian forces. The ridge was finally captured by the Australians on 9 February 1945.[13]

Another elaborate Japanese defensive position, crosscut with bunkers and pillboxes, awaited the Diggers on Bonis Peninsula, 15 kilometres south of Buka. As the Australian troops slogged it out in fetid jungle, their counterparts in Europe were jubilant about the end of the war in Europe on 8 May. By mid-May, the Australians had cut off the Bonis Peninsula, giving them an 8-kilometre front. A company was sent by sea to outflank the Japanese by landing on the Buka side. It quickly established a perimeter, but a barge carrying heavy weapons and reinforcements ran aground and was attacked by enemy machine-gun fire. Likewise, a company on the beach came under such heavy fire from snipers and machine guns that it was impossible for them to lift their heads, let alone move. To hold off the attackers, Australian artillery fire was called down from an adjoining battery, while low-flying Corsairs and Boomerangs attacked the Japanese positions. Attempts to save the Diggers resulted in chaos when two out of three rescuing barges also ran aground. After three exhausting terror-filled days, the survivors were finally rescued off the barges. Of the 190 in the company, 22 were killed and 62 wounded. The effort to capture Buka continued until Japan surrendered on 2 September 1945.[14]

The main effort on Bougainville was inevitably concentrated on Buin, where about 70 per cent of the Japanese strength on the island – believed to consist of around 28,000 fighters – was located. Malnutrition, malaria and dysentery had taken such a hold that only half the Japanese were able to fight. Those who could did so with typical fanaticism.

The 3rd Division set off overland from Torokina in late December 1944 with strict instructions from Savige to rotate its three brigades. Not more than a battalion was to be committed to the attack without his explicit approval. Nevertheless, the division endured a string of small, frequent, terrifying attacks by the Japanese, and by March 1945, nerves were stretched to breaking point.[15]

Travelling down the island was a two-pronged affair. In January 1945, a barge was sent carrying a battalion to rendezvous with an inland force around Buin. In early April, the two units combined at Slater's Knoll, 50 kilometres north-east of Buin, which was already under siege from a Japanese force arriving from the south. Matilda tanks proved a godsend when they reached the beleaguered Australians. In that action alone, 620 Japanese died, while the Australians suffered 106 killed and 414 wounded for the longer period of January to April.[16]

The Diggers at Slater's Knoll were exhausted. Savige ordered they be relieved and replaced by a fresh brigade for the final push to Buin. For the next four months, the various brigades slowly forced the Japanese into retreat, covering just 6.5 kilometres in 31 days. This slow advance was designed to maximise the use of firepower and minimise direct contact with the enemy, saving lives and reducing casualties. Nearly 40,000 mortar bombs, 70,000 artillery shells and 800 bombs were dropped between April and June.

Blamey received a warm welcome from the troops on Bougainville when he visited on 24 March. Nomimated to toss the coin at the start of a football match, he had walked out to the centre of the ground in front of 8000 or so Diggers. Mission accomplished, he returned to the stands to spontaneous cheers from the men.[17] In early June, he again went on a tour of the forward areas, meeting with different brigades, and advising the force still pursuing the Japanese to Buin to take their time and to use plenty of artillery.

As the Diggers moved forward, the weather deteriorated, bridges were washed out, corduroy surfaces floated off roads and tracks, men became sodden, eating grew difficult, and sleeping became almost impossible. Any poorly covered stores rotted and ammunition corroded. Meanwhile, the Japanese continued to attack, and set mines and booby traps. The closer the Australians got to Buin, the more frantically the Japanese pounded them with artillery, using over 200 shells a day. They were not yet at Buin when they got news that the atomic bombs had been dropped, on 6 and 9 August.[18]

In total, the Australian campaign on Bougainville led to the deaths of 8789 Japanese and left 516 Australians dead and 1572 wounded, amounting to around 17 Japanese deaths for every Australian. This does not take into account the unknown number of Japanese who died of starvation and disease as a result of Australian action, which is thought to be around 30,000, or the 23,800 who surrendered at the end of the war.

Of the local inhabitants, a quarter of the pre-war population died during the Japanese occupation.[19]

More than 30,000 Australians served on Bougainville Island, making this one of the largest Australian campaigns of the war.[20]

* * *

New Britain lies 100 kilometres off the coast of New Guinea, opposite the Huon Peninsula. The US Alamo Force had taken the south-western end of the 450-kilometre-long and 80-kilometre-wide island during Operation Cartwheel (30 June 1943 to 20 March 1944), and had been content to leave most of the island, particularly the fortress town of Rabaul, alone. US and Japanese troops had skirmished in the middle of the island, but ultimately, as on Bougainville, both sides had decided to live and let live.

The Australian 5th Division relieved the Americans on New Britain in October 1944, brought up by barge on both sides of the island. It was believed there were 38,000 Japanese on the island, but the Australians ultimately found 93,000. Blamey decided to concentrate his force on the Gazelle Peninsula, close to Rabaul on the island's northern tip, where the main Japanese base had previously existed.[21]

Pushing the Japanese ahead of them, they established a defensive line across the 50-kilometre-wide neck of the peninsula at the Tol Plantation. They arrived at Tol Plantation, where they uncovered the grisly remains of some of the Australian Lark Force, who had been captured and massacred in January 1942.

The 'battle' for New Britain stopped at Tol Plantation. The Diggers of the 5th Division sat out the last four months of the war in boredom and relative safety. This campaign cost the lives of 53 Australians killed in combat. The number of Japanese deaths is not known.[22]

It is interesting to note that, unlike in the Aitape–Wewak and Bougainville campaigns, Blamey did not push for complete annihilation of the Japanese here. This may have been because the 5th Division was a relatively inexperienced militia force.

* * *

The battle might have been over for the 5th Division, but the 'mopping up' was not. Yet events unfolding in Europe gave the Diggers in New Guinea hope that the end was now in sight.

18

Countdown to Surrender

March to 21 August 1945

On Tuesday, 8 May 1945, the Allies accepted the unconditional surrender of Germany, marking the end of World War II in Europe. The last shots were fired on 11 May on the Eastern Front.

It was good news for the Australians fighting with the Royal Air Force or in other British commands, but in the Pacific, the Japanese remained an undefeated – if retreating – enemy. While the Australians continued to 'mop up', US forces had been island-hopping towards the Japanese mainland, conducting the bloody Battle of Iwo Jima from 19 February to 26 March, followed by the Battle of Okinawa from 1 April to 22 June.

The value of what the Australians were doing was not always obvious to the public. It was not glorious offensive fighting that would force ultimate Japanese surrender. But it was necessary in terms of flushing out a dangerous enemy in neighbouring territories and ensuring that Australia remained strategically engaged.

Disquiet within the country about the human cost of the mopping up was simmering, with Blamey often the target of blame from both politicians and the public. But, whether

General Blamey's sea-going flag is unfurled and used for the first time during a lunch break from inspecting troops and equipment of Lieutenant General Morshead's Headquarters I Corps. Moratai Island, 25 April 1945. (AWM 090739)

Below: During a tour of inspection with Lieutenant General Berryman and Brigadier Whitehead, General Blamey passes tanks at the airport. Tarakan, Borneo, 8 May 1945. (AWM 089780)

he approved of the operations or not, Blamey was under the direction of the government and MacArthur.

* * *

On 24 February 1945, the Supreme Commander had triumphantly returned to Manila to wreak his vengeance on the Japanese after months of fighting. Blamey and Berryman flew there on 13 March to once again confer with him about the future disposition of Australian troops. MacArthur said he wanted the Australians, British and Dutch – the colonial power in what would soon become Indonesia – to take over all the South West Pacific Area except the Philippines. Blamey and MacArthur then agreed on a complex command structure; I Corps under Leslie Morshead would be under MacArthur's command to invade and liberate Borneo, currently occupied by approximately 35,000 Japanese marooned soldiers.[1]

As mentioned, Blamey had been doubtful about the Borneo campaign, but the government had agreed to it, still not wanting to jeopardise Australia's relationship with MacArthur.[2] As Berryman noted in his diary, it was now clear that MacArthur was planning to get into the real war against the Japan mainland and leave the Australians with the secondary role of clearing up the 250,000 Japanese in the South West Pacific Area.[3]

The staging areas for the invasion of Borneo were on the island of Morotai, some 300 kilometres to the east of Borneo. It had been invaded by US and Australian forces in September 1944 and used as a staging post for the US liberation of the

Philippines. Japanese resistance on the island was weak but would continue until the end of the war.

The invasion of Borneo, known as Operation Oboe, would proceed in three phases: to Tarakan Island off the north-east coast, then Balikpapan further south, followed by Brunei Bay on the west coast. Another three phases were planned but would not be executed.[4]

The transport of troops and materiel to Morotai began on 12 March 1945. Transport was mainly provided by the Americans. By the end of April, elements of the 9th Division and Morshead's HQ were in place on the island, while the 7th Division was preparing to move from the Atherton Tablelands.

Initially, the operation went smoothly. It benefited hugely from the Diggers' prior experience and training in amphibious operations, and from levels of equipment surpassing anything Australian forces had previously experienced in the war. Nearly 13,000 vehicles, plus stores, adding up to a total of 178,000 tons, were shipped from Australia and the USA within three weeks. The overall endeavour was so large that some of the convoys had to leave Morotai up to a week before the designated landings. Transport was organised by the US Army Services of Supply, with shipping provided by the US Navy, assisted by the Royal Australian Navy.

The invasion of Tarakan Island began on 1 May 1945. It was the first target in Borneo because its airfield was intended as a base from which the planes would provide close shore-based air cover for the rest of the invasion.[5]

Reconnaissance had been carried out, but had failed to discern the atrocious conditions on the island. The beaches were covered in mangroves and black, sticky mud, and protected by manmade obstacles and pillboxes. During the landings, ships stuck fast, while men and tanks struggled to get onto firm ground. Worse was yet to come.

The Japanese did not attack during the landing, but instead set themselves up at the end of the airfield and had to be laboriously flushed out. Prior to the invasion, the airfield had been overzealously bombed by Allied air forces. The badly cratered strip was continually flooded by torrential rain. During the day bomb craters were pumped out, but they rapidly refilled with seepage and rain; at night the Japanese infiltrated the airfield and did even more damage. The latter problem was slowly overcome as the Diggers gradually eliminated Japanese stragglers.

The first plane landed on 28 June, seven weeks later than planned, by which time most Japanese resistance on Tarakan had been defeated. In the short-term, air support was required to come from the Philippines. Aircraft from Morotai would provide help during Oboe 2, the invasion of Balikpapan.

Taking Tarakan involved an Allied force of around 15,000, of whom 225 were killed and 669 wounded against a Japanese force of 2400, of which 85 per cent, or 1920 Japanese, died, giving the Allies an efficiency ratio of 8.5 to 1.[6]

* * *

MacArthur's next objective for the Australians in Borneo was to take Balikpapan on the south-east coast. The campaign began on 1 July, using the 7th Division under Major General Edward Milford, and was marked by controversy from the start.

Heavy anti-aircraft battery on Tarakan Island, Borneo, 18 July 1945. (AWM 111687)

A Matilda (Frog) flamethrowing tank immolating a Japanese dugout in Balikpapan, Borneo, 3 July 1945. (AWM 111060)

MacArthur's general headquarters was of the opinion that oil refineries at Balikpapan were supplying enemy planes. In fact, the Japanese had relocated oil production to more secure oil fields elsewhere, and there had been no large tankers in dock at Balikpapan since late 1944. The US joint chiefs had decided that Balikpapan was not a strategic threat and did not need to be taken, nor did most Australian officers, from Blamey down, believe the operation was necessary. Orders had to be obeyed, but that didn't mean winning at any cost. Officers worked assiduously to achieve their ordered objectives with minimal casualties.[7]

The campaign at Balikpapan involved the last amphibious landing of World War II, and the largest under Australian command. The operation followed what was now a tried-and-true formula. Heavy, prolonged pre-landing bombardment of the town from the air and sea ensured that there was little resistance. However, time was of the essence, as there were strong Japanese emplacements behind the town. Tanks were brought up to clear Japanese positions, followed by a remorseless Australian onslaught. The Japanese withdrew from the town on 3 July and it was secured with only 22 Australian deaths compared with more than 500 Japanese, meaning that 22.7 times more Japanese died than Australians.

The Australians moved on through the island in a determined but cautious manner. Their advance was accompanied by naval gunfire and air strikes, including the use of napalm, followed by mortar and artillery fire. The fleet of tanks also included Matilda Frogs with mounted flamethrowers, which reached at least 80 metres ahead.[8] In all, 25 of these new weapons were used in Borneo. Their success made hand-held flamethrowers redundant.

As the fight passed beyond the open ground into the jungle, the Japanese set ambushes. By the time the Diggers had encountered a few of these, Milford decided he had achieved his objectives and discontinued the advance; the cost in Diggers' lives was becoming too great. The Australians continued to block the Japanese from leaving the jungle and maintained security with active patrolling.

During the whole of Oboe 2, the Australian Army lost 229 men and the Japanese 2032, meaning 8.9 times more Japanese deaths than Australian ones.

* * *

As with Balikpapan, a key objective of the invasion of Brunei Bay on the west coast of Borneo was to secure existing oil-production facilities. The overall planning concept was handed down from MacArthur's GHQ via I Corps and extensively modified by 9th Division commander Major General George Wootten and his planners, and reviewed and approved by Berryman and Blamey. The final plan was for the 9th Division to spread along 300 kilometres of coastline in a pattern that would give the invaders many opportunities to outmanoeuvre the Japanese.

Basic plans had to be adjusted several times because of shipping shortages. Embarkation from Morotai was delayed and Wootten used the time to train his men. The landings finally got underway on 10 June 1945 and went gratifyingly well.[9]

The first battalion to land was the 17th. They faced a weak opposition and had taken Brunei township by 13 June. Other battalions disembarked at various landing points around the bay and advanced on the oil-producing areas. In accordance with Wootten's demand that his commanders not take unnecessary risks, they paused when they met tough resistance and relied on coordinated long-distance fire by artillery, mortars and Matilda tanks – some equipped with flamethrowers – as well as naval and air fire. Progress was generally fast, because the Japanese were dispirited, weak and disorganised. Where pockets of resistance were particularly fierce, they were soon quelled when Matilda tanks with flamethrowers came through.

By 15 July, the Australians had achieved their objectives and become a garrison force.

* * *

Following the bombing of Hiroshima on 6 August and Nagasaki on 9 August, VJ (Victory over Japan) Day arrived on 15 August with the confirmation that Emperor Hirohito had accepted Allied surrender terms. Still, the Australians expected difficulties in ensuring that the Japanese in Borneo received and complied with surrender instructions. This proved to be a realistic forecast.

On 2 September 1945, Blamey achieved the great honour of accepting the Japanese surrender on behalf of Australia, aboard the USS *Missouri* in Tokyo Bay. That he was given a position in the centre of the front row at the ceremony speaks volumes about the regard in which MacArthur held him. This would not have happened without the Supreme Commander's specific instruction.

On his way home from Japan, Blamey visited the HQ of I Corps on Morotai. On the evening of 8 September, he held a dinner party for senior officers, and nursing matrons and sisters. As he wrote in his diary, Berryman turned in at midnight, but Blamey and a few others stayed on until 4 am. Perhaps on this occasion, the Commander in Chief deserved the celebration.[10]

The next day, Blamey accepted the surrender of the Japanese Second Army and its 126,500 soldiers on Morotai from Lieutenant General Futsataro Teshima. In the crowd were senior representatives of the Americans and the Dutch. In his address, Blamey said:

> In receiving your surrender I do not recognise you as an honourable and gallant foe, but you will be treated with due but severe courtesy in all matters ... I recall the treacherous attack made upon the British Empire and upon the United States of America in December 1941 ... I recall the atrocities inflicted upon the persons of our nationals as prisoners of war and internees, designed to reduce them by punishment and starvation to slavery. In the light of these evils, I will enforce most rigorously all orders issued to you, so let there be no delay or hesitation in their fulfilment at your peril.[11]

Blamey flew back to Australia the following day, leaving Berryman to wind down the Australian Army's Pacific operations, including the difficult job of rounding up the Japanese who had

General Blamey, as Australia's representative, preparing to sign the Japanese surrender document on the USS *Missouri*, Tokyo Bay, 2 September 1945. Japanese General Yoshijiro Umezo is on the far left in the foreground. (AWM 019131)

General Blamey accepting the surrender of 2 Japanese Army, Moratai, 9 September 1945. (AWM 115650)

not yet surrendered, either because they remained loyal to the old empire or they hadn't heard that the war had ended.

The last Australian military operation on Borneo was carried out on 6 October. In November, a program began to prepare soldiers in Borneo for the demobilisation process and return to civilian life. This included education and sport, to enhance both mental and physical wellbeing. Elements of the 9th Division would remain in place performing garrison duties until January 1946, when they too were shipped to Australia and disbanded.

During the entirety of Operation Oboe, the Australian Army suffered 568 deaths to around 7000 Japanese deaths, or 12.2 times as many. Blamey's instruction to keep casualties low had indeed been followed.

The Australian forces demobilised without waiting for all of the Japanese to be found. It was a mammoth job because there were 224,00 men and women serving in the SWPA area alone, with another 20,000 spread out in other areas including Britain. Prisoners of war, both Australian and Japanese, needed to be transported home as well. The process was slower than most people wanted because there was a bottleneck of shipping with all Allies doing the same thing at the same time. By year's end, only 76,000 Australians had been repatriated. Most had been returned to Australia by mid-1946.

The many hundreds of Japanese left spread around the Pacific would be tracked down over a long period of time and shipped back to Japan. The last Japanese soldier to formally surrender was Teruo Nakamura. He would be found on Morotai Island and surrendered to Indonesian armed forces on 10 March 1974.[12]

19
Fractious Finish

January 1945 to May 1951

In early 1945, there was a mood of disquiet in Australia. The dangers of 1942 were now well past. The Japanese were on the run in the extremities of New Guinea, Borneo and the Philippines. It was now widely accepted that they would be beaten. Yet the Australian people were restive, because their boys had been given the poor relation's role compared with the Americans, and the poor relation's media coverage too. All the while, it was becoming increasingly clear that Blamey was no longer required as a bulwark against the enemy. The politicians were becoming positively difficult. The nation seemed to be turning against the Commander in Chief.

During the final campaigns, Blamey spent more time in forward areas than in Australia. While forward, he set out to visit each of the Australian brigades. In his absence, his critics in Australia had a field day. Inevitably, others felt he did not visit his troops often enough. Even Curtin became concerned, and criticised the army public relations service for not doing its job properly. In one response to complaints that Blamey was not forward enough, an army spokesman noted that 'like all personal criticisms that have been directed against the Commander-in-Chief this allegation was notable only for its complete inaccuracy ... He had spent more than half of 1944 outside the mainland. Since April 1944 he had travelled 65,000 miles by air, 7000 miles by sea and 7500 miles on land.'[1]

Nothing Blamey, an army spokesman or the occasional politician said could moderate the attacks from the Opposition or the press about the way he ran operations from 1944 through to the end of the war. Maybe it was just politics as usual, but sniping about Blamey's perceived mistakes took its toll on his reputation and mood, and there seemed to be nothing he could do about it. Snapping back just made it worse.

Prime Minister John Curtin, Blamey's sometime buffer, became increasingly ill from the beginning of 1945 and died in office on 5 July 1945. From that point on, Blamey's problems became worse and his mood increasingly tetchy. Frank Forde took over for eight days then Ben Chifley was elected Prime Minister in a leadership ballot. Chifley disliked Blamey and, unlike Curtin, did little to protect him from Labor politicians who saw him as a class enemy and Opposition members playing the opposition game.[2]

Army Minister Forde increasingly picked fights with Blamey, who had long considered Forde incompetent and treated him with contempt. And Chifley would not allow Blamey to bypass Forde and go directly to him in the way that Curtin had.[3]

The final straw came when another politician wrote a report in April 1944 in which he was critical of ship cargo-loading practices following a trip to Aitape.[4] When Forde sent an inquiry, Blamey could easily have replied politely or delegated the matter to a more diplomatic subordinate, but instead, the two men carried on a snippy exchange for months. Through sheer bloody-mindedness, Blamey had turned a potential ally into a certain foe. This would go against him in the coming peace.

Official war historian Gavin Long has also stated, quite correctly, that 'from 1942 to 1945 the temperament of Blamey must be reckoned with'.[5] In other words, like most great commanders, Blamey was a hard man who, while not a poor speaker, called a spade a spade. He was not prepared to sacrifice Diggers' comfort or lives to political expediency. To put it mildly, Blamey was not popular with a number of ministers, and Chifley was no friend of soldiers.

Long has also suggested that Blamey was inadequate in managing his own publicity. This overlooks the demands of the job and other constraints on the man. Had he paid more attention to his public image, most likely he would have been despised by both his men and his commanders as a self-promoter, the type of person those in the army loathe. In any event, while the fighting continued, MacArthur controlled the news. Any leaks suggesting that his 'American' army owed much of its success to the more numerous and more experienced Australians would have risked retribution. Once Blamey gained MacArthur's confidence, rather than indulging in attempts at personal public relations, he invested his time in morale-boosting visits to the men at the front.

* * *

On 15 September 1945, Blamey all but resigned by sending Forde a letter that said: 'My task is now complete and there is no further occasion for the exercise of continuance of my powers of Commander-in-Chief ... I am desirous of laying down my office as early as possible'.[6] The government, however, asked him to stay to supervise demobilisation and other matters, which he did.

In September and October, he recommended 16 of his generals to receive honours. He later found that these recommendations had been ignored, as had his ideas about the future structure of the armed forces.[7]

On 10 October, he set off on his final tour of forward areas. A week later, he was in Balikpapan to review a parade of the 65th Battalion, newly formed as part of the British Commonwealth Occupation Force of Japan. Then he visited Australian forces at Ambon, Macassar and Timor.

Next stop was Wewak, where he reviewed a parade of the 6th Division and made a stirring speech to them on the airstrip in the blazing hot sun. He told them that there would be delays in their return to Australia, but that when they went home, they would find strong differences between themselves and the citizens who hadn't served.[8] As it happened, most of the division was returned to Australia by November 1945 and the infantry battalions disbanded in early 1946.

Blamey then moved on to Rabaul in New Britain. With him was the last general he had promoted in wartime, 44-year-old Major General Kenneth Eather, who had commanded the 25th Brigade on the Kokoda Track and at Lae and Borneo, and the 11th Division in New Britain for a few weeks before the Japanese surrender. The final stop before returning home was Torokina on Bougainville, where Blamey reviewed 5260 soldiers of the 3rd Division.

In the meantime, Blamey had asked for permission to travel to Chicago to take up the guest of honour's chair at the first post-war conference of the American Legion in November. He considered this to be a great honour both for him and the country, because no Australian had been invited before. His request was declined on 3 November in a telegram from Forde, saying that the complex army situation made him indispensable and he should remain at home. He accepted the refusal, but didn't understand the reasoning.

He was even more bemused when he received a letter from Forde nearly two weeks later, saying the government had accepted his resignation and that First Army commander Lieutenant General Vernon Sturdee had been chosen as Acting Commander in Chief.[9]

In his reply, Blamey voiced his 'surprise at the very short notice of the termination of my appointment',[10] which would give him insufficient time to complete all the necessary tasks. There were several constrained written interchanges between Forde and Blamey. Blamey's real feelings came out when Forde visited his office on 30 November, the general's last working day. Their increasingly heated exchange began with Forde offering Blamey a KCMG (Knight Commander of the Most Distinguished Order of Saint Michael and Saint George – the second highest award given for outstanding service). Blamey declined anything personal and asked only for the awards to bestowed on his generals. On being told that was impossible,

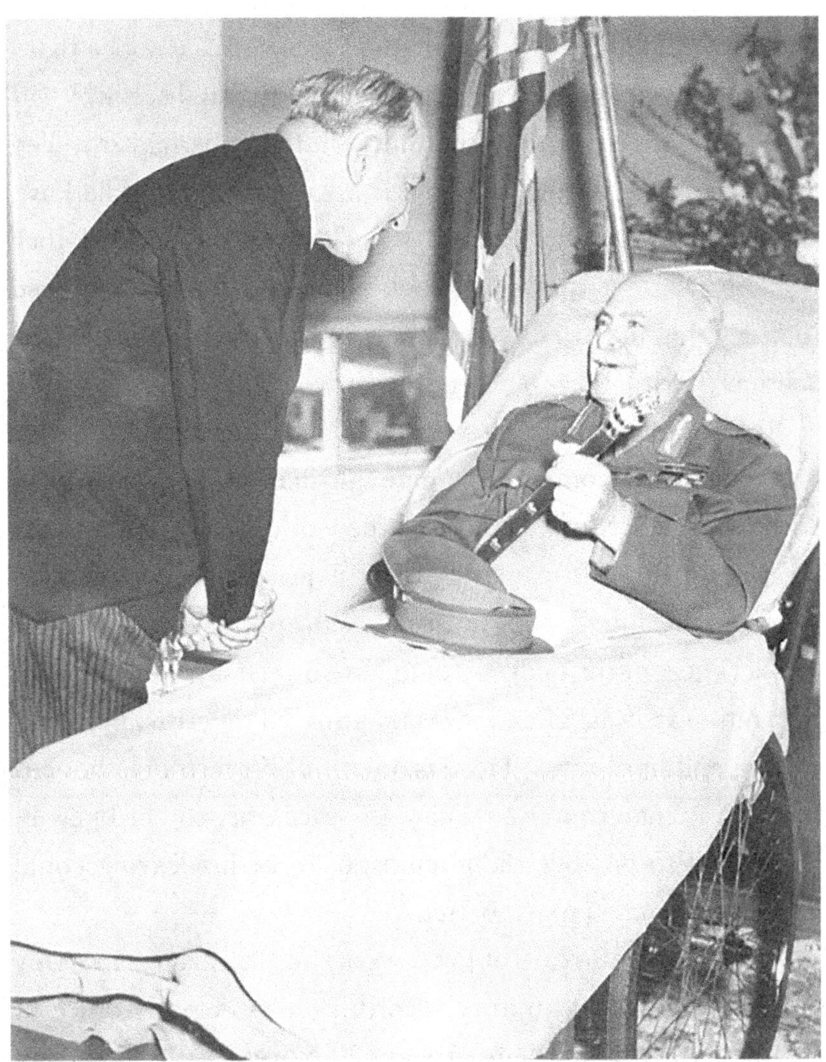

Blamey accepting his field marshal's baton from Governor-General William McKell at Heidelberg Repatriation Hospital, Melbourne, 16 September 1950. (AWM 135225)

he rounded on Forde, saying, 'You will concede that I have complete loyalty to you and your Government, and in fact all previous governments during my command. Today as I leave Barracks I am a free individual, and I give you due notice that I will attack you and your government in any way I see fit.'[11]

Blamey offered to buy the Buick staff car he had travelled 50,000 miles in around the Pacific areas and the Middle East. After a pause of some days, the Government decided they wanted to gift it to him. It took some convincing by Alfred Kemsley, his old friend from the pre-war radio days of 'The Sentinel', for Blamey to accept the car as a gift.[12]

Resigning had been exactly the right thing to do. Blamey was a wartime commander, a tough man who could mix it with the toughest of men around the world. But he had neither the finesse nor the patience to be a peacetime commander. Ceremonial duties and jousting with politicians for ever-smaller slices of the budget would have driven him madder with frustration than he already was. He thrived on crisis, problem-solving and hard work. He was a natural-born troubleshooter; that sort of man can be a menace in peacetime, and he knew it.

He had to go. But the circumstances of his leaving could have been handled much better.

After nearly 40 years of loyal service to the Australian Army and an impeccable military record, Blamey left his office at Victoria Barracks in Melbourne on 30 November 1945, having received no public recognition of any kind. He was pointedly not invited to the London victory celebrations or the national victory celebrations in June 1946, although he did lead the Victory Day march in Melbourne in that month.

A great military career had ended not with a bang but a whimper.

* * *

Blamey lived for only another five years, and he was sick for the final 11 months of his life. In those five years, he was left to wander in the political wilderness, with little to do but criticise the Chifley Government from the sidelines. While not seeking any honours for himself, he was bitter about the lack of honours for the generals who had fought under him.

After the war, without bothering to find out the facts of the matter, Chifley expressed strong sympathy for Sydney Rowell, saying of Blamey's dismissal of him: 'I hate bloody injustice.'[13] Rowell became Vice Chief of the General Staff from 1946 to 1950, overseeing the army's transition to peace, then Chief of the General Staff to December 1954.

Blamey, meanwhile, had few friends in power. Nevertheless, the Victorian Labor government made him Chairman of State Savings Bank Commissioners. He lent his name to, and sometimes chaired, charitable organisations including the Victorian Blinded Soldiers' Welfare Trust, the War Nurses' Memorial Centre and Australia's Battle Honours Committee, as well as keeping up his associations with old soldiers.

With Cold War paranoia running rife, he led the discussion on how to thwart the communist threat in Australia. He promised Chifley's government in an Anzac Day speech on 25 April 1947 that soldiers, airmen and sailors would stand behind them to beat this threat.

Following this promise, he was asked by various businessmen to lead a secret organisation called The Association, which aimed to prevent a communist coup. Blamey accepted and continued to talk publicly about the dangers of communism.[14]

The Association is believed to have had as many as 100,000 members, primarily made up of ex-servicemen and concentrated in Victoria and New South Wales. It was never called to action and Blamey's role in it is conjecture. It was disbanded in 1949 when Chifley's government set up the Australian Security Intelligence Organisation.[15]

* * *

With the war behind him, his position secure and Blamey no longer a competitor in the military prestige game, MacArthur was free to say exactly what he thought of the former Australian commander in chief. In his *Reminiscences*, published in 1964, he wrote of his early days in Australia: 'The picture was not all dismal ... General Sir Thomas Blamey, a veteran soldier of highest quality, was appointed to command the Allied Land Forces.'[16] In 1944, on his own authority, MacArthur had awarded Blamey and Generals Herring, Vasey and Eather the Distinguished Service Cross, the second-highest military award in the United States.

In September 1948, MacArthur invited Blamey to Tokyo to view the developments there since the war's end. This was an extraordinary honour: while MacArthur had many visitors, he was seldom the one to invite them. The Australian Government reluctantly organised Blamey's passage on a courier plane. By then, Blamey's health had begun to fail, and during the tour he complained of exhaustion and leg aches.

In December 1949, his old supporter, Robert Menzies, became Prime Minister again and immediately took steps to honour Blamey with a promotion. Blamey also wrote to Menzies, asking him to right the wrong of not honouring Australia's generals. The generals were Beavis, Berryman, Burston, Cannan, Chapman, Lloyd, Murray, Northcott, Savige, Simpson, Steele, Stevens, Sturdee and Wootten. Cannan was the only general on Blamey's list of 15 who was not subsequently knighted.

Blamey was promoted to field marshal on 8 June 1950. In order for this to be achieved, he was restored to active service for one day and the next day transferred to the Reserve of Officers. The government gave him an allowance of £3000 per annum: much needed, because by that point Blamey was somewhat impecunious.

Less than two weeks later, he became critically ill with pneumonia and also suffered a stroke. He was admitted to hospital, where he accepted the engraved field marshal's baton on 16 September 1950 from Menzies's delegate, Governor General William McKell. During the bedside ceremony he was too ill to complete his acceptance speech.

Blamey died from a stroke on 27 May 1951, at the age of 67. Despite his claim that he thrived on stress, the war years had obviously taken their toll, and the humiliating years of peace that followed probably contributed too. It is oft said that some people wither away in retirement if they have nothing meaningful to do. The problem is even greater for once-powerful people like Blamey, who struggle to find relevance as ordinary citizens.

A state funeral was held in Melbourne three days after Blamey's death. Some 300,000 Melburnians, or one-fifth of the population, lined the 11-kilometre route from the Shrine of Remembrance to the Fawkner Crematorium. He had 10 pall bearers, all lieutenant generals, including Rowell. Four thousand troops accompanied the gun carriage that carried his coffin.

At last he received the long overdue parade, and was honoured by the people he had really worked for: the citizens of Australia.

Commander in Chief General Sir Thomas Blamey at Bougainville where he visited forward troops in the south and headquarters 7th Infantry Brigade, 26 March 1945. (AWM 079976)

20
Blamey's Legacy

These days Blamey's reputation is dominated by two negatives. The most damaging is the 'rabbits' speech he gave on the Kokoda Track. Those unfortunate two minutes have distracted many commentators' attention from all that Blamey achieved in his two million or so minutes of command during the war. The other period in Blamey's life that has harmed his legacy is his 11 years as Victorian Police Commissioner. This was a turbulent era in Australia's history, and while some of Blamey's behaviour during that time was undoubtedly distasteful, it needs to be viewed separately from his achievements as Commander in Chief of the Australian Military Forces.

It is instructive to read the comments of official World War II historian Gavin Long, who supports the view that Blamey was a world-class general: 'From 1939 onwards in experience of staff and command problems he was seldom inferior and generally superior to his collaterals and superiors in the Middle East and South-West Pacific. The clarity and wisdom of his appreciations of such problems and the logic and far-sightedness of his strategical thinking have been illustrated through this history.'[1]

Australia was indeed lucky to have a soldier of Blamey's calibre ready and willing to command at the start of World War II, a soldier who had been trained and tested during the horrors of World War I by the great Monash.

The solution to commanding in an alliance while protecting your force was to have unity of command, formally backed up by government. Australia didn't have unity of command until late in World War I, when Monash was made corps commander, but even then, there wasn't strong political support from the Australian Government for dealing with the British. Monash compensated for this by creating authority through the force of his own personality. In contrast, Canadian forces in World War I had unity of command for longer than Australia and strong backing from their government, and had a much lower fatality rate than Australia (as will be seen in the Epilogue). Monash and Blamey knew of the advantage Canada enjoyed.

In preparation for leadership in World War II, Blamey set about implementing a formal charter with his government. That charter said that he and his delegated officers had authority to maintain unity of command, so that parts of their force could not be taken and used without agreement. In general, the Australian and British Governments had to agree on how the Australian force was to be used, but the Australian commander could act in an emergency if he informed the Australian Government of his actions. This offered Blamey considerable protection but didn't guarantee perfect control, particularly while he was under British authority. Maintaining unity of command in the South West Pacific Area campaigns was easier, because Prime Minister Curtin never wavered on backing Blamey in his demand for Australian command of the Australian Army.

Unity of command and government support go some of the way to explaining how Blamey saved the lives of 35,000 fighting men – as I have calculated in the Epilogue – over the course of the war. And since the leader determines an organisation's culture, the rest comes down to Blamey's character, capabilities and values.

Blamey was a hard man, as he needed to be. He could stand up to the toughest adversary if he had to. In the case of foreign command, he generally stopped just short of being insubordinate. He stood up to Churchill, thus bringing the 9th Division out of Tobruk before they were worn down, and he achieved an evacuation of the Anzac forces out of Greece when none was planned. In the Pacific war, his relationship with MacArthur had a rocky start, but it warmed over time to the considerable advantage of both the US and Australian forces. Blamey also had a frank and robust way with Australian prime ministers and government during the war that caused him strife in the following peace. Other generals under his command, such as Morshead, might have handled the government more diplomatically but would not have acted as firmly. Berryman had excellent relations with US officers but probably could not have handled MacArthur better than Blamey, particularly as he did not have the rank.

Despite his toughness and his necessary acts of discipline, Blamey was also compassionate. His values closely aligned with those of Monash. Both believed that 'the true rôle of the Infantry was not to expend itself upon heroic physical effort, nor to wither away under merciless machine-gun fire, nor to impale itself on hostile bayonets, nor to tear itself to pieces in hostile entanglements', as Monash wrote.[2] Obviously this command principle applied not only to infantry but also to the rest of the forces.

Blamey demonstrated his care for the men in ways other than assessing what the toll in lives was likely to be. He looked after the health of the men under his command, insisting they be relieved if they were in combat for too long; nor did he want them sitting around bored with no active duties. He was also sensitive to their leisure needs, as per his instructions early in the war regarding canteens.

While he worked hard to protect his men in the Middle East, Blamey was given no strategic role. The first time he was able to shine as a commander in planning a campaign was in 1943 before the battle for Lae. This battle started with Blamey's idea to blindside the defending Japanese. He was fortunate that there was sufficient transport available for men and materiel.

Of course, not all the campaigns in Papua and New Guinea could be supported like the battle for Lae. The fighting over the Kokoda Track to the beachheads was tough on the Diggers. This was because the campaigns were ordered by MacArthur prematurely, before the forces could be properly supplied.

Everyone, including Blamey, was playing catchup. With the exception of Milne Bay, there was insufficient shipping available to move men, heavy equipment and artillery onto the north coast of New Guinea until very late in the campaign. With that and a bit of patience, the Kokoda campaign may not have been necessary.

To compound the problem, no one knew how to fight the Japanese in the jungle. This was where the adaptability of the Diggers came into play. Through trial and error, they learned lessons in theatre that were shared and passed back, collated and used for training. This bottom-up learning was actively supported by Blamey and his senior officers, as evidenced by Blamey's rapid establishment in late 1942 of the Jungle Training Centre in Queensland with its sophisticated training programs.

Blamey's army developed a distinguished record in winning against the enemy and keeping casualties low. Obviously, this had a great deal to do with how Blamey selected his officers. His initial choices in the Middle East were officers he had known, or known of, in World War I with a record of looking after the men while being high-performance combat officers. Many of them remained in the fray until the end of World War II and attained high rank. This points to good decision-making. As the army grew, Blamey promoted an increasing number from the lower ranks, who were selected on performance. Most of the men holding ranks up to and including brigadier were from this cohort, while a few made it to the rank of lieutenant general.

Blamey's job was full of uncertainties. It is clear that he made mistakes, but there is no evidence that he deliberately did anything other than try to maximise the chances of success and survival of the men he was responsible for. He might have relieved a few good officers too soon, or for the 'wrong' reasons, but he replaced them with others who were at least as good and often better. Despite his achievements, Blamey's leadership record was under attack even before the war ended. As Gavin Long has remarked, 'on his head descended perhaps the strongest vituperation to which any military leader in the war was subjected by people on his own side, and at the end the Government terminated his appointment in a summary fashion'.[3]

On his retirement, though he had led the Australian Army efficiently and effectively, and enjoyed the respect of the general population, Blamey, as we have seen, was barely honoured by the government. In terms of public memorials, there is a statue of him close to Monash's near the Shrine of Remembrance in Melbourne, commissioned by the City of Melbourne and partly paid for by donations. It was unveiled by Menzies in 1960. In Canberra there is a square, a crescent and a place just off the crescent named after him. In Sydney there is a street and a park named after him. There is also the Blamey Barracks near Wagga Wagga. In the nation's war memorials, his presence is at best intermittent and usually nonexistent. It is not really enough for such an important historical figure.

Interestingly, though, he *is* remembered with some gratitude by the soldiers and their descendants, as suggested by this unexpected message sent to me after a presentation I gave:

> I guess I, my siblings, my children and grandchildren owe our lives to two top leaders, Sir Leslie Morshead and Blamey. If the 2/17 and the artillery hadn't stopped the Germans in the Easter battle at Tobruk (led by Morshead) and if Blamey hadn't had his way in withdrawing the 9th from Tobruk and if Blamey hadn't bullied McArthur into keeping to the Huon Peninsula plan and sent the 26th brigade and tanks to support the 20th I wouldn't be here to write this.

These days, popular Australian World War II histories tend to concentrate on the experience of the Diggers. Any mention of Blamey is usually minor and disparaging. As heroic as the Diggers were, they did not fight the war by themselves. There was a colossal enabling organisation behind them, with Blamey and his generals at its head.

The soldiers were world-class fighters under world-class Australian command, and the whole resulted in heroic achievement. Heroic achievement all too often comes with high casualty rates, but fortunately, in this case, that outcome was avoided by excellent command. Currently, there is little in the way of integrated narrative about how the Australian Army achieved its successes in World War II, and there cannot be unless Blamey and his generals are given recognition in our histories in a substantial and enduring way.

Historian David Horner has asserted that 'Field Marshal Sir Thomas Blamey was Australia's greatest and most important soldier.'[4] As would be expected of such an accomplished historian, he has used multiple sources and much narrative synthesis to support this conclusion.

In writing this book, I started from a somewhat different place. I was asked to write this history by a retired major general who wanted someone to have a fresh look at Blamey. I knew almost nothing about Blamey, but I accepted the challenge. My belief is that greatness should be measurable in some way, especially for occupations that rely on a great deal of physicality. The most obvious measures are battles won and lives saved. The first was easy. The Australians under Blamey had a superb record in World War II. The second required some rigour, and when I did the work I discovered a drop of 35,000 in the expected fatality number of Blamey's soldiers during World War II. A result like this could not be accidental; it demanded an explanation. My journey varied somewhat to that of Horner, but it ended up at the same point. The only credible explanation of the fatality figures is that Blamey was not only a great soldier but also a superb and visionary head of a vast organisation.

Through incredible leadership during the crisis of a world war, Blamey took a tiny, underprepared and poorly equipped force in 1939, and built it up into a three-quarters-of-a-million-strong, world-class fighting force. While it was always under foreign command of some sort, the Australian Army racked up an impressive number of firsts. Under Blamey's command it was the first to thwart the Germans on land (Rommel, at Tobruk) and beat the Vichy French in Syria. It also did worthy service in several other battles. It was the first force to beat the Japanese on land in a minor campaign (Milne Bay), in a moderate-sized campaign (Kokoda and the beachheads) and in a major campaign (Salamaua–Lae campaign then on to Madang). In fact, it never lost a battle to the Japanese. It also provided MacArthur with his tactical template for winning the war. And, as Blamey demanded of his generals, and as the numbers show, the casualties were kept low.

Blamey worked to supply the best training, the best health outcomes, the best equipment, and the best tactical and strategic planning given what was achievable at the time. He did all this while also doing what no other Australian commander has ever done: simultaneously fulfilling the roles of Commander in Chief of the Australian Military Forces and of operational commander in the South West Pacific Area (in the position of Commander, Allied Land Forces). In both those positions, he fulfilled Prime Minister John Curtin's vision of a successful strategic alliance with the United States in World War II, and provided a foundation that enabled this alliance to thrive in the future.

Blamey has the distinction of having led through the whole of World War II, under three prime ministers of both conservative and Labor governments, and gained the trust of his British and American superior commanders: all of which is a ringing endorsement of his leadership.

In the generally accepted Blamey narrative, his blemishes dominate the story while his many exceptional qualities are ignored. Yet a proper case study of leadership involves dispassionate analysis. This is what I have tried to provide in writing this book – hopefully proving the supreme benefits of Blamey's leadership throughout the crisis of World War II.

EPILOGUE

Fighting Efficiency: Bringing the Boys Back Home

There are very obvious reasons for a military commander to concentrate on fighting efficiency. It is humane to look after the wellbeing of the troops within a fighting force. And from a clinical, organisational point of view, it is efficient to do more with less, be it troops or materiel. In the case of troops, not only does every soldier lost need to be replaced, but their experience is also permanently gone. This degrades levels of both effectiveness and efficiency.

Concerns about keeping casualty rates low have not always been put into practice by the military, but they were emphasised by the Australian Army in World War II, and especially by Blamey.

Casualty figures are a strong indicator of command capability, all other things being equal. Better commanders do things better, which means less waste of everything, especially troops. This statement applies to all officers from the bottom up. It also applies to all organisations: the amount of time lost through accidents, labour turnover and absenteeism provides an excellent indicator of management capability in peacetime.

By and large in this book, I have used deaths as a measure because they are less subject to categorisation errors than total casualties. There are variations, however, in the time scale considered – that is, how long after a battle a death can take place and still be ascribed to that battle. Data for these analyses come from myriad sources. Most data points have been checked for plausibility more than once against other sources.

This epilogue presents evidence supporting the existence of a 'Blamey effect' throughout World War II, beginning with the first Australian campaigns in the Middle East and persisting through the Pacific campaigns until the conflict's end. The data suggests that General Blamey's emphasis on troop welfare significantly reduced casulaties. Of course, he had to balance that with his troops being an effective fighting force. The latter is self-evident in the results of the battles, and the former will be shown below.

Casualty comparisons within the Australian Army, World War II

The total Australian Army had 726,543 enlistments. The number of personnel under Blamey's control was 706,862, or 97.29 per cent of the total army compliment.[1] The remainder, not under Blamey's control, were those stationed in Malaya, Singapore and Java. This small proportion (2.71 per cent of the total army) contributed 44 per cent of the army's fatalities. Table 1 shows that 78 per cent of the fatalities of troops in Malaya, Singapore and Java happened while those men were prisoners of war under the Japanese. Despite being by far the largest force, the troops under Blamey's contingent accounted for 56 per cent of all Australian Army battle-related deaths from 1939 to 1945. Blamey's forces suffered only 37 per cent of the army's deaths in almost four years in the South West Pacific Area (SWPA) and 19 per cent during two years in the Middle East. In contrast, the battles in Malaya, Singapore and Java, which involved just over a division, accounted for around 44 per cent of army deaths, exceeding the deaths under Blamey in the SWPA and the Middle East combined.

Table 1: Battle-Related Australian Army Deaths in World War II Under Blamey Compared with Other Commands[2]		
	Number of deaths	% of total deaths
Blamey, Middle East (against Germany and Italy)	3,552	19%
Blamey and Malaya, Singapore and Java (against Japan)	15,161	81%
Total Army (all theatres)	**18,713**	100%
Separating Blamey and Malaya, Singapore and Java		
Total Blamey and Malaya, Singapore and Java (against Japan)	15,161	81%
Malaya, Singapore and Java (Table 2 below)	8253	44%
Blamey's army only in SWPA	**6908**	37%
Blamey total		
Blamey only in SWPA (against Japan)	6908	37%
Blamey, Middle East (against Germany and Italy)	3552	19%
Total Blamey Army (all theatres)	**10,460**	56%

This table only covers army deaths, but it is useful to compare them with deaths within other branches of the Australian armed forces. Between 1939 and 1945, around 10,000 Australians served in the Royal Air Force (RAF) Bomber Command, and sustained total combat fatalities of 4050.[3] Australian fatalities in Bomber Command were around 38 per cent of those under Blamey's command, or 22 per cent of the whole army. Clearly, it was much more dangerous to be in Bomber Command than in Blamey's army. The number of battle-related deaths of Australians in Bomber Command, just one branch of the RAF, is greater than those within the entire Australian Army in the Middle East.

Table 2 below provides more detail about Australian World War II deaths in Malaysia, Singapore and Java. The units involved were the Australian 8th Division under Major General Gordon Bennett based in Malaya and Singapore, and an ad hoc brigade from the 6th and 7th Brigades returning from the Middle East, which landed in Java and was trapped there. The table includes battlefield deaths, plus an estimate of the number of deaths in captivity.

Table 2: Australian Army Deaths in World War II in Malaya, Singapore and Java[4]

Theatre	Number of battlefield deaths	Number of POW deaths (estimate)	Total number of deaths
Malaya and Singapore	1789	5390	7179
Java	36	1038	1074
Total, Malaya, Singapore and Java	**1825**	**6428**	**8253**

Casualty comparisons between World War I and World War II

We can gain even greater insight into the existence of a 'Blamey effect' by comparing fatality data from World War I and World War II among the Allied nations of Australia, Canada, Great Britain, New Zealand and the USA. This is a standard benchmarking comparison. While nothing is ever exactly comparable, such comparisons are a powerful tool for uncovering gross differences.

The two measures generally used in such comparisons are total deaths from all causes, and battle deaths (including deaths of POWs). I have only included total deaths in the tables below, because information about combat deaths in World War I is not consistently available for all five nations. The other important point to note is that, unlike Tables 1 and 2 above, Tables 3 and 4 below include deaths across all services of the military forces.

Table 3: Fatality Rates in World War I of the Armed Forces of Australia, Canada, Great Britain, New Zealand and the United States[5]

Rank	Country	Years in theatre	Start event	Enlisted	Deaths	% deaths	% deaths per year
1	New Zealand	3.9	Arrive Egypt, 13 December 1914	105,986	18,058	17.04%	4.37%
2	Australia	3.9	Arrive Egypt, 13 December 1914	416,809	61,645	14.78%	3.79%
3	Great Britain	4.3	Battle of Mons, 4 August 1914	6,111,732	887,858	14.53%	3.36%
4	Canada	3.9	Arrive France, 1 December 1914	619,636	59,544	9.61%	2.45%
5	United States	1.4	Arrive France, 1 June 1917	4,734,991	116,516	2.46%	1.76%

Table 4: Fatality Rates in World War II of the Armed Forces of Australia, Canada, Great Britain, New Zealand and the United States[6]							
Rank	Country	Years in theatre	Start event	Enlisted	Deaths	% deaths	% deaths per year
1	Great Britain	5.5	Norwegian campaign, 9 April 1940	5,896,000	384,000	6.5%	1.18%
2	New Zealand	5.3	Egypt, June 1940	204,000	11,928	5.8%	1.10%
3	Canada	5.3	Fall of France, June 1940	1,100,000	45,400	4.1%	0.78%
4	Australia	5.4	6th Division arrives Middle East, May 1940	990,900	39,654	4.0%	0.74%
5	United States	3.8	Pearl Harbor bombing, 7 December 1941	16,112,566	405,399	2.5%	0.66%

Tables 3 and 4 compare the fatality rates (deaths per soldier per year) of Australian, Canadian, British, New Zealand and US soldiers in and between World War I and World War II. They show, firstly, that the fatality rates per year of all five nations substantially decreased between World War I and World War II. In total, the fatality rates in World War II are about one-third of those in World War I. Australia achieved the most significant reduction, with its World War II fatality rate about one-fifth of its World War I rate. What this reduction means in real terms is an estimated 35,000 lives saved. If deaths in World War II had continued at the World War I rate of 14.8 per cent of the total enlisted, Australia would have seen about 203,000 deaths instead of the 39,654 that are recorded. This theoretical increase in deaths is a result of the yearly death rate and reflects the fact that World War II was a longer war with more than twice the size of the armed forces than in World War I.

In comparing death rates between the two wars, one factor to be aware of is the number of years a country was involved. The United States entered World War II immediately after the Japanese attack on Pearl Harbour in December 1941 and participated in the fighting for almost four years, but was not seriously involved in action in World War I until May 1918, six months before the end of hostilities. Because in fact some scattered US soldiers became involved as early as June 1917, I have taken that as the US start date, but clearly the total American deaths in World War I are not comparable with the deaths in World War II because of the very different lengths of time the US was involved in either conflict.

Another point to note is that, while there can be action against the enemy as soon as war is declared, usually it takes some time for forces to assemble and be in a position to fight. The build-up of each nation's fighting force is not linear. Nor is each country's casualty rate: it usually consists of a small number when hostilities are declared, peaks sometime after what is called the 'start event' then largely stops at the official surrender. It is impossible to plot this build-up and decline for each nation, so I have had to assume that all casualties occurred at a uniform rate between the start event and the official surrender.

For both wars, the relevant date for the end of hostilities is the date of surrender, although sometimes the actual finish occurs later for a small proportion of the forces, as do the deaths counted.

* * *

The following table is the key to the benchmarking analysis. It compares the World War I and World War II losses across all the armed services of Australia, Canada, Great Britain, New Zealand and the United States, derived from the two tables above.

Table 5: Comparative Fatality Rates in World War I and World War II of the Armed Forces of Australia, New Zealand, Canada, Great Britain and the United States[7]

Country	% deaths per year, WWI	% deaths per year, WWII	Ratio, WWII to WWI
United States	1.76%	0.66%	37.67%
Great Britain	3.36%	1.18%	35.21%
Canada	2.45%	0.78%	31.77%
New Zealand	4.37%	1.10%	25.18%
Australia	3.79%	0.74%	19.54%

The key column in this table is 'Ratio, WWI to WWII'. It shows that all five nations were able to reduce casualties substantially between World War I and World War II. Table 5 shows that, on average, a person in the Australian armed forces in World War II would have only 20 per cent of the chance of dying per year compared to a person serving in World War I.

The UK and the US committed the largest number of men, enjoyed the greatest political and command influence, and achieved remarkably similar fatality ratios, on average: 36.44 per cent fewer deaths per year in World War II than they would have expected if the World War I rate applied. This figure has been taken as the interwar improvement benchmark because these two nations dominate the three smaller allies.

Obviously these figures, which use overall numbers for all services, are not perfectly comparable, because countries had different service mixes from each other, and these were different between the two wars. Nevertheless, the approximation can be taken as strongly indicative.

One other assumption I have made is that however much the weapons and machinery changed during and between the wars, the tactics, weapons type and mix became relatively uniform across the five nations, given the transfer of equipment and knowledge between the nations. There is also a high degree of interoperability between the services. They all help each other in many ways.

Some may question battle conditions in World War I versus World War II. They are obviously not identical but they are internally consistent within the wars. This means that the ratios developed are consistent. I believe that the statistical analysis validates the comparison, highlighting the effectiveness of Australian leadership.

Canada, New Zealand and Australia achieved greater reductions in their fatality rates than the two major Allies. In numerical terms, Australia's position improved from suffering the second-worst death rate per year of these Allies in World War I, to suffering a slightly smaller death rate than Canada in World War II and slightly more than the United States.

As previously stated, Canada had fewer proportional fatalities in World War I than Australia, almost certainly because Canada had very strong government support from the start of the war. Then, from 9 June 1917, its army came under the command of a strong national leader in Lieutenant General Sir Arthur Currie.[8]

This was not the case for the Australian Army. It did not enjoy strong political support from its government, which meant that it only came under a strong unifying commander in Lieutenant General Sir John Monash more than a year later than the Canadians.

Australia's total military deaths in World War II numbered 39,654. Had Australia merely achieved the benchmark fatality improvement ratio of 36.44 per cent, its World War II fatality numbers would have been approximately 73,947. Thus, we can say that Australia's World War II management represents a saving of around 35,000 Australian lives over what would have occurred if Australia had only achieved the benchmark figure. Given the number of Australian fatalities that occurred in theatres where Blamey did not have command, it is most likely that the figure of 35,000 Australian lives saved actually *underestimates* the Blamey effect.

A further test was added to the one above. Table 6, overleaf, shows that once the impacts of Malaya, Singapore and Java as well as Bomber Command are removed, then almost all the drop in Australian fatalities accrue to Blamey.

The calculation in Table 6 indicates that Blamey, with 73.5 per cent of the armed force numbers, saved close to 35,000 lives during World War II. He probably saved more lives because of his influence over the other services. As the table stands, the Royal Australian Air Force and the Royal Australian Navy collectively have been credited with savings of around 12,000 service men and women together.

In the calculation, the losses from Malaya, Singapore and Jarva and Bomber Command have been excluded as these are extraordinary losses in circumstances not under Australian commanders' influence when the losses occurred.

Table 6: Estimate of Lives Saved by Blamey	
	Benchmark
Average WWII v WWI GB & US benchmark rate	36.44%
Actual rate for Australia	19.54%
Scale factor calculates expected from achieved	1.86%

	Deaths
Australian WWII deaths	**39,654**
Deaths Malaya, Singapore and Java & Bomber command	**12,303**
Australian WWII deaths less Malaya, Singapore and Java & Bomber command	**27,351**
Expected Australian WWII deaths by applying the scale factor	**73,947**
Modified reduction in Australian WWII deaths ex Malaya, Singapore and Java	**46,596**
Blamey's Army component of the reduction: 73.5%	**34,248**

Plausibility test

It is always difficult to quantify something that didn't actually happen within different countries' armed forces at different times. None of the figures I have used can be precise. Nevertheless, such comparisons are possible, and are commonly used by organisations of many types to measure leadership and foresight.

To test my approach in a very human and anecdotal way, I approached 14 senior Australian Army officers – two chiefs of the defence force, five major generals, four brigadiers and three colonels – some of them currently serving and some retired. I asked them whether my calculation that Blamey saved 35,000 World War II Diggers' lives sounded plausible. Twelve of them said the figure was indeed plausible; one declined to hazard an opinion; and one said, 'Probably more.' These senior officers did not check the calculations behind that number. Rather, they offered a rapid confirmation of how they rated Blamey as a commander, and his effect on the lives of his men.

No test can definitively estimate how many men's lives Blamey saved. The balance of probability is that he saved at least 35,000 Diggers, but it could easily be more.

APPENDIX

Basic Army Structure, Australia[1]

Formations	Organisation	Strength	Made up of		Commanded by
	Army	n/a	Two or more corps		General
	Corps	30,000 or more	Two or more divisions		Lieutenant general
	Division	10,000–20,000	Three brigades		Major general
	Brigade	2500–5000	World War I	World War II	Brigadier general/ colonel
			Four battalions	Three battalions	
Sub-units	Battalion	550–1000	Four companies	Four companies	Colonel/lieutenant colonel
	Company	100–225	Four platoons	Three platoons	Major
	Platoon	30–60	Four (later three) sections	Three sections	Lieutenant
	Section	~9–16			Corporal/sergeant

Notes:

1. This table indicates the usual construction of the core of the unit; in larger formations there will be more supporting units, including units for headquarters, administration, signals, air defence, etc, which will increase the overall number of personnel involved.
2. A regiment is not usually deployed as a whole, but is more of a permanent label of a group's identity. Thus, units from a particular regiment may be spread around an army.
3. The establishment number of an Army is not specified.

ACKNOWLEDGMENTS

The author wishes to thank the people who contributed to the development of this book and its fruition. Major General Jim Barry AM MBE RFD ED (Retd) inspired me to begin this project. He helped me considerably along the way with his wise counsel and by explaining the finer points of the military. He also deserves thanks for passing the manuscript to General Sir Peter John Cosgrove AK CVO MC (Retd) who subsequently wrote the generous foreword.

Others have helped by reading the manuscript and offering constructive comments. These include fellow author Robert Hadler for his insights and advice over many hours. Colonel Marcus Fielding (Retd) offered advice and introduced me to Military Heritage and History Victoria whose span of interests in military matters has helped me immensely over the years. It is through this means that I met Professor David Horner AM FASSA, whose book on Blamey and other books on military command have been both an inspiration and a great source. I also thank him for allowing me to quote his work extensively. Sam Taylor provided me with valuable insights. Ted Blamey of the Blamey family gave support and willingly gave me access to family photographs and records.

Former Prime Minister the Honourable John Howard OM AC SSI took an interest in the book and generously introduced me to his publisher. Thanks also belong to my wife Merran Kelsall AO, who introduced the book to John Howard and who showed great patience and gave sage advice and guidance over the years it took to complete this book.

Thanks go to the folks at HarperCollins who supported and guided me while working hard on the manuscript and artwork.

ENDNOTES

Introduction

1 McCarthy, *South-West Pacific Area – First Year*, p. 334–335.
2 Carlyon, *I Remember Blamey*, p. 111.
3 Paull, *Retreat from Kokoda*, p. 258.
4 Reports of F.T. Smith (Collins Publishers), 23 July 1942, quoted in Horner, *Blamey*, p. 305.
5 Horner, *Blamey*, p. 162.

1. Building Character

1 Hetherington, *Blamey: Controversial Soldier*, p. 12.
2 Staff College Quetta, 'Final Report on T.A. Blamey', 10 July 1914, quoted in Horner, *Blamey*, pp. 21–22.
3 Blamey to his mother, 25 January 1914, quoted in Horner, *Blamey*, p. 22.

2. Hard Lessons

1 Hetherington, *Blamey: Controversial Soldier*, pp. 38–39.
2 *Ibid.*, p. 39.
3 Horner, *Blamey*, pp. 36–37.
4 Hetherington, *Blamey: Controversial Soldier*, p. 40.
5 'Gallipoli', dva.gov.au/media/media-backgrounders/gallipoli.
6 Walker to Bean, 16 August 1928, quoted in Horner, *Blamey*, p. 42.
7 Bean, *The Australian Imperial Force in France, 1916*, p. 862.
8 Recommendation, 6 October 1916, quoted in Horner, *Blamey*, p. 45.
9 Hetherington, *Blamey: Controversial Soldier*, p. 47.
10 Tibbitts, 'The Battles for Bullecourt', www.awm.gov.au/articles/blog/the-battles-for-bullecourt.
11 'Second Battle of Bullecourt', awm.gov.au/collection/E84360.
12 Horner, *Australia's Military History for Dummies*, p. 117.
13 Horner, *Blamey*, p. 49.
14 R. Perry, *Monash*, p. 193.
15 *Ibid.*, p. 247.
16 *Ibid.*, p. 247.
17 B. Lodge, *Lavarack: Rival General*, London: Robinson Reynolds, 2021, quoted in Henderson, 'A personal vendetta in Australian military history', thesydneyinstitute.com.au/blog/a-personal-vendetta-in-australian-military-history.

3. Monash's Apprentice

1 Monash to Major General George Johnston, 15 September 1918, quoted in Horner, *Blamey*, p. 50.

2 Bean, *The Australian Imperial Force in France: During the Allied Offensive, 1918*, p. 193.
3 Birdwood to Governor General Munro Ferguson, quoted in Horner, *Blamey*, p. 50.
4 Foott to Arthur Bazley (assistant to Charles Bean), 13 October 1939, quoted in *ibid.*, pp. 51–52.
5 Memoirs of Major General Sir Jack Stevens, p. 13, quoted in *ibid.*, p. 52.
6 Hetherington, *Blamey: The Biography of Field Marshall Sir Thomas Blamey*, pp. 47–48.
7 Monash, *The Australian Victories in France in 1918*, Kindle location 1071.
8 *Ibid.*, Kindle locations 1031–1048.
9 *Ibid.*, Kindle location 1162.
10 Bean, cited in Hetherington, *Blamey: Controversial Soldier*, p. 48.
11 Bean, *The Australian Imperial Force in France During the Allied Offensive, 1918*, pp. 326–327.
12 'Hamel: The textbook victory – 4 July 1918', awm.gov.au/visit/exhibitions/1918/battles/hamel.
13 Fleming, *The Australian Army in World War I*, p. 7.
14 Monash, *The Australian Victories in France in 1918*, Kindle locations 4513, 4332.
15 Horner, *Australia's Military History for Dummies*, p. 146.
16 'Mont St Quentin and Péronne: Australian victories', awm.gov.au/visit/exhibitions/1918/battles/mtstquentin.
17 Monash, *The Australian Victories in France in 1918*, Kindle location 4015.
18 *Ibid.*, Kindle locations 5050–5158.
19 *Ibid.*, Kindle location 5137.
20 *Ibid.*, Kindle location 5087.
21 Ludendorff, *Memoirs*, republished in *The Times*, 22 August 1919, quoted in Monash, *The Australian Victories in France in 1918*, Kindle location 2411.
22 R. Perry, *Monash*, p. 450.

4. Between the Wars

1 Blamey to Monash, 30 January 1919, quoted in Horner, *Blamey*, p. 60.
2 Blamey, 'The British Empire and the Pacific Problem', quoted in *ibid.*, p. 21.
3 Horner, *Blamey*, p. 82.
4 Hetherington, *Blamey: Controversial Soldier*, pp. 54–57.
5 R. Perry, *The Battle of the Generals*, Chapter 4.
6 Horner, *Blamey*, pp. 122–123.
7 'War Cabinet records', naa.gov.au/help-your-research/fact-sheets/war-cabinet-records.
8 Menzies, 'Foreword', in Hetherington, *Blamey: Controversial Soldier*, p. vii.
9 Gavin Long diary, interview with Menzies, 20 June 1946, AWM: AWM67, 1/11, quoted in Stockings and Connor (eds), *The Shadow Men*, p. 158.
10 Horner, *Blamey*, p. 129.

5. Australian Commander

1 R.R. Vial, *The War I Went To*, self-published, 1995, p. 4, quoted in Horner, *Blamey*, p. 134.
2 Wilmot to Bean, 14 August 1953, quoted in *ibid.*, p. 133.
3 Horner, *Blamey*, p. 134.
4 *Ibid.*, p. 153.
5 N. Carlyon, *I Remember Blamey*, p. 18.
6 *Ibid.*, pp. 20–21.
7 Hetherington, *Blamey: Controversial Soldier*, p. 106.
8 Horner, *Blamey*, p. 156.

9 Rowell, *Full Circle*, p. 50.
10 Freyberg, *Bernard Freyberg, VC*, p. 233.
11 Long, *To Benghazi*, p. 138.
12 Playfair, *The Early Successes Against Italy*, Kindle locations 5854–5902.
13 Long, *To Benghazi*, p. 203.
14 Stockings, *Bardia*, p. 276.
15 Playfair, *The Early Successes Against Italy*, Kindle location 6014.
16 Long, *To Benghazi*, p. 238.
17 Playfair, *The Early Successes Against Italy*, Kindle location 7411.
18 Horner, *Blamey*, p. 176.
19 *Ibid.*, p. 168.
20 Day, *Menzies and Churchill at War*, p. 43.
21 Rowell, *Full Circle*, p. 64.

6. A Lost Cause
1 Semmler, *The War Diaries of Kenneth Slessor*, p. 202, quoted in Horner, *Blamey*, pp. 160–161.
2 Long, *Greece, Crete and Syria*, p. 184.
3 *Ibid.*, pp. 182–183.
4 Dunnigan, *How to Make War*, p. 70; Haskew, *Artillery Compared and Contrasted: From World War 1 to the Present Day*, p. 60.
5 Long, *Greece, Crete and Syria*, p. 143.
6 N. Carlyon, *I Remember Blamey*, p. 42.
7 Long, *Greece, Crete and Syria*, p. 129.
8 N. Carlyon, *I Remember Blamey*, p. 42.
9 Special Order of the Day, 21 April 1941, War Diary, I Corps HQ, quoted in Horner, *Blamey*, p. 200.
10 N. Carlyon, *I Remember Blamey*, p. 43.
11 *Ibid.*, pp. 45–46.
12 *Ibid.*, p. 48.
13 Shedden, diary entry, recounting a conversation with Bridgeford on 5 June, quoted in Horner, *Blamey*, p. 198.
14 Olga Blamey, 'Shellfire and Orchids', c. 1951–1955, unpublished manuscript, quoted in Horner, *Blamey*, p. 198.
15 Ewer, *Forgotten Anzacs*, Kindle locations 3096–3099.
16 Rowell, *Full Circle*, p. 56.
17 Foott to Arthur Bazley (assistant to Charles Bean), 13 October 1939, quoted in Horner, *Blamey*, p. 51.
18 Notes by Savige on official history, quoted in *ibid.*, p. 195.
19 N. Carlyon, *I Remember Blamey*, p. 43.
20 *Ibid.*, p. 40.
21 Blamey to Sturdee, 26 June 1941, quoted in Horner, *Blamey*, p. 213.
22 Notes of interview with Wilson, undated, quoted in Horner, *Blamey*, p. 199.
23 Rowell, *Full Circle*, p. 79.
24 N. Carlyon, *I Remember Blamey*, p. 44.
25 *Ibid.*, p. 45.
26 *Ibid.*, p. 47.
27 Wavell, quoted in *ibid.*, p. 19.

7. Tragedy and Triumph
1 Dill to Wavell, 19 April 1941, quoted in Horner, *Blamey*, p. 210.
2 *Ibid.*
3 Notes of interview with Wavell's chief of staff, Lieutenant General Sir Arthur Smith, quoted in Horner, *Blamey*, p. 211.
4 Horner, *Blamey*, p. 211.

5 Herring, quoted in N. Carlyon, *I Remember Blamey*, p. 50.
6 Day, *Menzies and Churchill at War*, p. 160.
7 *Ibid.*
8 Beevor, *Crete*, p. 83.
9 Horner, *Blamey*, p. 218.
10 Blamey to Menzies, 7 June 1941, quoted in *ibid.*, p. 218.
11 N. Carlyon, *I Remember Blamey*, p. 59.

8. The Rats of Tobruk

1 Menzies to Chester Wilmot, 2 December 1948, quoted in Horner, *Blamey*, p. 170.
2 Bean, *The AIF in France, Vol V*, p. 301, cited in A. Hill, 'Lieutenant General Sir Leslie Morshead; Commander, 9th Australian Division', quoted in Horner, *The Commanders*, p. 184.
3 Maughan, *Tobruk and El Alamein*, p. 12.
4 A. Hill, 'Lieutenant-General Sir Leslie Morshead', in Horner, *The Commanders*, pp. 176–178.
5 Wavell, from Connell, *Wavell Scholar and Soldier*, pp. 385–386, quoted in Coombes, *Morshead*, p. 103.
6 Coombes, *Morshead*, p. 108.
7 Horner, *Blamey*, pp. 191–192.
8 Morshead, quoted in Horner, *The Commanders*, p. 181.
9 A. Hill, 'Lieutenant-General Sir Leslie Morshead', quoted in Horner, *Blamey*, pp. 180–81.
10 Miller, *The 9th Australian Division Versus the Africa Corps*, Kindle location 400.
11 *Ibid.*, Kindle locations 372–376.
12 Liddell Hart (ed.), *The Rommel Papers*, p. 132.
13 Corporal Allan Jones, letter, 14 May 1990, quoted in Johnston, *An Australian Band of Brothers*, p. 52.
14 A. Hill, 'Lieutenant-General Sir Leslie Morshead', in Horner, *The Commanders*, p. 181.
15 Miller, *The 9th Australian Division Versus the Africa Corps*, Kindle location 532.
16 Mitcham, *Triumphant Fox*, p. 88.
17 *Ibid.*, p. 86.
18 Freyberg, *Bernard Freyberg, VC*, p. 342.
19 Hetherington, *Blamey: The Biography of Field Marshall Sir Thomas Blamey*, p. 117.
20 Horner, *Blamey*, p. 231.
21 N. Carlyon, *I Remember Blamey*, p. 65.
22 *Ibid.*, pp. 66–67.
23 Freyberg, *Bernard Freyberg, VC*, p. 365.
24 N. Carlyon, *I Remember Blamey*, p. 68.
25 *Ibid.*, p. 69.
26 Horner, *Blamey*, p. 242.
27 N. Carlyon, *I Remember Blamey*, p. 72.
28 'Siege of Tobruk', awm.gov.au/articles/encyclopedia/tobruk.
29 N. Carlyon, *I Remember Blamey*, p. 75.
30 Horner, *Blamey*, p. 252.
31 N. Carlyon, *I Remember Blamey*, p. 79.

9. The Pacific War Begins

1 Young, 'The loss of Lark Force', awm.gov.au/articles/blog/the-loss-of-lark-force.
2 Horner, *Blamey*, pp. 258–260.

3 Calvocoressi, Wint and Pritchard, *The Penguin History of the Second World War*, p. 988.
4 *Ibid.*, p. 997.
5 'History of Australia–Malaysia defence relationship', malaysia.highcommission.gov.au/files/klpr/History%20of%20the%20Australia-Malaysia%20Defence%20Relationship.pdf.
6 Hetherington, *Blamey: Controversial Soldier*, p. 336.
7 Horner, *Australia's Military History for Dummies*, p. 234.
8 Curtin to Blamey, 20 February 1942, quoted in Horner, *Blamey*, p. 263.
9 Day, *John Curtin*, p. 453.
10 *Ibid.*, p. 456.
11 Horner, *Blamey*, p. 264.
12 *Ibid.*, p. 269.
13 N. Carlyon, *I Remember Blamey*, pp. 83–86.
14 'Japanese advance (December 1941 – March 1942)', anzacportal.dva.gov.au/wars-and-missions/world-war-ii-1939-1945/events/japanese-advance-december-1941-march-1942.
15 McCarthy, *South-West Pacific Area, First Year*, p. 24.
16 M. Perry, *The Most Dangerous Man in America*, p. 155.
17 Horner, *Blamey*, p. 274.
18 M. Perry, *The Most Dangerous Man in America*, p. 155.
19 *Ibid.*, p. 156.
20 *Ibid.*, p. 159.
21 *Ibid.*, p. 61.
22 Horner, *Blamey*, p. 264.
23 Press statement, 29 June 1942, cited in *ibid.*, p. 265.
24 Horner, *Blamey*, p. 267.
25 *Ibid.*, pp. 267–268.
26 Wilmot to his father, 2 January 1943, quoted in *ibid.*, p. 337.
27 R. Perry, *Pacific 360*, p. 168.
28 Perret, *Old Soldiers Never Die*, p. 286.
29 Wukovits, *Eisenhower*, pp. 74–76.
30 Horner, *Blamey*. pp. 283–284.
31 US Major General Thomas Handy to Marshall, 3 August 1942, quoted in Horner, *Blamey*, pp. 301–302.
32 Richardson to Marshall, 28 July 1942, and Minutes of Conference, 26 July 1942, quoted in *ibid.*, pp. 301–302.
33 Notes by Herring on draft official history, 19 March 1954, quoted in *ibid.*, pp. 395–396.
34 Horner, *The Evolution of Australian Higher Command Arrangements*, p. 14.
35 R. Perry, *The Battle of the Generals*, pp. 106–108.

10. 'Nobody in Their Right Senses Would Land There'

1 D. Horner, 'Australia in 1942: A pivotal year', in Dean (ed.), *Australia 1942*, pp. 21–22.
2 Calvocoressi, Wint and Pritchard, *The Penguin History of the Second World War*, pp. 1052–1058.
3 David Jenkins, 'Invasion warnings were ignored', *Sydney Morning Herald*, 14 August 1992, p. 6K., quoted in Horner, *Blamey*, p. 293.
4 K. James, 'On Australia's doorstep: Kokoda and Milne Bay', in Dean (ed.), *Australia 1942*, p. 202.
5 Horner, *Blamey*, p. 294.
6 Notes of discussion with MacArthur, 20 to 26 October 1942, cited in *ibid.*, p. 294.

7 Horner, *Blamey*, p. 296.
8 *Ibid.*, p. 299.
9 *Ibid.*, p. 302.
10 N. Carlyon, *I Remember Blamey*, p. 98.
11 McCarthy, *South-West Pacific Area, First Year*, p. 159.
12 K. James, 'On Australia's doorstep: Kokoda and Milne Bay', in Dean (ed.), *Australia 1942*, p. 202.
13 *Ibid.*, p. 202.
14 *Ibid.*, pp. 202–205.
15 R. Honner, 'The 39th at Isurava', in *Stand-To* magazine, July–August 1956, p. 12, quoted in K. James, 'On Australia's doorstep: Kokoda and Milne Bay', in Dean (ed.), *Australia 1942*, pp. 202–204.
16 Williams, *Japan's Pacific War*, p. 37.
17 Rowell, Wills to Gavin Long, 29 October 1942, G. Long Diary No. 9, p. 38, quoted in Horner, *Crisis of Command*, p. 126.
18 K. James, 'On Australia's doorstep: Kokoda and Milne Bay', in Dean (ed.), *Australia 1942*, p. 208.
19 Drea, *MacArthur's ULTRA*, pp. 44–46.
20 Brune, *A Bastard of a Place*, p. 297.
21 Johnston, *At the Front Line*, p. 41.
22 'List of casualties for Kokoda, Milne Bay and Buna–Gona', anzacportal.dva.gov.au/wars-and-missions/kokoda-track-1942-1943/resources/casualties-kokoda/list-casualties-kokoda-milne-bay-and-buna-gona.
23 McCarthy, *South-West Pacific Area, First Year*, p. 185.

11. Retreat to Victory

1 R. Honner, 'The 39th at Isurava', in *Stand-To* magazine, July–August 1956, p. 12, quoted in K. James, 'On Australia's doorstep: Kokoda and Milne Bay', in Dean (ed.), *Australia 1942*, p. 205.
2 K. James, 'On Australia's doorstep: Kokoda and Milne Bay', in Dean (ed.), *Australia 1942*, pp. 205–206.
3 Horner, *Blamey*, p. 323.
4 MacArthur to General George Marshall, 6 September 1942, quoted in McCarthy, *South-West Pacific Area, First Year*, p. 225.
5 Sadashige Imanishi, personal interview, quoted in Williams, *Japan's Pacific War*, pp. 34–35.
6 Ham, *Kokoda*, p. 243.
7 Reports of F.T. Smith (Collins Publishers), 11 September 1942, quoted in Horner, *Blamey*, p. 323.
8 George H. Johnston (war correspondent), *New Guinea Diary*, Sydney: Angus & Robertson, 1944, p. 156, quoted in Horner, *Blamey*, p. 324.
9 Kenney, *General Kenney Reports: A Personal History of the Pacific War*, Washington, D.C.: Office of Air Force History, 1987, p. 94, quoted in Horner, *Blamey*, p. 325.
10 Wilmot, 'Observations on the New Guinea campaign', quoted in Horner, *Blamey*, p. 324.
11 'Note of secraphone conversation between the Prime Minister and the Commander-in-Chief Southwest Pacific Area – 17/9/1942', quoted in Horner, *Blamey*, p. 326.
12 Horner, *Blamey*, p. 326.
13 K. James, 'On Australia's doorstep: Kokoda and Milne Bay', in Dean (ed.), *Australia 1942*, p. 212.
14 Horner, *Blamey*, p. 339.
15 Wilmot to Molesworth, 23 January 1943, quoted in *ibid.*, p. 328.
16 Blamey to Sturdee, 26 June 1941, quoted in *ibid.*, p. 213.

17 Rowell to Clowes, 22 September 1942, quoted in *ibid.*, p. 328.
18 N. Carlyon, *I Remember Blamey*, pp. 106–110.
19 Kenney, diary entry, 23 September 1942, quoted in Horner, *Blamey*, p. 330.
20 Rowell to Clowes, 27 September 1942, quoted in Horner, *Blamey*, p. 335.
21 Blamey, Rowell termination report, quoted in N. Carlyon, *I Remember Blamey*, p. 109.
22 Blamey to Curtin, 1 October 1942, quoted in Horner, *Blamey*, p. 334.
23 Rowell, *Full Circle*, p. 138.
24 Horner, *Blamey*, p. 339.
25 Eichelberger, *Our Jungle Road to Tokyo*, p. 29.
26 K. James, 'On Australia's doorstep: Kokoda and Milne Bay', in Dean (ed.), *Australia 1942*, p. 207.
27 Sublet, *Kokoda to the Sea*, p. 87.
28 Threlfall, *Jungle Warriors*, p. 92.
29 Horner, *Blamey*, p. 258.

12. Courting Controversy

1 Horner, *Blamey*, p. 348.
2 Herring's comments on draft official history, 15 May 1957, quoted in Horner, *Blamey*, p. 348.
3 Horner, *Blamey*, p. 349.
4 Russell, *The Second Fourteenth Battalion*, p. 183.
5 FitzSimons, *Kokoda*, p. 413, citing Jack Gallaway, *Odd Couple: Blamey and MacArthur at War*, p. 136.
6 Horner, *Blamey*, pp. 350–351.
7 Hetherington, *Blamey: Controversial Soldier*, p. 262.
8 *Horner, Blamey, p. 356.*
9 Russell, *The Second Fourteenth Battalion*, p. 219.
10 Eichelberger to Herring, letter, 27 November 1959.
11 Long, *The Final Campaigns*, p. 70.
12 Blamey to Birdwood, 20 November 1945, quoted in Horner, *Blamey*, p. 563.
13 Ham, *Kokoda*, pp. 278–279.
14 Horner, *Blamey*, p. 337.
15 K. James, 'On Australia's doorstep: Kokoda and Milne Bay', in Dean (ed.), *Australia 1942*, p. 212.
16 Horner, *Blamey*, p. 352.
17 N. Carlyon, *I Remember Blamey*, p. 111.
18 'Stanley Bisset (Stan) – Transcript of interview', australiansatwarfilmarchive.unsw.edu.au/archive/htmlTranscript/1223.
19 *Ibid.*
20 Sublet, *Kokoda to the Sea*, p. 88.
21 Horner, *Blamey*, p. 353.
22 I. Dougherty, quoted in McCarthy, *South-West Pacific Area, First Year*, pp. 334–335.
23 'Stanley Bisset (Stan) – Transcript of interview', australiansatwarfilmarchive.unsw.edu.au/archive/htmlTranscript/1223.
24 Russell, *The Second Fourteenth Battalion*, pp. 181–182.
25 Sublet, *Kokoda to the Sea*, p. 88.
26 I. Dougherty, quoted in McCarthy, *South-West Pacific Area, First Year*, pp. 334–335.
27 P.J. Dean, 'Anzacs and Yanks: US and Australian operations at the Beachhead battles', in Dean (ed.), *Australia 1942*, p. 236.
28 McCarthy *South-West Pacific Area, First Year*, pp. 146, 234, 334–335.
29 Williams, *The Kokoda Campaign, 1942*, p. 235.
30 Trelfall, *Jungle Warriors*, p. 83.

31 M.C.J. Welburn, 'The development of Australian Army doctrine 1945–64', Canberra: Australian National University, 1994, quoted in Trelfall, *Jungle Warriors*, p. 76.
32 Threlfall, *Jungle Warriors*, p. 95.
33 *Ibid.*, p. 111.
34 *Ibid.*, p. 145.
35 *Ibid.*, p. 144.
36 Johnston, *An Australian Band of Brothers*, p. 255.
37 Long, *The Final Campaigns*, p. 73.
38 Threlfall, *Jungle Warriors*, p. 174.
39 Bullard, 'Kokoda: A Japanese tragedy', p. 20.
40 Hetherington, *Blamey: Controversial Soldier*, p. 275.
41 Howie-Willis, *A Medical Emergency*, p. 315.

13. On the Ascendant
1 P.J. Dean, 'Anzacs and Yanks: US and Australian operations at the Beachhead battles', in Dean (ed.), *Australia 1942*, p. 219.
2 B. Lunney and R. Lunney, *Forgotten Fleet 2*, pp. 14–31.
3 Kenney, *General Kenney Reports*, quoted in Horner, *Crisis of Command*, p. 227.
4 Byers, diary, 30 November 1942; Eichelberger Dictations, I/7, Robert Eichelberger Papers, Duke University, Kenney, diary, 30 November 1942, quoted in Perret, *Old Soldiers Never Die*, p. 323.
5 Eichelberger, *Our Jungle Road to Tokyo*, p. 39.
6 Walker, *The Island Campaigns*, p. 121, cited in Howie-Willis, *A Medical Emergency*, p. 262.
7 Eichelberger, *Dictations, Book 4*, pp. VIII35, VIII36, quoted in Horner, *Blamey*, p. 302.
8 Eichelberger, *Our Jungle Road to Tokyo*, p. 48.
9 *Ibid.*
10 Blamey to Curtin, 4 November, quoted in Horner, *Crisis of Command*, pp. 236–237.
11 Dickens, *Never Late: The 2/9th Australian Infantry Battalion, 1939–1945*, p. 236, quoted in P.J. Dean, 'Anzacs and Yanks: US and Australian operations at the Beachhead battles', in Dean (ed.), *Australia 1942*, p. 234.
12 P.J. Dean, 'Anzacs and Yanks: US and Australian operations at the Beachhead battles', in Dean (ed.), *Australia 1942*, p. 234.
13 Horner, *Crisis of Command*, p. 241.
14 Blamey to MacArthur, 26 December 1942, quoted in *ibid.*, pp. 251–252.
15 Horner, *Blamey*, p. 376.
16 *Ibid.*
17 Vasey to his wife, 5 January 1942, quoted in *ibid.*, p. 380.
18 Luvaas (ed.), *Dear Miss Em: General Eichelberger's war in the Pacific, 1942–1945*, Greenwood Press, 1972, p. 54, quoted in Horner, *Blamey*, p. 381.
19 Eichelberger, *Our Jungle Road to Tokyo*, p. 54.
20 Williams, *Japan's Pacific War*, p. 63.
21 'List of casualties for Kokoda, Milne Bay and Buna–Gona', anzacportal.dva.gov.au/wars-and-missions/kokoda-track-1942-1943/resources/casualties-kokoda/list-casualties-kokoda-milne-bay-and-buna-gona.
22 Willoughby (ed.), *Reports of General MacArthur*, Vol. 2, Pt 2, p. 188.
23 Williams, *Japan's Pacific War*, pp. 53–54.
24 'List of casualties for Kokoda, Milne Bay and Buna–Gona', anzacportal.dva.gov.au/wars-and-missions/kokoda-track-1942-1943/resources/casualties-kokoda/list-casualties-kokoda-milne-bay-and-buna-gona.

25 Conlon, in Ryan, *Brief Lives*, pp. 34–35, quoted in Sligo, *The Backroom Boys*, pp. 29, 34.
26 McCarthy, *South-West Pacific Area, First Year*, p. 591.

14. Australia's Most Successful Year
1 Horner, *Blamey*, p. 385.
2 *Ibid.*, p. 391.
3 *Ibid.*, p. 388.
4 Notes of discussions with Commander-in-Chief South West Pacific Area, Brisbane, 16 to 20 January 1943, CRS A5954, box 2, quoted in *ibid.*, p. 389.
5 Horner, *Blamey*, pp. 389–399.
6 Hetherington, *Blamey: Controversial Soldier*, p. 292.
7 Morshead to Curtin, quoted in Hetherington, *Blamey: Controversial Soldier*, p. 301.
8 D. Coombes, *Morshead: Hero of Tobruk and El Alamein*, Oxford University Press, 2001, p. 163, cited by Horner, 'Deciding Australian War Strategy in 1943' in Dean (ed.), *Australia 1943: The Liberation of New Guinea*, p. 44.
9 Hamilton, *Monty: The Making of a General 1887–1942*, p. 817; Hamilton, *The Man Behind the Legend*, p. 135, quoted in Coombes, *Morshead*, p. 153.
10 Forde to Blamey, 9 April 1943, BP, 4/17; Blamey to Forde, 9 April 1943, BP, 4/17, quoted in Horner, *Blamey*, p. 397.
11 P.J. Dean, 'Strategy, Command and Plans for the 1943 Offensives', in Dean (ed.), *Australia 1943: The Liberation of New Guinea*, Kindle locations 1434–1438.
12 B. Nelson, 'Foreword', in Dean (ed.), *Australia 1943: The Liberation of New Guinea*, Kindle locations 66–72.
13 R. Mallet, 'Logistics and the Cartwheel operations', in Dean (ed.), *Australia 1943: The Liberation of New Guinea*, Kindle location 3416.
14 Horner, *Blamey*, p. 407.
15 P.J. Dean, 'MacArthur's War Strategy, Command and Plans for the 1943 Offensives', in Dean (ed.), *Australia 1943: The Liberation of New Guinea*, Kindle location 1453.
16 Horner, *Blamey*, pp. 415–416.
17 *Ibid.*, pp. 416, 418.
18 Williams, *Japan's Pacific War*, p. 78.
19 K. James, 'Salamaua Magnet', in Dean (ed.), *Australia 1943: The Liberation of New Guinea*, Kindle location 4079.
20 *Ibid.*, Kindle locations 4054–4059.
21 *Ibid.*, Kindle locations 4126–4128.
22 P.J. Dean, 'From the Air, Sea and Land: The Capture of Lae', in Dean (ed.), *Australia 1943: The Liberation of New Guinea*, Kindle locations 4516–5737.
23 Dean (ed.), *Australia 1943: The Liberation of New Guinea*, Kindle location 231.

15. The High Point of Australian Military Operations
1 L. Grant, 'Operations in the Markham and Ramu Valleys', in Dean (ed.), *Australia 1943: The Liberation of New Guinea*, Kindle locations 4746–4747.
2 Dexter, *The New Guinea Offensives*, p. 422.
3 *Ibid.*, p. 689.
4 Vasey to his wife, 24 December 1943, Vasey Papers, quoted in Horner, *Blamey*, p. 432.
5 Vasey, quoted in Dexter, *The New Guinea Offensives*, p. 761.
6 Bradley, *The Battle for Shaggy Ridge*, p. 273.
7 *Ibid.*, p. 219.
8 G. Pratten, 'Securing the Huon Peninsula', quoted in Dean (ed.), *Australia 1943: The Liberation of New Guinea*, Kindle location 5387.

9 *Ibid.*, Kindle locations 5268–5270.
10 *Ibid.*, Kindle locations 5344–5358.
11 *Ibid.*, Kindle locations 5658–5659.
12 Dexter, *The New Guinea Offensives*, pp. 727, 734.
13 P.J. Dean, 'Securing the Huon Peninsula', quoted in Dean (ed.), *Australia 1943: Liberation of New Guinea*, Kindle location 5975.
14 Dexter, *The New Guinea Offensives*, p. 817.
15 *Ibid.*
16 B. Nelson, 'Foreword', in Dean (ed.), *Australia 1943: Liberation of New Guinea*, Kindle locations 66–72.
17 P.J. Dean, 'Conclusion: 1943 and Beyond', in Dean (ed.), *Australia 1943: The Liberation of New Guinea*, Kindle location 5993.

16. Fighting for a Place at the International Table

1 K. James, 'The unnecessary waste: Australians in the late Pacific campaigns', in Stockings (ed.), *Anzac's Dirty Dozen*, p. 143.
2 Minutes of War Cabinet meeting, October 1943, quoted in D. Horner, 'Advancing National Interests: Deciding Australia's War Strategy, 1944–45', in Dean (ed.), *Australia 1944–45*, p. 13.
3 Hillgarth, report on a visit to Australia, 6 to 28 March 1944, quoted in Horner, *Blamey*, p. 447.
4 Unless otherwise indicated, the following account of Blamey's trip to the US and UK relies on Horner, *Blamey*, pp. 447–453.
5 Day, *Curtin*, pp. 592–595.
6 D. Horner, 'Advancing National Interests: Deciding Australia's War Strategy, 1944–45', in Dean (ed.), *Australia 1944–45*, p. 16.
7 Brooke, diary, quoted in Horner, *Blamey*, pp. 454, 455.
8 Horner, *Blamey*, pp. 487, 458.
9 Shedden, diary, cited in Horner, *Blamey*, p. 459.
10 'Much Yet to Do', *Age*, 28 June 1944, quoted in Horner, *Blamey*, p. 463.
11 D. Horner, 'Advancing National Interests: Deciding Australia's War Strategy, 1944–45', in Dean (ed.), *Australia 1944–45*, p. 17–19.
12 Minutes of Prime Minister's War Conference, Canberra, 27 September 1943, NAA: A5954, 4/2, quoted in D. Horner, 'Advancing national interests: Deciding Australia's war strategy, 1944–45', in Dean (ed.), *Australia* 1944–45, p. 14. 4
13 D. Clayton James, *The Years of MacArthur, Volume Two: 1941–1945*, Boston: Houghton Mifflin, 1975, pp. 716–17, quoted in D. Horner, 'Advancing national interests: Deciding Australia's war strategy, 1944–45', in Dean (ed.), *Australia* 1944–45, p. 22.
14 Blamey to Berryman, letter, AWM: 3DRL6643, 2/43.68; Curtin to MacArthur, letter, AWM: 3DRL6643, 2/23.11, quoted in D. Horner, 'Advancing national interests: Deciding Australia's war strategy, 1944–45', in Dean (ed.), *Australia 1944–45*, p. 21–22.

17. 'Mopping Up'

1 L. Grant, '"Given a second rate job": Campaigns in Aitape–Wewak and New Britain, 1944–45', in Dean (ed.), *Australia 1944–45*, p. 214.
2 *Ibid.*, p. 216.
3 *Ibid.*, pp. 217–218.
4 Horner, *Blamey*, p. 489.
5 Williams, *Japan's Pacific War*, p. 116; L. Grant., '"Given a second rate job": Campaigns in Aitape–Wewak and New Britain, 1944–45', in Dean (ed.), *Australia 1944–45*, p. 220.

6 L. Grant, '"Given a second rate job": Campaigns in Aitape–Wewak and New Britain, 1944–45', in Dean (ed.), *Australia 1944–45*, p. 219.
7 Australian Field Censorship Coy Report, 27 April 1945, quoted in *ibid.*, p. 221.
8 L. Grant, '"Given a second rate job": Campaigns in Aitape–Wewak and New Britain, 1944–45', in Dean (ed.), *Australia 1944–45*, p. 222.
9 *Ibid.*, p. 225.
10 K. James, 'More than Mopping Up: Bougainville', in Dean (ed.), *Australia 1944–45*, p. 225.
11 *Ibid.*, p. 233.
12 *Ibid.*, p. 234.
13 *Ibid.*, p. 239.
14 *Ibid.*, p. 241.
15 *Ibid.*, pp. 242–244.
16 *Ibid.*, p. 245.
17 *Ibid.*, p. 246.
18 Horner, *Blamey*, p. 515.
19 K. James, 'More than Mopping Up: Bougainville', in Dean (ed.), *Australia 1944–45*, p. 248.
20 *Ibid.*, p. 232.
21 L. Grant, '"Given a second rate job": Campaigns in Aitape–Wewak and New Britain, 1944–45', in Dean (ed.), *Australia 1944–45*, p. 225.
22 *Ibid.*, p. 226.

18. Countdown to Surrender
1 Long, *Final Campaigns*, p.329.
2 D. Horner, 'Advancing national interests: Deciding Australia's war strategy, 1944–45', in Dean (ed.), *Australia 1944–45*, pp. 23–24.
3 Berryman, diary, quoted in Horner, *Blamey*, p. 513.
4 Unless otherwise noted, information regarding planning and transport to Borneo comes from R. Crawley and P. Dean, 'Amphibious warfare: training and logistics, 1942–45', in Dean (ed.), *Australia 1944–45*, pp. 257–277.
5 Unless otherwise noted, information regarding the invasion of Tarakan comes from T. Hastings and P. Stanley, '"To capture Tarakan": Was Operation Oboe I unnecessary?', in Dean (ed.), *Australia 1944–45*, pp. 278–297.
6 *Ibid.*, p. 293.
7 G. Pratten, '"Calling the tune": Australian and Allied operations at Balikpapan', in Dean (ed.), *Australia 1944–45*, p. 323. (Unless otherwise noted, information regarding the Balikpapan campaign comes from this source, pp. 320–340.)
8 Anderson, 'Matilda Frog and "Murray FT" flame tank', tanks-encyclopedia.com/ww2/australia/matilda-frog-and-murray-ft-flame-tank/.
9 G. Pratten, '"Unique in the history of the AIF": Operations in British Borneo', in Dean (ed.), *Australia 1944–45*, p. 300. (Unless otherwise noted, information regarding the invasion of Brunei Bay comes from this source, pp. 298–319.)
10 Berryman, diary, 9 September 1945, quoted in Horner, *Blamey*, p. 554.
11 Surrender of Japanese forces: Address delivered by General Sir Thomas Blamey, Morotai, 9 September 1945, quoted in Horner, *Blamey*, p. 555.
12 'Never happier, says Japanese soldier', *Canberra Times*, 12 March 1974, p. 5.

19. Fractious Finish
1 Long, *The Final Campaigns*, p. 61.
2 Horner, *Blamey*, p. 548.
3 *Ibid.*

4 *Ibid.*, pp. 548–541.
5 Long, *The Final Campaigns*, p. 585.
6 Blamey to Forde, 15 September 1945, quoted in Horner, *Blamey*, p. 557.
7 Horner, *Blamey*, pp. 559, 560, 562, 573.
8 Dan Dwyer (Blamey's military assistant), 'Interlude with Blamey', unpublished typescript, 1970, p. 71, quoted in Horner, *Blamey*, p. 559.
9 Horner, *Blamey*, p. 561.
10 Blamey to Forde, 17 November 1945, quoted in Horner, *Blamey*, pp. 557–558.
11 Dwyer, 'Interlude with Blamey', pp. 93–94, quoted in Horner, *Blamey*, p. 562.
12 Hetherington, *Blamey: Controversial Soldier*, p. 380.
13 Rowell, *Full Circle*, p. 159.
14 Hetherington, *Blamey: Controversial Soldier*, pp. 389–392.
15 *Ibid.*
16 MacArthur, *Reminiscences*, p. 157.

20. Blamey's Legacy
1 Long, *The Final Campaigns*, pp. 585–586.
2 Monash, *Australian Victories in France in 1918*, Kindle location 1804.
3 Long, *The Final Campaigns*, p. 586.
4 Horner, *Blamey*, p. xv.

Epilogue
1 Long, *The Final Campaigns*, p. 635.
2 Source: Long, *The Final Campaigns*, pp. 633–634.
3 Horner, *Australia's Military History for Dummies*, p. 215.
4 Sources: Horner, *Australia's Military History for Dummies*, pp. 228, 234; Long, *The Final Campaigns*, p. 634; Battle for Singapore, Australian War Memorial, awm.gov.au/collection/E84308; Fall of Singapore, Department of Veterans' Affairs, www.dva.gov.au/newsroom/media-centre/media-backgrounders/fall-singapore.
5 Source: see Bibliography, 'Enlistment and Casualty Sources, World War I'.
6 Source: see Bibliography, 'Enlistment and Total Deaths Sources, World War II'.
7 Source: Tables 3 and 4.
8 Cook, *The Madman and the Butcher*, pp. 1–10.

Appendix
1 Source: 'Structure', awm.gov.au/learn/understanding-military-structure/army/structure.

BIBLIOGRAPHY

General Sources

Books

Appleman, Roy E.; Burns, James M.; Gugeler, Russell A.; and Stevens, John. *Okinawa: The Last Battle*. Washington, D.C.: Center of Military History, United States Army, 1948.

Arnold, Michael. *Hollow Heroes: An Unvarnished Look at the Wartime Careers of Churchill, Montgomery and Mountbatten*. Havertown, Philadelphia, and Oxford: Casemate, 2015.

Battistelli, Pier Paolo. *Afrikakorps Soldier 1941–43*. Oxford: Osprey, 2010.

Bean, Charles. *The Story of Anzac, From 4 May, 1915, to the Evacuation of the Gallipoli Peninsula*. Official History of Australia in the War of 1914–1918, Volume II. Sydney: Angus & Robertson, 1924.

_____ *The Australian Imperial Force in France, 1916*. Official History of Australia in the War of 1914–1918, Volume III. Sydney: Angus & Robertson, 1929.

_____ *The Australian Imperial Force in France During the Allied Offensive, 1918*. Official History of Australia in the War of 1914–1918, Volume VI. Sydney: Angus & Robertson, 1942.

Beevor, Antony. *Crete: The Battle and the Resistance*. London: John Murray, 2005.

Bradley, Phillip. *The Battle for Shaggy Ridge*, Sydney: Allen & Unwin, 2021.

Brune, Peter. *A Bastard of a Place: The Australians in Papua*. Sydney: Allen & Unwin, 2003.

Burns, John Henry. *The Brown and Blue Diamond at War: The Story of the 2/27th Battalion AIF*. Adelaide: 2/27th Battalion Ex-Servicemen's Association, 1960.

Byrd, Martha. *A World in Flames: A Concise History of World War II*. New York: Smithmark, 1992.

Calvocoressi, Peter; Wint, Guy; and Pritchard, John. *The Penguin History of the Second World War*. London: Penguin, 1999.

Carlyon, Les. *The Great War*. Australia: Picador, 2007.

Carlyon, Norman. *I Remember Blamey*. Australia: Sun, 1981.

Cathcart, Michael. *Defending the National Tuckshop: Australia's Secret Army Intrigue of 1931*. Melbourne: McPhee Gribble, 1989.

Chalfont, Alun. *Montgomery of Alamein*. London: Weidenfeld & Nicolson, 1976.

Coatney, Careyn. *John Curtin: How He Won Over the Media*. Melbourne: Australian Scholarly Publishing, 2016.

Cook, Tim. *The Madman and the Butcher: The Sensational Wars of Sam Hughes and General Arthur Currie*. Toronto: Allen Lane, 2010.

Coombes, David. *Morshead: Hero of Tobruk and El Alamein*. Melbourne: Oxford University Press, 2001.

Corrigan, Gordon. *Blood, Sweat and Arrogance and the Myths of Churchill's War*. London: Phoenix, 2007.

Coulthard-Clark, Chris. *Where Australians Fought: the Encyclopaedia of Australia's Battles*. Sydney: Allen & Unwin, 1998.

Curran, Tom. *The Grand Deception: Churchill and the Dardanelles*. Kindle edition. Sydney: Big Sky, 2015.

Davies, Norman. *Europe at War 1939–1945: No Simple Victory*. London: Pan MacMillan, 2006.

Day, David. *Menzies and Churchill at War*. Sydney: Angus & Robertson, 1986.

_____ *John Curtin: A Life*. Kindle edition. Sydney: HarperCollins, 2014.

De Groot, Gerard J. *Douglas Haig, 1861–1928*. London: Unwin Hyman, 1988.

Dean, Peter J. (ed). *Australia 1942: In the Shadow of War*. Kindle edition. Melbourne: Cambridge University Press, 2013.

_____ *Australia 1943: The Liberation of New Guinea*. Kindle edition. Melbourne: Cambridge University Press, 2014.

_____ *Australia 1944–45: Victory in the Pacific*. Kindle edition. Melbourne: Cambridge University Press, 2016.

Deighton, Len. *Blood, Tears and Folly*. London: Vintage, 2007.

D'Este, Carlo. *Warlord: A Life of Churchill at War, 1874–1945*. London: Allen Lane, 2009.

Dexter, David. *The New Guinea Offensives*. Australia in the War of 1939–1945, Series One: Army, Volume VI. Canberra: Australian War Memorial, 1961.

Dougherty, Martin J. *Tanks Compared and Contrasted: From World War I to the Present Day*. Melbourne: Hinkler, 2010.

Douglas-Home, Charles. *Rommel*. London: Weidenfeld & Nicolson, 1973.

Drea, Edward J. *MacArthur's ULTRA: Codebreaking and the War Against Japan, 1942–1945*. Lawrence, Kansas: University Press of Kansas, 1992.

Duffy, James P. *War at the End of the World: Douglas MacArthur and the Forgotten Fight for New Guinea*. New York: New American Library, 2016.

Dunnigan, James F. *How to Make War: A Comprehensive Guide to Modern Warfare*. London: Quill, 2003.

Eichelberger, Robert L. *Our Jungle Road to Tokyo*. Kindle edition. New York: Viking, 1950.

Eisenhower, Dwight D. *Crusade in Europe*. Baltimore and London: John Hopkins University Press, 1948.

Ellis, John. *World War II: A Statistical Survey*. New York: Facts on File, 1993.

Evans, Richard J. *The Third Reich at War*. London: Penguin, 2006.

Ewer, Peter. *Forgotten Anzacs: The Campaign in Greece, 1941*. Kindle edition. Melbourne: Scribe, 2016.

Fay, Peter W. *The Forgotten Army: India's Armed Struggle for Independence 1942–1945*. Ann Arbor, Michigan: University of Michigan Press, 1995.

Fleming, Robert. *The Australian Army in World War I*. Oxford: Osprey, 2012.

Frank, Richard B. *MacArthur*. New York: Palgrave MacMillan, 2007.

Freyberg, Peter. *Bernard Freyberg, VC: Soldier of Two Nations*. London: Hodder & Stoughton, 1991.

Gallaway, Jack. *The Odd Couple: Blamey and MacArthur at War*. St Lucia: University of Queensland Press, 2000.

Grant, Ulysses S. *Personal Memoirs of U. S. Grant*. Volume 1. Kindle edition. New York: Charles L. Webster, 1886.

Griffith, Paddy. *Battle Tactics on the Western Front: The British Army's Art of Attack 1916–1918*. New Haven and London: Yale University Press, 1994

Guderian, Heinz. *Panzer Leader*. Kindle edition. London: Penguin, 2009.

Ham, Paul. *Kokoda*. Sydney: HarperCollins, 2004.

Hamilton, Nigel. *Monty: The Making of a General 1887–1942*. London: Hamish Hamilton, 1981.

_____ *Master of the Battlefield: Monty's War Years 1942–1944*. New York: McGraw-Hill, 1983.

_____ *Monty: Final Years of the Field-Marshall 1944–1976*. New York: McGraw-Hill, 1987.

_____ *Montgomery: D-Day Commander*. Washington, D.C.: Potomac, 2007.

Hammel, Eric. *Islands of Hell: The US Marines in the Western Pacific 1944–1945*. Minneapolis: Zenith, 2010.

Haskew, Michael E. *Artillery Compared and Contrasted: From World War 1 to the Present Day*. Melbourne: Hinkler, 2010.

Herman, Arthur. *Freedom's Forge: How American Business Produced Victory in World War II*. Kindle edition. New York: Random House, 2012.

_____ *Douglas MacArthur*. Kindle edition. New York: Random House, 2016.

Herwig, Holger H. *The Marne, 1914: The Opening of World War I and the Battle that Changed the World*. New York: Random House, 2009.

Hetherington, John. *Blamey: The Biography of Field-Marshal Sir Thomas Blamey*. Sydney: F.W. Cheshire, 1954.

_____ *Blamey: Controversial Soldier*. Canberra: Australian War Memorial and Australian Government Publishing Service, 1973.

Horner, David. *Crisis of Command: Australian Generalship and the Japanese Threat.* Canberra: Australian National University Press, 1978.

_____ *The Gunners: A History of Australian Artillery.* Sydney: Allen & Unwin, 1995.

_____ *Blamey: The Commander-in-Chief.* Sydney: Allen & Unwin, 1998.

_____ *Australia's Military History for Dummies.* Milton, Queensland: Wiley, 2010.

_____ *The War Game: Australian War Leadership From Gallipoli to Iraq.* Sydney: Allen & Unwin, 2022.

_____ (ed). *The Commanders: Australian Military Leadership in the Twentieth Century.* Sydney: Allen & Unwin, 1984.

Howie-Willis. *A Medical Emergency: Major General 'Ginger' Burston and the Army Medical Service in World War II.* Sydney: Big Sky, 2012.

James, Andrew. *Stan Bisset: Kokoda Wallaby.* Melbourne: Allen & Unwin, 2011.

James, D. Clayton. *The Years of MacArthur, Volume 1: 1880–1941.* Boston: Houghton Mifflin, 1970.

Janowitz, Morris. *The Professional Soldier.* New York: The Free Press, 1971.

Jans, Nicholas. *Leadership Secrets of the Australian Army.* Sydney: Allen & Unwin, 2018.

Johnston, Mark. *At the Front Line: Experiences of Australian Soldiers in World War II.* Melbourne: Cambridge University Press, 1996.

_____ *The Silent 7th: An Illustrated History of the 7th Australian Division 1940–46.* Sydney: Allen & Unwin, 2005.

_____ *An Australian Band of Brothers.* Sydney: University of New South Wales Press, 2018.

Kennedy, Paul. *Engineers of Victory: The Problem Solvers Who Turned the Tide in the Second World War.* Kindle edition. London: Penguin, 2013.

King, Michael. *The Penguin History of New Zealand.* Auckland: Penguin, 2003.

Liddell Hart, Basil H. (ed). *The Rommel Papers.* London: Hamlyn, 1984.

Lindsay, Patrick. *The Coast Watchers: Behind Enemy Lines – The Men Who Saved the Pacific*. Sydney: William Heinemann, 2010.

Livesey, Jack. *The Illustrated Guide to Armoured Fighting Vehicles of the World*. London: Hermes House, 2007.

Long, Gavin. *To Benghazi*. Australia in the War of 1939–1945, Series One: Army, Volume I. Canberra: Australian War Memorial, 1961 (reprint).

_____ *Greece, Crete and Syria*. Australia in the War of 1939–1945, Series One: Army, Volume II. Canberra: Australian War Memorial, 1953.

_____ *The Final Campaigns*. Australia in the War of 1939–1945, Series One: Army, Volume VII. Canberra: Australian War Memorial, 1963.

Lunney, Bill; and Lunney, Ruth. *Forgotten Fleet 2*. Medowie, New South Wales: Forfleet, 2004.

MacArthur, Douglas. *Reminiscences*. New York: McGraw-Hill, 1964.

McCarthy, Dudley. *South-West Pacific Area, First Year: Kokoda to Wau*. Australia in the War of 1939–1945, Series One: Army, Volume V. Canberra: Australian War Memorial, 1959.

McDonald, Neil. *Damien Parer's War*. Melbourne: Lothian, 2003.

Manchester, William. *American Caesar: Douglas MacArthur 1880–1964*. Richmond, Virginia: Hutchinson, 1978.

Marston, Daniel (ed). *The Pacific War: From Pearl Harbor to Hiroshima*. Oxford: Osprey, 2010.

Maughan, Barton. *Tobruk and El Alamein*. Australia in the War of 1939–1945, Series One: Army, Volume III. Canberra: Australian War Memorial, 1966.

Miller, Ward A. *The 9th Australian Division Versus the Africa Corps: An Infantry Division Against Tanks – Tobruk, Libya, 1941*. Fort Leavenworth, Kansas: US Army Command and General Staff College, 1986.

Mitcham Jr, Samuel W. *Rommel's Desert War: The Life and Death of the Afrika Korps*. Mechanicsburg, Pennsylvania: Stackpole, 2007.

_____ *Triumphant Fox: Erwin Rommel and the Rise of the Afrika Korps*. Kindle edition. Mechanicsburg, Pennsylvania: Stackpole, 2009.

Monash, John. *Australian Victories in France in 1918*. London: Hutchinson & Co., 1920.

Montgomery, Bernard L. *Normandy to the Baltic*. London: Hutchinson & Co., 1947.

_____ *El Alamein to the River Sangro*. London: Hutchinson & Co., 1948.

_____ *El Alamein to the River Sangro and Normandy to the Baltic*. London: Barry & Jenkins, 1973.

_____ *The Memoirs of Field Marshal Montgomery*. Kindle edition. Barnsley, South Yorkshire: Pen & Sword, 2012.

Mosier, John. *The Blitzkrieg Myth: How Hitler and the Allies Misread the Strategic Realities of World War II*. New York: Perennial, 2004.

Mueller, Joseph. *Guadalcanal 1942: The Marines Strike Back*. Oxford: Osprey, 1992.

Overy, Richard. *War in the Pacific*. Sydney: Allen & Unwin, 2010.

Perret, Geoffrey. *There's a War to Be Won: The United States Army in World War II*. New York: Random House, 1991.

_____ *Old Soldiers Never Die: The Life of Douglas MacArthur*. London: Andre Deutsch, 1996.

Perry, Mark. *Partners in Command: George Marshall and Dwight Eisenhower in War and Peace*. New York: Penguin, 2007.

_____ *The Most Dangerous Man in the World: The Making of Douglas MacArthur*. Kindle edition. New York: Basic Books, 2014.

Perry, Roland. *Monash: The Outsider Who Won the War*. Sydney: Random House, 2007.

_____ *Pacific 360: Australia's Battle for Survival in World War II*. Sydney: Hachette, 2012.

_____ *Monash and Chauvel: How Australia's Two Greatest Generals Changed the Course of World History*. Kindle edition. Sydney: Allen & Unwin, 2017.

_____ *Anzac Sniper*. Sydney: HarperCollins, 2018.

_____ *The Battle of the Generals: MacArthur, Blamey and the Defence of Australia in World War II*. Kindle edition. Sydney: Allen & Unwin, 2024.

Paull, Raymond. *Retreat from Kokoda*. Melbourne: Heineman, 1958.
Pfennigwerth, Ian. *The Royal Australian Navy and MacArthur*. Sydney: Rosenberg, 2009.
Playfair, I.S.O. *The Early Successes Against Italy (To May 1941)*. History of the Second World War, United Kingdom Military Series, The Mediterranean and Middle East, Volume I. Kindle edition. London: Her Majesty's Stationery Office, 1954.
_____ *The Germans Come to the Help of Their Ally (1941)*. History of the Second World War, United Kingdom Military Series, The Mediterranean and Middle East, Volume II. Kindle edition. London: Her Majesty's Stationery Office, 1954.
_____ *British Fortunes Reach their Lowest Ebb*. History of the Second World War, United Kingdom Military Series, The Mediterranean and Middle East, Volume III. Kindle edition. London: Her Majesty's Stationery Office, 1960.
_____ *The Destruction of Axis Forces in Africa*. History of the Second World War, United Kingdom Military Series, The Mediterranean and Middle East, Volume IV. Kindle edition. London: Her Majesty's Stationery Office, 1966.
Plowman, Jeffrey. *Greece 1941: The Death Throes of Blitzkrieg*. Barnsley, South Yorkshire: Pen & Sword, 2018._
Ray, John. *The Battle of Britain: Dowding and the First Victory, 1940*. London: Cassel, 2009.
Rogan, Eugene. *The Fall of the Ottomans: The Great War in the Middle East 1914–1920*. Kindle edition. Penguin, 2015.
Rommel, Erwin. *Infantry Attacks*. London: Greenhill, 1990.
Rottman, Gordon L. *Saipan & Tinian 1944*. Oxford: Osprey, 2002.
_____ *Okinawa 1945*. Oxford: Osprey, 2005.
_____ *US Combat Engineer 1941–45*. Oxford: Osprey, 2010.
Rowell, Sydney F. *Full Circle*. Melbourne: Melbourne University Press, 1974.
Russell, W.B. *The Second Fourteenth Battalion: A History of an Australian Infantry Battalion in the Second World War*. Sydney: Angus & Robertson, 1948.
Sears, David. *The Last Epic Naval Battle: Voices from Leyte Gulf*. New York: Nal Caliber, 2007.

Serle, Geoffrey. *John Monash: A Biography*. Melbourne: Melbourne University Press, 1982.

Showalter, Dennis. *Patton and Rommel*. New York: Berkeley, 2005.

_____ *Hitler's Panzers: The Lightning Attacks that Revolutionized Warfare*. New York: Berkeley, 2009.

Sligo, Graeme. *The Backroom Boys*. Sydney: Big Sky, 2013.

Smith, Peter. *Dive Bomber: Aircraft, Techniques, and Tactics in World War II*. London: Casemate, 2008.

Stevenson, David. *1914 –1918: The History of the First World War*. London: Penguin, 2005.

Stockings, Craig. *Bardia: Myth, Reality and the Heirs of Anzac*. Sydney: University of New South Wales Press, 2009.

_____ (ed). *Anzac's Dirty Dozen: 12 Myths of Australian Military History*. Sydney: NewSouth, 2018.

Stockings, Craig; and Connor, John (eds). *The Shadow Men: The Leaders Who Shaped the Australian Army from the Veldt to Vietnam*. Sydney: NewSouth, 2017.

Sublet, Frank. *Kokoda to the Sea: A History of the 1942 Campaign in Papua*. Mornington: Slouch Hat, 2000.

Tanaka Kengoro. *Operations of the Imperial Japanese Armed Forces in the Papua New Guinea Theater during World War II*. Tokyo: Japan Papua New Guinea Goodwill Society, 1980.

Taylor, Brent D. *The Outsider's Edge: The Making of Self-Made Billionaires*. Melbourne: Wiley, 2007.

_____ *The Creative Edge: Insights from the Lives of the World's Most Famous Outsiders*. Melbourne: Wiley, 2008.

Threlfall, Adrian. *Jungle Warriors*. Sydney: Allen & Unwin, 2014.

2/17 Battalion History Committee. *'What We Have ... We Hold!' A History of the 2/17 Australian Infantry Battalion, 1940–1945*. Sydney: Australian Military History Publications, 1990.

Unger, Debi; Unger, Irwin; and Hirshson, Stanley. *George Marshall: A Biography*. Kindle edition. New York: HarperCollins, 2014.

Uren, Malcolm. *A Thousand Men at War: The Story of the 2/16th Battalion, AIF*. London and Melbourne: Heinemann, 1959.

Watson, Bruce Allen. *Exit Rommel: The Tunisian Campaign, 1942–43*. Mechanicsburg, Pennsylvania: Stackpole, 2007.

Wiest, Andrew A. *Haig: The Evolution of a Commander*. Washington, D.C.: Potomac, 2005.

Wigmore, Lionel Gage. *The Japanese Thrust*. Australia in the War of 1939–1945, Series One: Army, Volume IV. Canberra: Australian War Memorial, 1957.

Williams, Peter. *Japan's Pacific War: Personal Accounts of the Emperor's Warriors*. Barnsley, South Yorkshire: Pen & Sword, 2021.

_____ *The Kokoda Campaign, 1942: Myth and Reality*. Melbourne: Cambridge University Press, 2012.

Willoughby, Charles (ed). *Reports of General MacArthur: Japanese Operations in the Southwest Pacific Area*, Volume II, Part II, Washington, D.C.: United States Army Center of Military History, 1994.

Wolmar, Christian. *Engines of War: How Wars Were Won and Lost on the Railways*. London: Atlantic, 2010.

Wright, Derrick. *Tarawa 1943: The Turning of the Tide*. Oxford: Osprey, 2000.

Wukovits, John. *Eisenhower*. New York: Palgrave MacMillan, 2006.

Journals and Journal Articles

Australian Defence Force Journal. No 148, May/June 2001 (Special Blamey Edition). Canberra: Australian Government Department of Defence.

Bridge, Carl. Review of David Horner, *Blamey: The Commander-in-Chief* (Sydney: Allen & Unwin, 1998). *Journal of the Australian War Memorial*, Issue 34. awm.gov.au/articles/journal/j34/bridgerev.

Bullard, Steve. 'Kokoda: A Japanese tragedy'. *Wartime*, Issue 20, September 2002, pp. 20–21.

McMullin, Ross. 'Disaster at Fromelles'. *Wartime*, Issue 3, Spring 2006, '1916: A Terrible Year'. awm.gov.au/wartime/36/article/.

Young, Gabrielle. 'The loss of Lark Force'. Australian War Memorial, 20 March 2024. awm.gov.au/articles/blog/the-loss-of-lark-force.

Newspaper and Other Articles

'Never happier, says Japanese soldier', *Canberra Times*, 12 March 1975, p. 5.

Australian High Commission Malaysia. 'History of the Australia–Malaysia defence relationship'. malaysia.highcommission.gov.au/files/klpr/History%20of%20the%20Australia-Malaysia%20Defence%20Relationship.pdf.

Blainey, Geoffrey. 'As the Pacific theatre opened, the nation was ill-prepared'. *The Australian*, 15 August 2020.

Hetherington, John. 'What did Tom Blamey think of MacArthur? The story of Australia's highest ranking soldier'. *Sunday Mail*, 6 December 1953.

Jenkins, David. 'Invasion warnings were ignored'. *Sydney Morning Herald*, 14 August 1992.

Webpages

Anderson, Thomas. 'Matilda Frog and "Murray FT" flame tank'. The Online Tank Museum, 22 July 2017. tanks-encyclopedia.com/ww2/australia/matilda-frog-and-murray-ft-flame-tank/.

Anzac Portal, Australian Government Department of Veterans' Affairs. 'Japanese advance (December 1941 – March 1942)'. anzacportal.dva.gov.au/wars-and-missions/world-war-ii-1939-1945/events/japanese-advance-december-1941-march-1942.

_____ 'List of casualties for Kokoda, Milne Bay and Buna–Gona'. anzacportal.dva.gov.au/wars-and-missions/kokoda-track-1942-1943/resources/casualties-kokoda/list-casualties-kokoda-milne-bay-and-buna-gona.

Australian Government Department of Veterans' Affairs. 'Bomber command', 31 January 2020. dva.gov.au/newsroom/media-centre/media-backgrounders/bomber-command

_____ 'Fall of Singapore', 31 January 2020. dva.gov.au/newsroom/media-centre/media-backgrounders/fall-singapore.

_____ 'Gallipoli', 25 March 2025. dva.gov.au/media/media-backgrounders/gallipoli.

Australian War Memorial. 'Australian military statistics: World War II – a global perspective.' web.archive.org/web/20100527221139/http://awm.gov.au/atwar/statistics/ww2.asp.

_____ 'AWM52 8/2/21 – 21 Infantry Brigade' (war diaries). awm.gov.au/collection/C1360843.

_____ 'Capture of Lae'. awm.gov.au/collection/E84347.

_____ 'Field Marshal Thomas Albert Blamey'. awm.gov.au/collection/P10676218.

_____ 'Hamel: The textbook victory – 4 July 1918'. awm.gov.au/visit/exhibitions/1918/battles/hamel.

_____ 'Mont St Quentin and Péronne: Australian victories'. awm.gov.au/visit/exhibitions/1918/battles/mtstquentin.

_____ 'Second battle of Bullecourt'. awm.gov.au/collection/E84360.

_____ 'Siege of Tobruk'. awm.gov.au/articles/encyclopedia/tobruk.

_____ 'Structure' (Australian Army). awm.gov.au/learn/understanding-military-structure/army/structure.

Australians at War Archive, University of New South Wales Canberra. 'Stanley Bisset (Stan) – Transcript of interview', 12 December 2003. australiansatwarfilmarchive.unsw.edu.au/archive/htmlTranscript/1223.

Felton, Mark. 'Death march: 1945's forgotten tragedy', 26 August 2015. markfelton.co.uk/publishedbooks/death-march/.

Grant, Lachlan. 'Remembering the fall of Singapore'. Australian War Memorial, 15 February 2021. awm.gov.au/collection/E84347.

Henderson, Anne. 'A personal vendetta in Australian military history'. Review of Brett Lodge, *Lavarack: Rival General* (London: Robinson Reynolds, 2021). The Sydney Institute. thesydneyinstitute.com.au/blog/a-personal-vendetta-in-australian-military-history/.

Horner, David. 'Blamey: The Commander in Chief', 17 August 2020. Shrine of Remembrance (Melbourne). shrine.org.au/blamey-commander-chief.

National Archives of Australia. 'War Cabinet records'. naa.gov.au/help-your-research/fact-sheets/war-cabinet-records.

Tibbitts, Craig. 'The battles for Bullecourt'. Australian War Memorial, 3 April 2007. awm.gov.au/articles/blog/the-battles-for-bullecourt.

Enlistment and Casualty Sources, World War I

Anzac Portal, Australian Government Department of Veterans' Affairs. 'List of casualties for Kokoda, Milne Bay and Buna–Gona'. anzacportal.dva.gov.au/wars-and-missions/kokoda-track-1942-1943/resources/casualties-kokoda/list-casualties-kokoda-milne-bay-and-buna-gona.

_____ 'Timeline of Australians and the Gallipoli campaign'. anzacportal.dva.gov.au/wars-and-missions/ww1/where-australians-served/gallipoli/timeline.

Australian War Memorial. 'Deaths as a result of service with Australian units'. awm.gov.au/articles/encyclopedia/war_casualties.

_____ 'Enlistment statistics, First World War'. awm.gov.au/articles/encyclopedia/enlistment/ww1.

Canadian War Museum. 'The cost of Canada's war'. warmuseum.ca/firstworldwar/history/after-the-war/legacy/the-cost-of-canadas-war/.

The Long, Long Trail. 'Some British Army statistics of the Great War'. longlongtrail.co.uk/army/some-british-army-statistics-of-the-great-war/.

Shoebridge, Tim. 'First World War by the numbers'. New Zealand History, 2015. nzhistory.govt.nz/war/first-world-war-by-numbers.

UK Parliament. 'The fallen'. parliament.uk/business/publications/research/olympic-britain/crime-and-defence/the-fallen/.

US Department of Veterans Affairs. 'America's wars'. department.va.gov/american-wars/.

Enlistment and Total Deaths Sources, World War II

Anzac Portal, Australian Government Department of Veterans' Affairs. 'List of casualties for Kokoda, Milne Bay and Buna–Gona'. anzacportal.dva.gov.au/wars-and-missions/kokoda-track-1942-1943/resources/casualties-kokoda/list-casualties-kokoda-milne-bay-and-buna-gona.

Australian War Memorial. 'Deaths as a result of service with Australian units'. awm.gov.au/articles/encyclopedia/war_casualties

_____ 'Enlistment statistics, Second World War'. awm.gov.au/articles/encyclopedia/enlistment/ww2.

Canadian War Museum. 'Canada and the Second World War'. www.warmuseum.ca/remembrance-day-resources/canada-and-the-second-world-war.

Ellis, John. *World War II: A Statistical Survey*. New York: Facts on File, 1993.

The National WWII Museum, New Orleans.'Research starters: Worldwide deaths in World War II'. nationalww2museum.org/students-teachers/student-resources/research-starters/research-starters-worldwide-deaths-world-war.

UK Parliament. 'The fallen'. parliament.uk/business/publications/research/olympic-britain/crime-and-defence/the-fallen/.

US Department of Veterans Affairs. 'America's wars'. department.va.gov/american-wars/.

Enlistment and Combat Deaths Sources, World War II

Australian War Memorial. 'Battle for Singapore'. awm.gov.au/collection/E84308.

_____ 'Deaths as a result of service with Australian units'. awm.gov.au/articles/encyclopedia/war_casualties

_____ 'Enlistment statistics, Second World War'. awm.gov.au/articles/encyclopedia/enlistment/ww2.

Canadian War Museum. 'Canada and the Second World War'. www.warmuseum.ca/remembrance-day-resources/canada-and-the-second-world-war.

Ellis, John. *World War II: A Statistical Survey*. New York: Facts on File, 1993.

McGibbon, Ian. 'Second World War – overview'. New Zealand History. nzhistory.govt.nz/war/second-world-war.

US Department of Veterans Affairs. 'America's wars'. department.va.gov/american-wars/.

INDEX

Note that page numbers with photos are rendered in **bold** type.

Entries beginning 'acting commander ...', 'Colonel, promotion to ...', 'as General Staff Officer ...', 'knighted', 'transfers to ...', 'writes letters to ...', '1st Div, transfers to ...' and so on refer to Blamey.

Post-World War II